The Study of Culture—Revised Edition

Chandler & Sharp Publications in Anthropology
and Related Fields
General Editors: L. L. Langness and Robert B. Edgerton

THE STUDY OF CULTURE

REVISED EDITION

L. L. Langness

University of California, Los Angeles

Chandler & Sharp Publishers, Inc.
Novato, California

Notices of Copyright and Literary Property appear on pages 251 and following.

Library of Congress Cataloging in Publication Data

Langness, L. L. (Lewis L.), 1929–
 The study of culture.

 (Chandler & Sharp publications in anthropology and
related fields)
 Bibliography: p.
 Includes index.
 1. Ethnology—History. 2. Culture. I. Title.
II. Series.
GN17.L36 1987   306'.09   86–32716
ISBN 0–88316–556–2

Book design by Joe Roter.
Cover design and art by Jacki Gallagher.
Edited by W. L. Parker.
Composition by Publications Services of Marin.

This book is dedicated to the memory of my
mother, Judith Ellen Otterson

Contents

Illustrations

Preface

Although this book is primarily intended to be an historically focused introduction to the study of cultural anthropology it should also be of use to anyone who deals with the concept of culture. Since culture can well be regarded as the key concept of anthropology (Devereux 1956), and since it has been said that "we could define an anthropologist as someone who uses the word 'culture' habitually" (Wagner 1975:1), an examination of the history and development of the concept is of obvious significance for anyone interested in anthropology. More broadly, however, in the slightly more than one hundred years since its introduction into the English language, the culture concept has come to be regarded as "the foundation stone of the social sciences" (Chase 1948:59), and as "the most central problem of all social science" (Malinowski 1939:588). A. L. Kroeber and Clyde Kluckhohn, two of America's most distinguished anthropologists, argued in their definitive survey of the concept (1963:3) that "in explanatory importance and in generality of application it [culture] is comparable to such categories as gravity in physics, disease in medicine, evolution in biology." Huxley (1960:19) has asserted that man's acquisition of culture "enabled him to cross the barrier set by biological limitations and enter the virgin fields of psycho-social existences [which implies that] man's true destiny emerges in a startling new form. It is to be the chief agent for the future of evolution on this planet." More recently has appeared a volume, *The Idea of Culture in the Social Sciences* (Schneider and Bonjean 1973), which emphasizes the enormous influence of the concept of culture on sociology, political science, geography, and history. It also makes clear that there is a budding field of cultural economics! The term culture has now, of course, become part

of standard English. It is commonplace to hear educated people everywhere preface their statements with the phrase "in this culture," and the
like. Thus the study of culture must be seen not as the unique occupation
of a few professors interested in the academic and esoteric but rather as
one of the major ingredients in any basic educational program and as one
of the keys to the understanding of the human being's place on earth and
in the biosphere.

Because the development of the culture concept occurred simultaneously with the development of anthropology it is treated here in its relevant historical context: that is, as part of the history of anthropology.
Until fairly recently no comprehensive histories of anthropology were
available. Such history of the profession as there was tended to be passed
along orally in classrooms or informally from one generation of students
to the next. This lack led to a number of oversimplifications, half truths,
and even untruths, which are just now beginning to sort themselves out.
Only because of recent work in the history of anthropology, most importantly by George W. Stocking, Jr., Marvin Harris, Fred W. Voget, John
J. Honigmann, Margaret T. Hodgen, Murray Leaf, Adam Kuper, Ian
Langham, and others has it now become possible to attempt a shorter
and more precise version of the development of anthropological ideas.
The debt owed to these scholars — and to earlier students of the history of
anthropology, most notably A. I. Hallowell — is apparent on virtually
every page of this volume. Since it is meant for the general student rather
than for the professional, I have often favored these recent sources rather
than the earlier.

Although this is not meant to be the definitive, comprehensive, and
original work on the history of anthropology, it does introduce the most
significant figures, terms, and concepts of cultural anthropology in the
order in which they emerged and became of significance.

I have used quotations liberally. In some cases the quotation makes
the point far more parsimoniously than I can make it; in others I believed
it was better to let the author speak for himself; and in still others I
simply felt the quotation was interesting or provocative enough to stimu-
late students to want to look further.

Contemporary interest in the history of anthropology is only part of a
broader interest in the history of science in general, which has produced
some recent books of much value in the preparation of this volume. The
collection *The Wild Man Within,* edited by Maximillian E. Novak and
Edward Dudley, Ernest Becker's stimulating work *The Lost Science of
Man,* and Sidney Pollard's *The Idea of Progress* come particularly to
mind. There are also *The Idea of Prehistory* by Glyn Daniel (1964),

Growth of a Prehistoric Time Scale by William Berry (1968), Muhsin Mahdi's *Ibn Khaldun's Philosophy of History* (1971), and B. V. Street's fascinating work, *The Savage in Literature* (1975).

This historical approach has been deliberately chosen. It is important for students not only to understand the concept of culture as it is presently employed, but also to understand that it developed out of a series of real problems that people were attempting to cope with in the eighteenth and nineteenth centuries. Many of these problems are with us yet. Further, it is necessary and worthwhile to emphasize that no science, cultural anthropology included, developed independently of other sciences or of the important inventions and discoveries that were being made during the period of its emergence. Suggested links between developments in the history of anthropology and other disciplines have been pointed out whenever possible. Finally, the exceedingly comprehensive scope of anthropology itself must be made clear. Cultural anthropology is only one subfield of the larger whole that also includes archeology, physical anthropology, linguistics, social anthropology, and psychological anthropology. Although these other subfields are not all dealt with directly, an attempt has been made to show how developments in each of them have affected the others.

I have attempted to present the history of the culture concept in such a way as to illustrate the arguments and counterarguments that were involved in its emergence and change. Naturally there was more overlapping of ideas and arguments over time than I have been able to make clear. And, concededly, the views presented in this account are somewhat oversimplified. By focusing on the concept of culture I have tried to eliminate the problem of having to be encyclopedic. Since the earlier history of anthropology is inseparable from the history of the social and behavioral sciences in general, the tendency has often been to start with Herodotus and move forward from there so slowly that by the time the introduction of the culture concept is reached the history of anthropology since then becomes a mere afterthought.

Anthropology does have its own history, however brief—a very interesting history worthy of treatment in its own right. This history is virtually synonymous with the history of the culture concept. Thus in this account the early history of anthropology is passed over relatively quickly in favor of the past roughly one hundred years. I believe it is most important for students to have a brief overview of this type. Too often we hear from students that they do not see how things fit together, or why certain things are important, or why they should study anthropology or social science at all. If this book gives them a broader perspective and helps them to answer these questions it will have fulfilled its purpose. It if leads them to an appreciation of anthropology and stimulates them to pursue further studies in the social and behavioral sciences, so much the better.

L.L.L.

April, 1986

Acknowledgments

I am indebted to many friends and colleagues who read the manuscript for the first edition of this book: in particular Robert B. Edgerton, Carol Eastman, Paul Preuss, George Guilmet, and Gilbert Herdt. For this version I am grateful in addition for the advice of Jill E. Korbin, John G. Kennedy, Harold G. Levine, and Jorja Manos-Prover. I would also like to thank Ms. Ellen Watnofsky for help in all aspects of the preparation of this revision and, finally, I express my genuine gratitude to Willis L. Parker, quite simply the best editor anyone could have.

Naturally, I am alone responsible for whatever shortcomings the book may have.

The Study of Culture—Revised Edition

INTRODUCTION

A Human Science of Human Beings

Anthropology is the scientific study of *human beings*—that is, of the human creature viewed in the abstract: male, female, all colors and shapes, prehistoric, ancient, and modern. Anthropology, then, most fundamentally viewed, is simply the attempt of human beings to study and hence to understand themselves at all times and all places.

Cultural anthropology, the subject of this book, is only one part of man's efforts to know himself—that part which deals with culture. Although the concept of culture was introduced into the English language only in the 1880s by Matthew Arnold and Edward B. Tylor, the study of cultural anthropology has existed for much longer than that. It has been suggested, for example, that the metaphysical foundation upon which the definition of culture depended can be found in John Locke's *An Essay Concerning Human Understanding* (1690), and the concept itself was first given clear expression in Europe in 1750 by Anne Robert Jacques Turgot:

> Possessor of a treasure of signs which he has the faculty of multiplying to infinity, he [man] is able to assure the retention of his acquired ideas, to communicate them to other men, and to transmit them to his successors as a constantly expanding heritage. (Quoted in Harris 1968:14)

This definition does have a surprisingly contemporary character.

1

Rousseau, too, at the same period of time, developed a systematic theory of the transition from "nature to culture" (Lévi-Strauss 1962) although he did not use those terms and has been often misunderstood (Wokler 1978).

Muhsin Mahdi's study of Ibn Khaldun, however, discloses roots of the idea of culture at least as early as the fourteenth century. Ibn Khaldun, an Arab historian, Mahdi proposes, founded a science of culture at that time. Ibn Khaldun's idea of culture has the same surprisingly modern character as Turgot's:

. . . Culture is not an independent substance, but a property . . . of another substance which is man. Hence the natural character of culture must have reference to what is natural to man, i.e., to his nature and what differentiates him from the rest of the animal world.

The essential differentia of man is the power or faculty of intellect or mind . . . reflection . . . or deliberation . . . Through his intellect man can understand; he can know both particular objects embedded in matter and universals abstracted from matter. (Mahdi 1971:173)

No doubt one could find evidence for some notion of culture even further back, in Herodotus or Tacitus for example. Even so, the history of cultural anthropology as we now conceive it is scarcely more than one hundred years old, a brief period indeed in the course of human history and prehistory.

Although at least some human beings seem always to have been interested in reflecting upon themselves, what we now consider the "scientific" study of the world's peoples—that is, anthropology—could not have come into being until realistic notions had been framed about the age of the planet and the myriad things found upon it. Geology, stimulated early primarily because of the economic interests of mining, was developing rapidly throughout the nineteenth century. As the various strata of the earth were exposed along with occasional accompanying fossils, it became apparent to some that the earth was much older than was popularly supposed. The new evidence did not fit well with the established idea of an independent creation of fixed and unchanging species. Also increasingly demanding explanation were the stone and bone tools being unearthed by a number of scholars who were then generally referred to as antiquarians. As men were not believed to have been on earth for very long, and as no human fossils had been recovered up to this time, there was no satisfactory explanation for the presence of such artifacts deep in the earth. Midway in the seventeenth century, Archbishop James Ussher had worked out a Biblical chronology in which the six-day creation of all things had taken place in 4004 B.C. and the flood had occurred in 2501

B.C. Charles Lyell, one of the foremost British scientists of his day, noted in his *Principles of Geology* in 1830 that remains of life were rare in the deepest geological strata, that immediately above these came shells and vegetable remains, then bones of fishes and reptiles, then remains of birds and, finally, remains of mammals. Human beings were much more recent.

So far as fossil men were concerned:

Ignorance and prejudice combined to assert that man was created a few thousand years ago in a state of physical perfection. The possibility of the discovery of fossil man was therefore inconceivable to most people, and those early writers who entertained the idea were generally inclined to deny it. Cuvier, limiting the age of the earth to the orthodox 6000 years, had stated that fossil bones of man did not exist. Moreover, up to the time of his death (1832) nothing had been found to disturb this generally received opinion. (Haddon 1934:48)

But the geologists of the time knew the earth had to be older than 6000 years. They also knew that Biblical chronologies of man did not fit properly into the scheme they were busily developing. But they were also for the most part very religious men. It was a controversial situation in which the scholars of the day moved slowly and with caution; the churchmen were powerful. Scientists were aware of what had happened to Copernicus (who allowed his "heretical" view of the universe to be published only while on his deathbed), to Giordano Bruno (who had been burned alive for his impiety), to Galileo (imprisoned and humiliated), to Kepler and Newton (both bitterly attacked and denounced for challenging scriptural authority), and to others less well known. But even so:

. . . The most conservative geologists were gradually obliged to admit that man had been upon the earth not merely six-thousand, or sixty-thousand, or one-hundred-and-sixty thousand years. And when, in 1863, Sir Charles Lyell, in his book on the *The Antiquity of Man*, retracted solemnly his earlier view—yielding with a reluctance almost pathetic, but with a thoroughness absolutely convincing—the last strong-hold of orthodoxy in this field fell. (A. D. White 1955:241)

Even more pathetic were the last-ditch attempts being made to somehow reconcile the findings of geology with those of scripture. Perhaps the best example of these is the book *Omphalos* by Philip Henry Gosse (1857) which attempted to argue that although the Almighty had in fact created everything in six days, He made it appear (for reasons that are never quite explained) that it had taken much longer. Thus glacial marks, various kinds of tilted and uplifted strata, fossils of all kinds, and all other geological data were believed to have been created overnight. Using capital letters, Gosse closed his book, "IN SIX DAYS JEHOVAH MADE HEAVEN AND EARTH, THE SEA, AND ALL THAT IN THEM IS," his ultimate refutation of geology (A. D. White 1955:242).

As another example of the climate of opinion, consider briefly the problems of Jacques Boucher de Perthes (1788–1868) who, according to Robert H. Lowie's *The History of Ethnological Theory* (1937), was largely responsible for bringing about the revolution in our ideas about the age of the earth. Boucher de Perthes was a French amateur antiquarian who, in the 1830s, argued that man must at one time have been contemporaneous with extinct mammals. In 1838, he argued that stone axes he had unearthed were proof of human craftsmanship in the Pleistocene (a geological period which, in the thinking of that time, antedated human creation). Most of the authorities were unconvinced. Some argued the artifacts had sunk to the strata where they were found simply because of their weight. Others doubted they were of human origin at all. Still others denied the stratum was as old as Boucher de Perthes claimed it was. Boucher de Perthes himself later commented on his experiences as follows:

Practical men disdained to look; they were afraid; they were afraid of becoming accomplices in what they called a heresy, almost a mystification: they did not suspect my good faith, but they doubted my common sense. (Quoted by Lowie 1937:7)

At last, in 1854, Dr. Rigollot, a countryman and an antagonist of Boucher de Perthes, after carefully examining the sites and the evidence, announced his conversion. By 1859 a number of English scholars, including Hugh Falconer and Joseph Prestwich, had similarly acknowledged their belief in Boucher's finds. A short time later the greatest and most influential geologist of the time, Charles Lyell, who had vigorously resisted the evolutionary theory of Lamarck as long as possible, announced his complete acceptance of the new view.

If we remember the reaction that Charles Darwin's *Origin of Species* provoked when it was published at about this same time (1859), we glimpse the truly revolutionary nature of the changes that were occurring in the way human beings thought about themselves: the belief in the immutability of species was being broken, the concept of biological evolution was becoming more widely accepted, the antiquity of man and the duration of culture were being extended backward to a more remote time. While it is convenient to say, as T. K. Penniman does (1935:20), "with Darwin, the history of anthropology as a single, though many-sided science begins," the statement grossly overemphasizes Darwin's contribution and ignores the many other scientists who labored to bring about this remarkable departure in human thought. In fact, the idea of evolution, in its primary sense of change over time, had been fundamental to virtually all philosophy at least since Lucretius in the first century B.C. Darwin's contribution was to bring the notion of evolution to biology from social science, where it had already gained prominence, not to discover it for the first time (Harris 1968:122). Further, as Jacob Gruber has shown (1965), the discovery of the antiquity of the human species, contrary to what we might ordinarily believe, was made quite independently of Darwin.

Geology, antiquarianism, and Darwin were not the only challenges to traditional authority. The age of exploration had been under way for some time. Travelers were beginning to visit even the most remote parts of the globe. But since Saint Augustine, about 400 A.D., had denied in *The City of God* that men could inhabit the far corners of the earth, the religious explorers of the day were confronted with a remarkably confused situation. There were people of some sort where none should have been; moreover, it was not clear whether they should be considered men or, more properly, animals. During the Middle Ages, descriptions had been circulated of men with only one eye in the center of their foreheads, hermaphroditic people, people without mouths, people with their feet backward, people with eyes in their shoulders and no heads at all, and still others who, instead of speaking, barked like dogs (H. White 1972). These notions were still influential when the new world was being discovered:

Spanish captains went forth to their conquest expecting to encounter many kinds of mythical beings and monsters depicted in medieval literature: giants, pygmies, dragons, griffins, white-haired boys, bearded ladies, human beings adorned with tails, headless creatures with eyes in their stomachs or breasts, and other fabulous folk. For a thousand years a great reservoir of curious ideas on man and semi-men had been forming in Europe, and was now freely drawn upon in America . . .

Governor Diego Velazquez, despite his years of experience in Cuba, instructed Cortez to look for strange beings with great flat ears and others with dog-like faces whom he might expect to see in Aztec lands. Francisco de Orellana was so positive that he had encountered warrior women on his famous voyage of 1540 that the mightiest river in South America was named the Amazon. The Devil himself was to be found, some believed, on a certain island in the Caribbean Sea . . . . (Hanke 1959:3-5)

Likewise, the discovery of subhuman primates—gorilla, orangutan, chimpanzee, and others—posed unprecedented problems of classification and understanding. There were arguments over whether "savages"

A

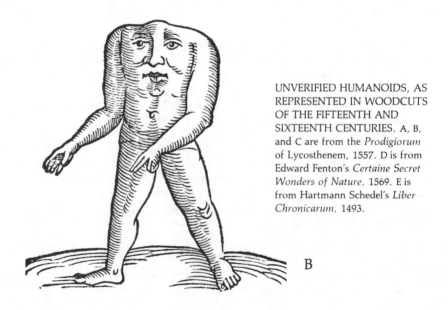

UNVERIFIED HUMANOIDS, AS
REPRESENTED IN WOODCUTS
OF THE FIFTEENTH AND
SIXTEENTH CENTURIES. A, B,
and C are from the *Prodigiorum*
of Lycosthenem, 1557. D is from
Edward Fenton's *Certaine Secret
Wonders of Nature*, 1569. E is
from Hartmann Schedel's *Liber
Chronicarum*, 1493.

B

C

D

E

and orangutans could breed with each other, whether chimpanzees could use fire and dance, whether gorillas were some form of grotesque human or merely some kind of animal, and so on:

> It is today much less widely appreciated . . . that one of the main points at issue in the Enlightenment controversies about human nature and culture was the character of the relation between mankind and the great apes. In the 1670's Sir William Petty was still able to argue that the second place in Nature's ladder was actually filled by elephants rather than apes, since, apart from their shape, elephants displayed greater signs of humanity. Yet by the 1680's and 1690's few commentators on the subject still doubted that apes resembled men more closely than did any other creature, and the anthropological interest over the next century came to be directed largely to the question of how we might be connected with, or distinguished from, those animals most immediately adjacent to us in the natural world. (Wokler 1978:109)

It is even less widely appreciated, as Robert Wokler has recently shown (1978), that Rousseau's famous portrait of the "noble savage" was actually based upon descriptions of the orangutan!

Eventually, of course, as more and more information on people from other parts of the globe was accumulated, as more was learned of various exotic animals, attention became drawn away from the distinction between apes and men and more and more to the subtle differences between various groups of people. It became evident that the people, at least, were capable of taking over ideas, including Christianity. Indeed, this ability was used to define humanness. So the question shifted from whether they were people to what their origins were. Paracelsus, in 1520, had first voiced the notion of a polygenist theory—that is, the idea that perhaps not everyone was descended from Adam and Eve. Around this issue, as well as the dispute over the age of the earth, battle was joined and the science of anthropology began to emerge.

The first anthropological society—the Société des Observateurs de l'Homme—was formed in Paris in 1800. Although it had a distinguished membership including Cuvier, Lamarck, Geoffroy Saint-Hilaire, Pinel, Bougainville, and others equally famous, it lasted only until 1804 when Napoleon apparently withdrew his support—an early example of the continuing conflict between government and the social sciences. The ambitions of the Society's founders were large. One, Jauffret, suggested in 1802 no less than a comprehensive classification of races, a complete comparative anatomy, a comparative dictionary of all languages, a complete anthropological topography of France, and a museum of comparative ethnography. It is interesting, if depressing, to speculate about how all of this information might have helped to ease the genocidal colonialism that was continually expanding at precisely this time. Jauffret also suggested an experiment (which, fortunately, was not carried out):

. . . possible only in "a century as enlightened as ours"—to determine the characteristics of "natural man" by observing through adolescence infants "placed from their birth in a single enclosure, remote from all social institutions, and abandoned for the development of ideas and language solely to the instinct of nature." (Stocking 1964:135)

In the virtual absence of any reliable or systematic information about non-European peoples, this experiment was in its way perhaps an advanced and humane proposal.

A major effort during the short-lived existence of the Society was collaboration in a grandiose but ill-fated scientific expedition to the south coast of Australia. One of the expedition members was François Péron, a medical student and self-styled "anthropologist." Interestingly enough, although information was sadly lacking, both doctors and travelers were asserting at this time that "savages" were superior in health, strength, and general physical perfection to Europeans. Simultaneously, however, it was commonly accepted that the same "savages" were almost totally lacking in manners, religion, and, above all, morals. Thus Péron set out to test his hypothesis that "moral perfection must be in inverse ratio to physical perfection." He also carried with him two outlines for how to study "savage peoples," one by Citizen Degérando (Joseph Marie de Gérando), *Considerations on the diverse methods to follow in the observations of savage peoples,* and one by George Cuvier, *Instructive note on the researches to be carried out relative to the anatomical differences between the diverse races of man.* Degérando's instructions were in many ways remarkably insightful. He insisted, first of all, on careful observation; having made such observations, one could then proceed with comparisons. From careful comparisons one could derive general laws of human behvior. It was easier to derive them by observing "primitive" people, Degérando argued, because such people were less modified by outside influences. He also believed, as anthropologists still believe, that one could understand "savages" only by learning their language and becoming "fellow citizens." He cautioned that numerous observations would be necessary (sex, age, and other factors must be considered) and that one should not assume that all such peoples would be of a single type (Stocking 1968:23–24).

Though Degérando's memorandum had flaws, it was nonetheless very far ahead of its time. One of its most interesting features was its humanitarianism. It lacked any reference at all to the idea of race or the permanence of hereditary differences between peoples of the earth (Degérando

1969). Cuvier's memorandum, on the other hand, was little more than instructions for grave-robbing, being mainly a plea for skeletons and especially skulls, obtained "in any manner whatever." In the light of how little was available at the time for students of comparative anatomy, Cuvier's instructions made sense, but when they are seen from an ethical or even from a local point of view their ethnocentric and essentially racist character becomes obvious (Stocking 1968:30).

Péron found on his journey, much to his satisfaction it appears, that the assertions of travelers and doctors were incorrect—that, in terms of his own work at least, Europeans were not only more moral but also stronger than savages. His conclusions are amusing now but at the time were taken more seriously:

> In interpreting his results, Péron argued that the lush bounty of their natural habitat had made the Malayans lethargic. But only the poverty of their social status could explain the weakness of the Australians and Tasmanians. If "these disinherited children of nature gave up their ferocious and vagabond customs" and gathered in villages, if "the rights of property excited in them a happy emulation"—then the effective resources of their physical environment would multiply, their social state improve, and their "temperament become more robust." Nor were these the only virtues of the civilized state. Commenting elsewhere on the surprise evinced by Tasmanians at the sexual virility of a French sailor who ravished a Tasmanian woman immediately upon stepping ashore, Péron hypothesized that Tasmanian sexual desire was, like that of animals, periodic. The sustained ability and interest of the European were environmental —the product of warm rooms, good food, spirituous liquors, more complex social relations, and leisure. (Stocking 1964:145)

That morals cannot be measured quite as easily as physical strength seems not to have occurred to Péron. He measured physical strength through a variety of tests he devised specifically for that purpose. He "measured" morals simply by arbitrarily comparing the "savage" to Europeans. This was a mistake which continued in anthropology for many years and continues even now among many nonanthropologists.

Sometime late in the seventeenth century a curious paradox arose in which two contradictory views of "savages" began to exist simultaneously. On the one hand was the traditional view of them as wild men, grotesque, nonhuman, immoral, disgusting, and variously objectionable. But a new view regarded such creatures as "noble savages"—happy, cooperative, carefree children of nature living lives uncluttered with the woes and cares of civilization. It has been suggested that the concept of the noble savage was created and popularized, mostly by Rousseau, as a convenient fiction that influential writers of the period could employ to

NOBLE SAVAGE. "Tragedy of the Stone Age," an engraving from an exhibit at the 1889 Exposition Universelle. (Print courtesy of David H. Spain)

make people aware of the flaws in their own culture (H. White 1972). Be that as it may, it was this contradiction that oriented Péron's quest; and it was his work, and this period of time, that ushered in the decline of the concept of the noble savage. What is even more important is that Péron and others, unlike Degérando, increasingly hinted that the differences found between peoples were due to race. Prior to the fifteenth century the idea of race had not been employed as an explanation for cultural differences; the known world was not large and the differences could be regarded as being between Christians and non-Christians. By the nineteenth century the concept of race grew increasingly in importance and was invoked to explain the differences that were being constantly discovered. The concept of culture emerged against this background, in part at least as an alternative to race for explaining differences in behavior.

It is highly important to recognize that cultural anthropology emerged in the nineteenth century as part of an attempt to create a new and comprehensive "science of man." It emerged out of a crisis of the eighteenth century, a crisis that continued into the nineteenth century and is still with us now in the twentieth century. The Industrial Revolution had brought with it changes in human behavior so unprecedented and drastic they have been described by at least one scholar as qualitative rather than quantitative (Polanyi 1944)—different, that is, in kind, not just in degree. The structure and coherence of medieval society had collapsed. There was, as Ernest Becker has eloquently stated,

. . . a moral crisis. The medieval view had loosened its hold on society, and now there was nothing to replace it. Whereas the church had offered the one thing that man needs as much as the air he breathes—a dependable mode of behavior for himself and his fellow men—it was precisely this that was now wanting. Society was headed for the kind of chaos *Homo sapiens* fears most: the chaos of undependable and immoral behavior in his fellow men, the chaos of unregulated, irresponsible social life.

The science of man, let it be emphasized once and for all, had the solution of this moral crisis as its central and abiding purpose. Why build a science of man in society? In order to have a sound basis for a new moral creed, an agreed, factual body of knowledge that men of good will could use to lay down laws for a new social order. (1971:11)

That anthropology or any wider "science of man" has not resolved this crisis is a different story, one that will become clearer as we proceed with our investigation. The concept of culture emerged from this crisis as an aid to the understanding of it, as a way of understanding human variation, and as a tool for the examination of human nature itself.

Degeneration and Progress

This chapter deals with what can be regarded as the first substantial systematic body of anthropological theory. This is usually referred to as "evolutionism" and the scholars who promoted it as "evolutionists." To distinguish these scholars from contemporary evolutionists we often emphasize that they were "early evolutionists."

Before this period the existence of "savage" people was usually explained by saying such people had descended from ancestors who had fallen from grace. Even earlier, some had denied that such peoples were human at all. The early evolutionists attempted to disprove the degeneration theory and substituted in its place a belief in "progress." The theory they suggested fitted nicely with other prevailing beliefs of the time and gave rise to a series of related ideas—among them "survivals," the so-called "biogenetic law" (ontogeny recapitulates phylogeny), the idea that it was possible to compare existing "savages" with our earliest ancestors. In this chapter I will attempt to show that many of the ideas of this formative period are with us yet, if not in anthropology then in related fields such as psychology and psychoanalysis. I will also mention examples of how evolutionary theory was applied to various dimensions of culture, particularly to religion.

13

SAVAGERY TO CIVILIZATION. The Early Anthropologists' Model

The relationship of anthropology to the notion of evolution is a fact of great importance in the study of culture, not only because all of the early anthropologists were influenced by the belief in evolution, but also because it continues to affect the ways we think about ourselves to the present day. This influence was so pronounced during the formative years of anthropology that we typically refer to the founders of anthropology as evolutionists. It matters little which of the early anthropological scholars one has in mind, or even what, specifically, they happened to be interested in; they invariably used essentially the same evolutionary idea. The most basic form of this model can be shown as in the diagram.

This scheme was suggested fairly early (1748) by Montesquieu, then elaborated by both A. R. J. Turgot (1750) and Adam Ferguson (1789). Even so, it has often been taught in anthropology that it was initiated by Lewis Henry Morgan (Harris 1968:28). In any case, as we will see below, the most fundamental idea was to distinguish different types of societies on the basis of different levels of *technology* or *material culture.* Unfortunately, it appears that this hierarchical view of technological achievement has always been linked either implicitly or explicitly with another more basic hierarchical view, one that appears to be universal in human thought. All peoples must distinguish at least two categories, a "we" and a "they." And this distinction, as Hayden White has pointed out (1972:8), is essentially a difference between beliefs in an achieved and an imperfect humanity—very often a "we" who are humans or "people" and a "they" who are nonhuman or nonpeople. The idea that all people are fundamentally the same, if it is conceived at all, is usually seen as meaning only all people of a single group. In Christianity this view is given an even greater emphasis (1) because of the belief that mankind had been originally created as one but had subsequently fragmented as the result of improper human actions; and also (2) because of the idea of a vertical chain of being, embracing all of creation, but leading up to the Creator himself. It is absolutely crucial to understand that this distinction between people is made most fundamentally on moral and ethno-centric grounds. This fact can be seen very clearly in the following:

> . . . As long as men appeared different from one another, their division into higher and lower forms of humanity had to be admitted; for, in a theonomic (one subject to the authority of God) world, variation—class or generic—had to be taken as evidence of species corruption. For if there was one all-powerful and just God ordering the whole, how could the differences between men be explained, save by some principle which postulated a more perfect and less perfect approximation to the ideal form of humanity contained in the mind of God as the paradigm of the species? Similarly, in a universe that was thought to be ordered in its essential relationship by moral norms rather than by immanent physical causal forces, how could radical differences between men be accounted for, save by the assumption that the different was in some sense inferior to what passed for the normal, that is to say, the characteristics of the group from which the perception of differentness was made? (H. White 1972:9)

The scheme thus places people on a continuum which in this case is a scale of value with "savages" on the bottom, "barbarians" somewhat higher, and "civilized" people at the very top. As it was seen in the context of evolution, it implies a time dimension as well as a scale of value—"savages" changed over time into "barbarians" and eventually might attain the "higher" stage of "civilization." That it is not necessary for this scheme to be linked to Christianity can be seen in the fact that Ibn Khaldun conceived precisely the same idea from an Islamic point of view:

> The most important distinction made by Ibn Khaldun in his study of the development of culture is the distinction between "primitive culture" . . . and "civilized culture" . . . or "civilization" . . . . Primitive culture is defined primarily in terms of an economic way of life, which, in turn, colours the other aspects of a community, and distinguished it from civilization. (Mahdi 1971:193)

There is no evidence to suggest that Ibn Khaldun was not impressed by civilization as were his western European counterparts although his *ethnocentrism* would, of course, have had quite a different flavor.

It is most important that no one underestimate the significance of this basic mode of thought. Although it has tended to disappear from anthropology (indeed, one could argue that this may well be anthropology's most distinguishing feature), because of what might be termed *cultural lag* it survives even now in other disciplines and in the minds of many "nonanthropologists" everywhere. Although it was obviously not Lewis Henry Morgan's creation, we can say for our purposes here that it was

Morgan who developed and elaborated it into what in social science are now regarded as *evolutionary stages*.

LEWIS HENRY MORGAN

Although it is most questionable to assert as does Carl Resek, Lewis Henry Morgan's biographer, that Morgan "created the science of anthropology," there is no question that he was a unique and towering figure in American history. His book *The League of the Iroquois* (1851) has been called the "first scientific study of an American Indian tribe" (Meggers 1946). Darwin called him the New World's first social scientist. Henry Schoolcraft said he was the greatest authority on Indians in America. Henry Adams went even further, saying Morgan's work was the "foundation of all future American historical scholarship." Some argued that he was a socialist, others that his work was, in fact, a defense of capitalism. The truth about Morgan is not easy to come by because most of his personal papers were, unfortunately, destroyed at the time of his death (Resek 1960). But whatever he was, it was Morgan's *Ancient Society* (1877) that influenced Karl Marx and through him Frederick Engels, a development of significance to which we will subsequently return.

Morgan was a New Englander. He attended Union College in Schenectady, New York, taking his degree in law. But for a number of years he could find no work so he read widely, lectured on temperance, and wrote scholarly articles and books on philosophy, the nature of society, instinct, and other related subjects. He went on to become a banker and railroad magnate as well as an ("amateur") anthropologist. He was also a great organizer and lodge member, which led him in 1843 to form "The Great Order of the Iroquois," which was to be modeled on the customs of the Iroquois. At first it was mostly just youthful exuberance: members dressed in Iroquois costumes and even carried tomahawks to their meetings. But this soon gave way to a more serious interest in American Indians. A chance meeting in a bookstore with a young Seneca Indian, Ely Parker, gave additional impetus to what was to become Morgan's lifelong devotion to *ethnology*. With a curious mixture of scholarship, romanticism, and paternalism, Morgan worked diligently all his life for various Indian causes and was instrumental in aiding Indian education, in preserving Indian tradition, and insofar as it was possible during his time in protecting Indians from the greed of those who were attempting to take over their lands. Although Morgan's evolutionary scheme was subsequently challenged and profoundly modified by succeeding generations of anthropologists, his impact upon American ethnology remains.

LEWIS HENRY MORGAN (1818–1881). (Smithsonian Institution; National Anthropological Archives)

Some appreciation of the virtually unlimited application of the basic evolutionary scheme can be gained from considering *Ancient Society* itself. Morgan was interested in the evolution of a number of specific things. He listed them as follows: Subsistence, Government, Language, the Family, Religion, House Life and Architecture, and Property (1877:5). There is probably no clearer statement anywhere describing the model to be employed for investigating these diverse things than Morgan's opening statement:

The latest investigations respecting the early condition of the human race, are tending to the conclusion that mankind commenced their career at the bottom of the scale and worked their way up from savagery to civilization through the slow accumulations of experimental knowledge.

As it is undeniable that portions of the human family have existed in a state of savagery, other portions in a state of barbarism, and still other portions in a state of civilization, it seems equally so that these three distinct conditions are connected with each other in a natural as well as necessary sequence of progress. Moreover, that the status attained by each branch respectively, is rendered probable by the conditions under which all progress occurs and by the known advancement of several branches of the family through two or more of these conditions.

An attempt will be made in the following pages to bring forward additional evidence of the rudeness of the early condition of mankind, of the gradual evolution of their mental and moral powers through experience, and of their protracted struggle with opposing obstacles while winning the way to civilization. It will be drawn, in part, from the great sequence of inventions and discoveries which stretch along the entire pathway of human progress; but chiefly from domestic institutions, which express the growth of certain ideas and passions. (1877:3)

Morgan then went on to attempt to demonstrate that subsistence had developed through five successive "arts of subsistence": "Natural Subsistence Upon Fruits and Roots on a Restricted Habitat," "Fish Subsistence," "Farinaceous Subsistence Through Cultivation," "Meat and Milk Subsistence," and "Unlimited Subsistence Through Field Agriculture."

The family, Morgan argued, had likewise evolved through five forms: the first type, "Consanguine," as based on the "intermarriage of brothers and sisters in a group," the second, called "Punaluan," was based on the "intermarriage of several brothers to each other's wives in a group; and of several sisters to each other's husbands in a group" (the term brother here included male cousins, the term sister, female cousins). The third form, an intermediate one called "Syndyasmian," was "founded upon the pairing of a male with a female under the form of marriage, but without an exclusive cohabitation." The "Patriarchal" type "was founded upon the marriage of one man to several wives," and finally, "Monogamian" families were, predictably enough "pre-eminently the family of civilized society, and . . . therefore essentially modern" (1877:27–28). Morgan regarded the family as the most important element in the evolution of society and believed that the first stage in the process was the *matrilineal clan*. He thought that *kinship systems* were related to marriage forms and could change over time. And, as he felt *kinship terminologies* would change more slowly than practices, if you found one in disharmony with current marriage forms you should be able to reconstruct what previous forms had been. Morgan did not consider the fact that kinship might be related to conditions other than marriage and thus was in serious error. Nonetheless, Morgan's early contribution was

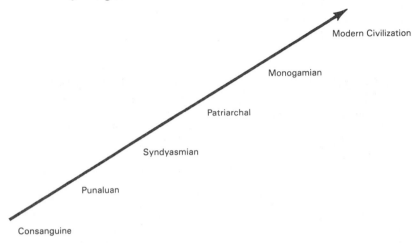

EVOLUTION OF THE FAMILY. Morgan's Model

of significance and stimulated much further work on the subject. We need not go into the details of Morgan's arguments here and, of course, his terminology is outdated, but notice in the diagram, again, the basic form of the argument.

It should not be assumed that Morgan's theory of cultural evolution was quite as simpleminded as it appears here. Morgan believed, as is currently believed by a great many scholars, that the most satisfactory criterion for creating classifications or divisions of mankind would ultimately be on the basis of subsistence (the technoeconomic base, as it is sometimes called in anthropology). He felt, however, that investigation had not been carried far enough at his time to demonstrate this clearly. He thus attempted to link his stages of evolution to important inventions and discoveries and in the process of doing this he further subdivided each of the three main stages into a number of "statuses." The recapitulation of Morgan's scheme, as he presented it in *Ancient Society* (1877:12), is shown overleaf.

Compared to what had come before, Morgan's "grand design" was most innovative and ambitious. Unfortunately, the scheme worked well enough for the positioning of some peoples but not at all for others. Hawaiian society, for example, which by most criteria would rank as a "high" culture, lacked both pottery and the bow and arrow and thus ranked low (Goldman 1959). There were many other such cases as well.

Morgan's most valuable and lasting contribution was in the theory of social organization. His realization that the important issue in social evolution was to account for the change of kinship-based societies into territorial or politically based ones was the seed from which virtually all

RECAPITULATION

Periods.	Conditions.
I. Older Period of Savagery,	I. Lower Status of Savagery,
II. Middle Period of Savagery	II. Middle Status of Savagery,
III. Later Period of Savagery,	III. Upper Status of Savagery,
IV. Older Period of Barbarism,	IV. Lower Status of Barbarism,
V. Middle Period of Barbarism,	V. Middle Status of Barbarism,
VI. Later Period of Barbarism,	VI. Upper Status of Barbarism,

VII. Status of Civilization

I. Lower Status of Savagery,	From the Infancy of the Human Race to the commencement of the next period.
II. Middle Status of Savagery,	From the acquisition of a fish subsistence and a knowledge of the use of fire, to etc.
III. Upper Status of Savagery,	From the Invention of the Bow and Arrow, to etc.
IV. Lower Status of Barbarism	From the Invention of the Art of Pottery, to etc.
V. Middle Status of Barbarism,	From the Domestication of animals on the Eastern hemisphere, and in the Western from the cultivation of maize and plants by Irrigation with the use of adobe-brick and stone, to etc.
VI. Upper Status of Barbarism,	From the Invention of the process of Smelting Iron Ore, with the use of iron tools, to etc.
VII. Status of Civilization,	From the Invention of a Phonetic Alphabet, with the use of writing, to the present time.

(Morgan 1877:12)

subsequent work grew. Morgan's work here was historical as well as *ethnographic* and he made widespread use of materials on the classical civilizations of the Greeks, Romans, and Hebrews as well as on cultures in Germanic tribes and others.

Although Morgan claimed he would present evidence of human "progress" on all seven of the themes mentioned above, he did not really treat them all equally. His ideas on kinship and the evolution of government, as we have seen, were well thought out, presented in detail, and quite influential; but when he came to religion he excused himself with what has since become one of the most widely known and quoted ethnocentric statements in anthropology:

The growth of religious ideas is environed with such intrinsic difficulties that it may never receive a perfectly satisfactory exposition. Religion deals so largely with the imaginative and emotional nature, and consequently with such uncertain elements of knowledge, that all primitive religions are grotesque and to some extent unintelligible. (1877:5)

As a further example of the fundamental theoretical position of evolutionism let us examine the work of perhaps the greatest early evolutionist of all, one who did not dismiss the subject of primitive religion in quite so cavalier a manner.

EDWARD BURNETT TYLOR

Edward Burnett Tylor was a Quaker son of a successful and liberal English Quaker father who owned a brass foundry. When threatened with tuberculosis in 1855 he was sent on a trip to the United States—to remove him from the English climate so that he might recover. While traveling in Cuba he met a somewhat eccentric but wealthy, enthusiastic, and intelligent antiquarian named Henry Christy. Christy was an avid collector of archaeological specimens and items of "primitive" art and manufacture. He soon interested Tylor in such things and the two of them set off on an adventurous journey through Mexico. Tylor, who incidentally had no university degree, soon wrote a successful book on the basis of his travels, *Anahuac or Mexico and the Mexicans, Ancient and Modern* (1861). This early interest, primarily in travel and sightseeing, led Tylor to more serious but related interests. He eventually became keeper of the University Museum at Oxford University, Reader, and then Professor of Anthropology, also at Oxford (Haddon 1930).

In a later book, Tylor provided what is usually understood as the first English-language definition of the culture concept:

Culture, or civilization, taken in its wide ethnographic sense, is that complex whole which includes knowledge, belief, art, morals, law, custom, and any other capabilities and habits acquired by man as a member of society. (1903:1)

Notice here that the term culture is used synonymously with civilization. Thus, as Stocking (1963) has made clear, Tylor was not using the term culture in its modern anthropological sense, but, rather, introducing into anthropology Matthew Arnold's notion of culture (in the

EDWARD BURNETT TYLOR (1832–1917). (National Portrait Gallery, London; Copyright Photograph)

sense of the appreciation of the fine arts, etiquette, fashion, etc.—in other words, civilization). This was quite a contribution in its day, however, because Tylor was implying that savages could at least potentially attain the civilized state like Europeans, an idea that had certainly not occurred to many western Europeans previously. We will return to this point later.

Like Morgan, Tylor appears to have been interested in virtually everything about man; but we will restrict ourselves here to a brief examination of his theory of religion. Like all the scholars of his time, Tylor was naturally interested in evolution and also in origins—hence, in the origin of religion. His explanation for religion, correct or not, must be appreciated as a truly remarkable intellectual achievement.

Many of the scholars of Tylor's day had asserted that "savages" simply had no religious beliefs, or, like Morgan, that they were "grotesque" and/or "unintelligible." Some of these writers, Tylor argued, gave evidence of inconsistency in their works. He decided their understanding of what constituted religion must be faulty—that it was ethnocentric:

Lang, Moffat, and Azara are authors to whom ethnography owes much valuable knowledge of the tribes they visited, but they seem hardly to have recognized anything short of the organized and established theology of the higher races as being religion at all. (1903:419)

Tylor decided religion would have to be defined more generally, as "the belief in Spiritual Beings" (1903:419), and, although he was willing to concede that men could have emerged from some "non-religious condition," he knew of no contemporary men without religion (1903:425). He associated religion with the fact that all men, everywhere, confronted directly two fundamental biological experiences: death and dreams. What was the difference between a live body and a dead one? And what, or who, were the creatures that appeared in dreams? Tylor postulated that humans, in reflecting upon these two experiences, would inevitably be led to invent the concept of the soul. His description of the soul is worth quoting:

It is a thin unsubstantial human image, in its nature a sort of vapour, film, or shadow; the cause of life and thought in the individual it animates; independently possessing the personal consciousness and volition of its corporeal owner; past or present; capable of leaving the body far behind, to flash swiftly from place to place; mostly impalpable and invisible, yet also manifesting physical power, and especially appearing to men waking or asleep as a phantom separate from the body of which it bears the likeness; continuing to exist and appear to men after the death of that body; able to enter into, possess, and act in the bodies of other men, of animals, and even of things. (1903:429)

Tylor believed that "savages" thought about animals differently from "civilized" man, that they did not distinguish an absolute or qualitative difference between men and animals. From the idea of human souls, therefore, the idea of souls of animals would follow as a simple and natural step. And since plants likewise partake of life—they grow, reproduce, and die—it would not be unnatural to attribute souls to them also. Finally, since savages are anthropomorphic, they would also attribute souls to objects such as tools and weapons, sticks and stones. Likewise, Tylor believed that savages did not distinguish subjective from

THE
STORY OF MAN:

A HISTORY OF THE HUMAN RACE,

FROM THE CREATION TO THE PRESENT TIME, EMBRACING AN ACCOUNT OF THE ORIGIN OF RACES
AND THEIR DISPERSION OVER THE GLOBE;

ALSO,

The Wondrous Story of Prehistoric Man, the Cave, Lake and Tree Dwellers, and
the Strange Wild People who Inhabit Africa, Asia, Arabia,
Egypt, Syria, South America, and

THE ISLANDS OF THE SEA,

With a Thrillingly Picturesque Record of the Mighty Convulsions of Nature that
Destroyed Continents, Threw Up Mountain Peaks, Established Lakes and
Oceans, and Buried Beneath the Waves the Ancient Splendors of

THE LOST ATLANTIS;

Showing Man's Advancement from His Low Condition of Barbarism after the Sin
of Disobedience in the Garden of Eden, Including

THE AGES OF STONE, BRONZE, IRON AND STEEL,

Embracing also a Full History of the Ancient Druids, Celts and Norsemen, and those
Bold Rovers of the Sea—the Vikings.

EMBELLISHED WITH

Many Curious Facts Singular Customs, Wonderful and Weird Adventures, and a
Multitude of Marvellous Incidents Connected with

THE HISTORY OF ANCIENT PEOPLES AND WILD RACES OF MODERN TIMES.

BY J. W. BUEL,

AUTHOR OF

"The Beautiful Story,"   "The Living World,"   "Sea and Land,"   "The World's Wonders,"
"Exile Life in Siberia," Etc.

ILLUSTRATED WITH NEARLY 600 SPLENDID ENGRAVINGS,

From Scenes and Incidents Described in this Marvellous Record,

AND

MAGNIFICENT COLORED PLATES.

NORTH AMERICAN PUBLISHING CO.,
ST. LOUIS, MO.
1889.

TITLE PAGE, *THE STORY OF MAN*, BUEL, 1889.

objective experience: "Even in healthy waking life, the savage or barbar-
ian has never learnt to make that rigid distinction between subjective and
objective, between imagination and reality, to enforce which is one of
the main results of scientific education" (1871:445). In consequence of
this lack of judgment, savages would believe that the various phantoms
and figures who visited them during their dreams and trances were real.

Eventually these two beliefs—in souls and phantoms—would be joined together to produce what Tylor termed *animism*. He believed that "Animism is, in fact, the groundwork of the Philosophy of Religion, from that of savages up to that of civilized men" (1903:426).

Animism eventually evolves into two great dogmas, forming parts of one consistent doctrine. The first is the belief in the souls of individual creatures which can survive after death; the second, a belief concerning spirits up to the rank of powerful deities who are believed "to affect or control the events of the material world and man's life here and hereafter" (1903:426). The second, the belief in spirits, comes later in human development and can be traced to the belief in souls upon which it is based:

> It seems as though the concept of a human soul, when once attained by man, served as a type of model on which he framed not only his idea of the souls of lower grade, but also his ideas of spiritual beings in general, from the tiniest elf that sports in the long grass up to the heavenly Creator and Ruler of the World, the Great Spirit. (1903:110).

Having thus established the basic evolutionary sequence involved in the history of religion, Tylor posed related questions. If one has a belief in souls this leads, of course, to further questions—what, for example, happens to souls after death? Tylor suggested that two general answers to this question had evolved. The first and earliest was the idea of the transmigration of souls; the second, the belief in the independent existence of souls after death. Transmigration, he thought, was a system of belief associated with "high" levels. A belief in the independent existence of souls leads to a further question: Where do they go? Tylor argued that three alternatives had been used to explain this: first, and most "primitive," a belief in a land of souls on earth; next, an intermediate notion, that of a subterranean Hades; and, finally, the highest-order belief, that of Heaven.

The doctrine of spirits undergoes a series of changes, too, leading always, of course, from lower to higher. One who has evolved to the level of a belief in spirits must also, according to Tylor, come to believe they can "hover about" people, animals, and objects, and thus act through them and affect them. This idea, in turn, allows the "savage" to carry a useful spirit about with him (since it is believed to be hovering around some object he can move about—a charm, an amulet, an effigy, or the like). It also allows him to place a harmful spirit somewhere else if he wishes. This notion also allows him to set up a spirit (deity) for worship in the body of an animal, in a shrine, or in a temple. For Tylor, this chain of thought explained *fetishism* and *idolatry*, fetishism being the "doctrine of spirits embodied in, or attached to, or conveying influence through, certain material objects" (1903:144). Idolatry was regarded by Tylor as being fundamentally the same, with fetishism lower on the scale fading imperceptibly into idolatry. Idolatry was regarded as an intermediate form of belief, being found neither among very "low" peoples nor among the "highest."

There are times, it seems, when a person's own soul serves him satisfactorily enough, but there are also times when he has a need for far more than that. This need led eventually, Tylor argued, to the idea of personal or guardian spirits—"the interventions of . . . a second superior soul" (1903:v.2,200). But "To the minds of lower races it seems that all nature is possessed, pervaded, crowded, with spiritual beings" (1903:v.2,185)—a vast number of spirits of all kinds. There could be spirits of almost every thing that "savages" used. Personality, we might say, was applied to natural things. This belief led, in Tylor's scheme, to tree worship, animal worship, water worship, patron animals, totemism, and the like.

At first a spirit was ascribed to each individual thing—each oak tree, for example, would be believed to have its own spirit. But this association gave way eventually to what Tylor called "species deities," an idea he developed from a clue he found in Auguste Comte, the famous French philosopher. Comte had distinguished deities from fetishes partly on the grounds that fetishes governed a single object and were inseparable from it, whereas deities (or gods) controlled a number of different objects simultaneously. "Thus . . . when . . . the similar vegetation of the different oaks of a forest led to a theological generalization from their common phenomena, the abstract being thus produced was no longer the fetish of a single tree, but became the god of the forest; here, then, is the intellectual passage from fetishism to polytheism, reduced to the inevitable preponderance of specific over individual ideas" (Tylor 1903:243).

Ultimately out of polytheism arose the concept of a supreme deity, more powerful than the others and in some way having control of all of them. Tylor insisted that the notion of a supreme deity did not necessarily imply monotheism. He felt that any discussion of this problem would hinge on the definition of the relation of the Christian God to its host of supporting saints and angels, as well as the relation of the high god of polytheistic religions to the minor deities of those religions.

Tylor's theory of religion has been criticized as being over intellectualistic. That is, he was concerned almost solely with what people must have been thinking when someone died and paid too little attention to the practical, emotional, and social factors that must also have been

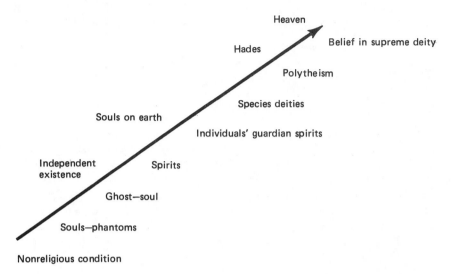

EVOLUTION PARADIGM FOR RELIGION. Tylor's terms

involved. R. R. Marett, another distinguished English anthropologist, brought up the question of practical considerations:

> The mourner has to act as undertaker as well. Here is the dead man's body; what, then, are we to do with it? Here is the dead man's gear, with the smell of him, as the Australian natives say, still in it—that smell which itself testifies to his change of condition. Will he want this gear any longer; or, in any case, do we dare to use it ourselves? (1936:110)

JAMES GEORGE FRAZER, J. J. BACHOFEN, HENRY MAINE, AND OTHERS

Sigmund Freud and Emile Durkheim, respectively, brought up the questions of emotional and social factors. The point here, however, is not to dissect in detail Tylor's theory of religion, but rather to demonstrate again the ubiquitous evolutionary paradigm and how western European civilization (culture) was used as the standard toward which all cultural forms were constantly seen to be striving.

Bear in mind that Morgan and Tylor are here being used merely as examples of a way of thinking about culture and evolution. All of the scholars of the period thought in essentially the same way. James George Frazer, who had been stimulated by Tylor, in his classic work *The*

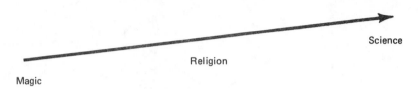

PROGRESSION TO SCIENCE. Frazer's concept

Golden Bough (1890), not only set forth the principles of magic for the first time, but argued that magic was an early form of science based upon incorrect notions of cause and effect—basically that things which were similar or had once been in contact with each other could affect or continue to affect each other at a distance. Out of this faulty magical belief, Frazer argued, arose religion, a higher achievement but one still trying to cope with the question of causality. Finally, he felt, science would inevitably emerge as the correct way of dealing with this question. Indeed, Frazer ends *The Golden Bough* with this rather optimistic prose which gives much insight into the mood of the period:

> The abundance, the solidity, and the splendour of the results already achieved by science are well fitted to inspire us with a cheerful confidence in the soundness of its methods. Here at last, after grasping about in the dark for countless ages, man has hit upon a clue to the labyrinth, a golden key that opens many locks in the treasury of nature. It is probably not too much to say that the hope of progress—moral and intellectual as well as material—in the future is bound up with the fortunes of science, and that every obstacle placed in the way of scientific discovery is a wrong to humanity. (1890:825)

It has been said that Frazer was "the last of the scholastics" and actually wrote *The Golden Bough* "as an extended footnote to a line in Virgil he felt he did not understand . . ." (LaBarre 1954:344). It appears, however, that Frazer thought of himself more as a writer than as a scholar (Leach 1966), which role perhaps explains his remarkable prose style. It also makes the point that anthropology in this early period was less a profession than the hobby of a number of gentlemen of leisure. In fact, there was as yet no profession of anthropology. Nevertheless, at that same time more and more data about non-Western peoples were accumulating, more and more information from geology and archaeology, and more and more knowledge in general.

At this time the term *culture* was used only in the singular and synonymously with the term *"civilization."* But if there was only a single grand tradition—civilization—how was it that people could be so different from one another? Why had some people attained the apex of civilization while others remained "savages" or "barbarians?" The primary concern of all of the scholars of the period was to explain the process of becoming "civilized," and to reconcile, classify, and make sense out of the wealth of information that was so rapidly accumulating. Modern anthropology is much indebted to the gentlemen scholars who attempted to do this, whatever their excesses and shortcomings.

One piece of information acquired by these early students of man was that in some places people did not inherit rights in property and other things through their fathers, as "civilized" people did, but rather through females. J. J. Bachofen, another evolutionist, was one of the first to attempt to deal with this question of *matrilineal descent*. In his 1861 book *Das Mutterrecht* (mother-right), Bachofen argued that social life for humans began with a period of sexual promiscuity. Women were entirely at the mercy of males. In such a situation the only parent relationship that could be determined with certainty was the physical (material) fact of motherhood. But women struggled to liberate themselves and eventually succeeded because of their religiosity. Matrilineality now prevailed for a time, and, in addition, female deities were believed to be more important than male: the moon was considered more important than the sun, the earth took precedence over the sky, and in general the order we now tend to think of was reversed. During this time women established the institution of the family by obliging men to marry them. But, as it turns out, according to Bachofen's speculations, the reign of women was predicated on an inferior principle—the basic and somewhat animal-like material ties between mother and child. Men established the higher religious principle of fatherhood and eventually took control. Thus *patrilineality* (tracing descent only through males) evolves out of *matrilineality* (tracing descent through females).

Henry Maine's *Ancient Law* appeared in the same year as *Das Mutterrecht*. Maine argued precisely the reverse of Bachofen—that originally the family must have been patrilineal and *patriarchical!* Nonetheless, the basic evolutionary point of view remained secure. Maine contended that whereas the unit of ancient society was the family, this evolved in such a way that in modern society the unit was the individual. There were corresponding changes from the common ownership of property to private ownership, and from a social organization based upon principles of kinship to a form based upon territory. It must be pointed out that these basic ideas set out by Maine are widely accepted today. Many scholars are attempting to deal with the implications of changing from kinship-based obligations to those that result from legal contracts. A great many more are still wrestling with the pros and cons of group versus individual ownership of land, of the means of production, and the like. There are many in modern society who decry the breakdown of the family that they believe to have accompanied the process of becoming "civilized." Even Lewis Henry Morgan's basic findings about kinship remain current and constitute the basis for one important school of thought on that subject (Fortes 1969).

There are many other examples of the scholarship of this period —Herbert Spencer, perhaps the greatest evolutionist of all, John Lubbock (Lord Avebury), J. F. McLennan, Andrew Lang, R. H. Codrington, Edward Westermarck, W. Robertson Smith, and more. But let us shift from the men and their particular interests to the questions, problems and implications of the evolutionary scheme itself.

QUESTIONS AND PROBLEMS OF EARLY EVOLUTIONISM

Obviously, when dealing with such things as stages, development, periods, successions, and sequences, there is the problem of when one begins and when another one ends. It was not supposed by any of the evolutionist scholars that the changes they dealt with were clear-cut and precisely defined. Indeed, the very fact that they were not was cleverly used as proof for the general evolutionary notion involved. This argument can be seen in the concept of *survivals* first employed by Tylor:

Among evidence aiding us to trace the course which the civilization of the world has actually followed is that great class of facts to denote which I have found it convenient to introduce the term "survivals." These are processes, customs, opinions, and so forth which have been carried on by force of habit into a new state of society different from that in which they had their original home, and they thus remain as proofs and examples of an older condition of culture out of which a newer has been evolved. (1903:16)

The notion of survivals allowed the evolutionists to explain the presence of certain things—"processes, customs, opinions, and so forth" —in European societies in particular, that would otherwise seem totally inconsistent with their evolutionary framework. If, for example, religion and science had evolved out of a previous belief in magic, how did one explain the fact that in Europe many people nailed iron horseshoes over their doors? Tylor was able to show that in European folklore iron doors kept away fairies and rendered them powerless. This fact he could relate in turn to earlier beliefs about witchcraft. Thus he could argue that the custom of nailing up horseshoes was a survival of previous beliefs in magic and witches. Likewise, he was able to explain palmistry,

astrology, and indeed the entire range of superstitious beliefs and practices of his day. Everything could be neatly fitted into a single theory of
history and culture.

Another question which arose from the use of stages and periods had
to do with the order of various steps. Was it necessary for certain stages
to precede others? Could a society simply bypass one stage altogether?
Did all societies necessarily evolve through all of the same stages? Was
the process, in short, one of *unilineal evolution?* This was an obviously
crucial issue but one that has never been completely clarified in the
history of anthropology. The early evolutionists have often been accused, rather unjustly, of being invariable unilineal evolutionists. The
facts are not so simple. Some of the scholars of the period, such as J. F.
McLennan (1876), appear to have been fairly insistent upon fixed
sequences; others, such as Maine, Morgan, and Tylor, were either not
certain or not completely consistent on this point.

Considerable consequences follow from a belief that the stages of
evolution are fixed and immutable so that one of them must be attained
before the next one becomes possible. Such a belief, for example, allows
one to predict accurately not only the direction of change but also what
form each change would take. Further, although not absolutely crucial to
either of them, the belief in fixed sequences is particularly congruent with
both the monogenic and polygenic theories (that man descended either
from one or from several origins). It is also consistent with what came to
be known as the *psychic unity of mankind,* a position we will discuss
later.

But all of the above notions—evolution, survivals, and unilineal
stages—were linked to still another, namely the idea of *progress.* As
Marvin Harris has indicated, the word progress was a standby of the
Enlightenment, being used to convey "a sense of moral satisfaction with
certain evolutionary trends" (1968:37). The term implies, then, not only
that demonstrable change is present but also that it is in a specific
direction—and this direction is arbitrarily defined as good. Here is the
moral dimension of which we spoke earlier. Even though some of the
evolutionists did not insist on unilineal steps, they almost all appear to
have assumed progress. The progress they saw, of course, led from a
previous condition (a "state of nature," "savagery," or the like) out of
which the contemporary one (nineteenth-century European society) was
believed to have evolved. Thus nineteenth-century western European
civilization was the standard by which change was evaluated—and thus
also science was "higher" than magic, monogamy "higher" than
polygyny, patriliny more "progressive" than matriliny, and territory a
more desirable criterion for political organization than kinship. It is a

"PROGRESS"

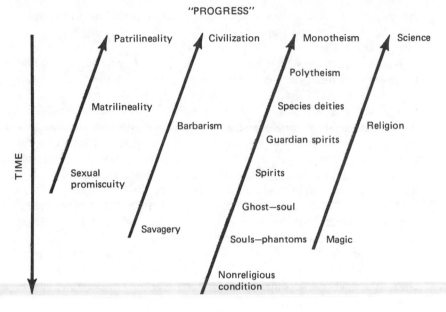

TIME AND "PROGRESS." Evolution model

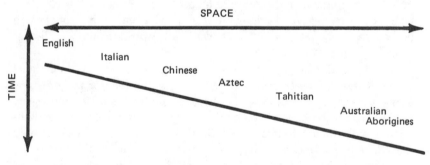

SOCIETIES IN TIME AND SPACE. Evolution model

powerful and insidious notion and one that influences our thinking even yet. The problem is that the notion of progress is fairly easily applied to those closely interrelated aspects of western European culture we call technology, science, and knowledge (although even here there are difficulties), but far less easily applied to anything else. One of the better descriptions of this problem is from the economic historian Sidney Pollard:

Improvement, or progress, has been understood in many different senses. Since the Renaissance, few men in the West, at least, have doubted the continued

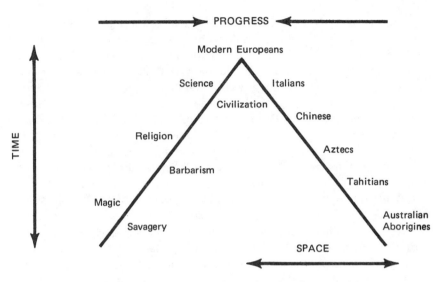

PROGRESS, TIME, AND SPACE. Combined evolution model

progress in knowledge of the environment of man, in the natural sciences, and more recently, few have doubted the continued improvement in technology derived from them. This is the base of the pyramid of the believers in progress and includes all those who believe in progress of some kind. There are almost as many who would add that this technological improvement will also lead, in the future, to greater wealth, to an improvement in the material conditions of life, and this may be said to form the next higher, and scarcely narrower, layer of the pyramid. . . .

There would, however, be considerably fewer, and perhaps a minority only, who would feel equally persuaded that the tendency of the past, to be continued into the future, includes the improvement of social and political organization, and that human societies will become better governed, more just, freer, more equal, more stable or in other ways better equipped to permit a higher development of the human personality. (1971:12)

Pollard goes on to observe that there would be still fewer who believe that people will actually learn to control their institutions more effectively or that human nature will change for the better, or that people will become kindlier or more moral. As he says, too little change has been observed along these lines to give cause for this type of optimism.

Nevertheless, to our earlier paradigms we must add direction—the further dimension "progress," as in the progress-time diagram.

All of this outlook becomes more clear, perhaps, when we consider how these scholars used the basic *comparative method* involved. This method is based most fundamentally upon the assumption that present-day cultures bear resemblances to cultures of the past. Some present-day cultures ("savages" and "barbarians") resemble those of the past much more clearly than do others ("civilization"), so the former, it was argued, could be used to understand the evolutionary processes involved in the development of the latter. To do so it is first necessary to arrange contemporary cultures along a continuum from more recent to more ancient. Such a series, as in the space-time diagram, would have been widely acceptable to the evolutionists. And, as the basic idea is that some societies are more ancient than others, the line on which societies are arranged in space must also slope downward a bit to indicate time (p. 32).

When the distance-ethnic axis and the progress-cultures axis are joined at their high points, the resulting scheme exhibits space-ethnic categories and progress-culture categories in what appear to be corresponding levels, as the combined progress-time-space diagram shows (p. 33).

With this scheme in mind, the evolutionists suggested, the inquirer desiring to know something about the earliest stages of modern European culture (civilization) could gain such knowledge by examining the current stages of existing "savage" societies—Tahitians, Australian Aborigines, or others. That is, one could equate existing "primitives" with prehistoric cultures. This position can be seen clearly in the following by A. Lane-Fox Pitt-Rivers, a well-known English archaeologist:

. . . the existing races, in their respective stages of progression, may be taken as the bona fide representatives of the races of antiquity. . . . They thus afford us living illustrations of the social customs, the forms of government, laws, and warlike practices, which belong to the ancient races from which they remotely sprang, whose implements, resembling with but little difference, their own, are now found low down in the soil. . . . (1906:53)

Archaeologists had conclusively demonstrated that stone tools and other implements of the past did appear in a certain sequence and were also still being used by contemporary peoples. And, since paleontologists had likewise shown that many extinct animals could be understood only through a knowledge of contemporary animals found in distant parts of the globe, the equation of savages with ancestors came to be widely accepted and firmly held. This is not to say that all of the evolutionists accepted this equation literally. Many of them—certainly Morgan, Tylor, and Lubbock/Avebury—knew that existing peoples could be regarded only as *approximating* ancestral groups. In any case, in a revised form, we still retain and use this idea, and there are contemporary evolutionary theories in anthropology that are considerably more sophisticated.

The difficulties with the comparative method, as the early evolutionists employed it, may have had less to do with the method itself than with the absence of solid information about non-Western peoples and with the blatantly ethnocentric, even downright racist, tendencies of the anthropologists themselves. Lord Avebury is usually cited as the best example of both. His works abound with instances of the uncritical acceptance of the statements of travelers and missionaries. The fact that he could accept such statements must be attributed to his beliefs about racial superiority. Thus in *The Origin of Civilization and the Primitive Condition of Man* (1912/1870) we find him asserting that "savages" often have "absurd reasons for what they do and believe" (p. 5), and he acceptingly quotes another "authority" that: "The mind of the savage then appears to rock to and fro out of mere weakness, and he tells lies and talks nonsense" (p. 7). "The lowest races have no institution of marriage; true love is almost unknown among them . . ." (p. 54). They have "no religion" (p. 184), and are "entirely wanting in moral feeling" p. 324). And so on. We have already noted Lewis Henry Morgan's attitude, even though unlike his contemporaries he had actually encountered "savages" first hand, that "all primitive religions are grotesque and to some extent unintelligible" (1877:5). Morgan also argued, in a different context, for the intellectual inferiority of Negroes, saying "It is too thin a race intellectually to be fit to propagate . . ." (Resek 1960:63). Ironically, one might observe that the anthropologists' ethnocentrism was mild when compared to some of the more popular accounts of "odd" people:

In his personal habits no human being is more filthy than the Fuegian. He never uses water for washing purposes, nor cleans the dirt from his skin in any way. He has no more idea of putting water to such use, than he has of drowning himself in it; and in respect to cleanliness, he is not only below most other savages, but below the brutes themselves: since even these are taught cleanliness by instinct. But no such instinct exists in the mind of the Fuegian; and he lives in the midst of filth. The smell of his body can be perceived at a considerable distance; and Hotspur's fop might have had reasonable grounds of complaint, had it been a Fuegian who came between the "wind and his nobility." To use the pithy language of one of the old navigators, "The Fuegian stinks like a fox." (Reid 1861:460)

Mayne Reid, author of the above, seems to have been a traveler and writer. It is difficult to assess the influence of such people but certainly there were many of them during the nineteenth century and much of what people think they know of each other must have come from their popular literature.

The ubiquitous racism of the time enabled the evolutionists to ignore what would otherwise have been a number of more troublesome questions. Virtually all of the early anthropologists seem to have believed in racial determinism, however implicit rather than explicit it may have been in their work. The effect of this belief was on the one hand to keep them from seeing the limitations of their evolutionary theory and on the other to let them ignore questions they might well have had to ask had they not assumed racial superiority.

To understand this distortion properly it is necessary to look at the criticisms of those who followed the evolutionists. But note that the concept of culture, although introduced and defined for the first time, is not further developed. "Culture," as used by the evolutionists, is no more than a synonym for "civilization." The scholars we have discussed do not speak of individual cultures but, rather, of the evolution of culture, or aspects of it, in a generic sense. They were primarily interested in how they, Europeans, arrived at their "higher," "civilized" state. It remains for those scholars who follow to speak of cultures—that is, to speak in the plural, to concentrate on individual cases, and to further elaborate the concept of culture.

IMPLICATIONS OF EVOLUTIONISM

The influence of the evolutionary mode of thought cannot be overstated. It influenced not only anthropology but also psychology, psychoanalytic theory, criminology, theories of art, and even medicine. As the notions involved here survive to the present day, and are related to current racist and sexist positions, we need to consider how this mode of thought came about.

When a powerful new theory comes along it inevitably generates a number of related ideas. One such idea generated by the theory of evolution was Haeckel's "biogenetic law." This was based upon work in embryology, in which it had been observed that features in the embryonic development of individual organisms sometimes resemble those which appear in adult individuals of earlier zoological form. For example, the human fetus at one period of development has gill slits similar to those of fishes. And, because such features sometimes appear in the individual in the same order in which they arose in the ancestral series, the phenomenon was generalized as the "recapitulation hypothesis"— "ontogeny recapitulates phylogeny." That is, the development of an individual organism (ontogenetic development) repeats the development of the species (phylogenetic development). This idea was quickly extended to the postnatal period as well. It was said by some, for example, that the grasping reflex in newborn human infants was a "simian phase in development as well as proof of the arboreal ancestry of man," and that the explanation of children sometimes walking on all fours is that this behavior represents an earlier mode, and the like (Hallowell 1955:15). It was further suggested that the development of the child exhibited recapitulation with respect to thinking as well as other forms of behavior. Thus the development of thought in the child could be equated with the development of thought in the species—the evolution of intelligence, that is.

Once the scholars of the time had this idea it was a simple step to link it to the evolutionary paradigm we have already discussed. This association allowed people to believe that the idea of development sequences found in individuals, particularly in the development of thinking, was supported by anthropology:

> Contemporaneously with the formulation and application of the recapitulation hypothesis, some anthropologists of the late nineteenth century were attempting to apply the biological concept of evolution to nonbiological phenomena. It was thought that human culture had evolved through a unilinear series of states culminating in occidental civilization. Hence the aboriginal peoples that still survived represented arrested stages of cultural development that the more advanced races had passed through.
>
> Usually the backwardness of these savage peoples, implicitly, if not explicitly, was interpreted as an index of their limited mental capacities. Hence, the idea of different levels of mental development within the human race as a whole was supported by anthropology, despite the fact that there was no direct evidence that this was true and that the stages of evolutionary cultural development postulated were arrived at by analogical reasoning rather than by actual historical investigation. (Hallowell 1955:15)

In the hands of certain psychologists of the period—most notably G. Stanley Hall, who was the first child psychologist to give explicit psychological content to such stages as infancy, childhood, and adolescence —this idea permitted the direct equation of "savage" thought with the thought of children. And it allowed people to believe that children's drawings, for example, were like the drawings of "primitive" people. This likening, in turn, was associated with the Lamarckian belief in the inheritance of acquired characteristics.

It is possible to see how simple patterns of behavior in the postnatal period might be accounted for via inheritance without the idea of acquired characteristics—such things, for example, as simple reflexes. But it is difficult indeed to understand how more complicated types of behavior, including thought, can be thus accounted for. If the development of thought and behavior in children parallels the evolution of culture, what can the mechanism be that allows that to happen? The

easiest answer, of course, is that the infant inherits acquired characteristics that were developed by his ancestors in the past. As the recapitulation theory came into prominence and was developed at the end of the
nineteenth century and prior to the discovery of modern genetics, this
was by no means an untenable assumption.

It is from this procedure that people have developed the ideas of such
things as memory traces in the species (Freud 1939), archetypes (Jung
1959), and so on. This is seen clearly throughout the work of G. Stanley
Hall:

. . . We are influenced in our deeper, more temperamental dispositions by the
life-habits and codes of conduct of we know not what unnumbered hosts of
ancestors, which like a cloud of witnesses are present throughout our lives. . . .
Our souls are echo-chambers in which their whispers reverberate. . . . We have
to deal with the archaeology of mind, with zones or strata which precede consciousness as we know it, compared to which even it, and especially cultured
intellect, is an upstart novelty. (1904:61)

As for the stages of development, Hall felt they were a function of
maturation and racial inheritance:

. . . Adolescence is a new birth, for the higher and more completely human traits
are now born. The qualities of body and soul that now emerge are far newer. The
child comes from and harks back to a remoter past; the adolescent is neo-
atavistic, and in him the later acquisitions of the race slowly become prepotent.
Development is less gradual and more saltatory, suggestive of some ancient
period of storm and stress when old moorings were broken and a higher level
attained. (Hall 1904:xiii)

Hall did not give much weight, if any at all, to social, cultural, or
environmental factors in development. He believed the individual
became what he or she was because of the racial past and the level of
maturity. He also held, as crucial to his theory, the notion that the child
had to pass through each stage in order, as one was the necessary stimulus for the next. This is similar to what we find in psychoanalytic theory
and obviously parallels the belief in unilineal cultural evolution. While
there may well be some stages of development in children as a result of
the limitations of physical maturation, this is a matter entirely different
from the evolution of "civilization." Nonetheless, the original theory was
constructed by analogy with the idea of cultural evolution and not on the
basis of independent work.

G. Stanley Hall was a very influential psychologist and this mode of
thinking about the development of children became widespread. But

even more unfortunate is the fact that Freud himself fell under the influ-
ence of the evolutionists' theorizing. It is no accident, perhaps, that G.
Stanley Hall was responsible for first inviting both Freud and Jung to the
United States.

Freud had read all of the major anthropologists of his day; these were,
for the most part, those mentioned in this chapter. There is no doubt that
he was familiar with evolutionism. That he was familiar with and used
both the recapitulation hypothesis and the notion of the inheritance of
acquired characteristics is demonstrated repeatedly throughout his work:

. . . The era to which the dream-work takes us back is "primitive" in a two-fold
sense: in the first place, it means the early days of the individual—his
childhood—and secondly, in so far as each individual repeats in some abbrevi-
ated fashion during childhood the whole course of the development of the human
race, the reference is phylogenetic. (Freud 1920:177)

And again:

. . . The experiences undergone by the ego seem at first to be lost to posterity;
but, when they have been repeated often enough and with sufficient intensity in
the successive individuals of many generations, they transform themselves, so to
say, into experiences of the id, the impress of which is preserved by inheritance.
Thus in the id, which is capable of being inherited, are stored up vestiges of the
existences led by countless former egos; and, when the ego forms its super-ego
out of the id, it may perhaps only be reviving images of egos that have passed
away and be securing them a resurrection. (1935:52)

There is no need to dwell upon the overwhelming influence of Freud
and psychoanalytic theory on the twentieth century. Some of Freud's
followers, particularly Sandor Ferenczi and Marie Bonaparte, have carried the recapitulation notion to even further extremes. Indeed, Otto
Fenichel, in his influential *The Psychoanalytic Theory of Neurosis* (1945)
goes so far as to assert: "Animal crackers, loved by children, are significant remnants of early cannibalistic fantasies" (1945:63). Jung's commitment to this point of view is also well known and can be seen throughout
his work, from the earliest to the latest:

All this experience suggests to us that we draw a parallel between the phan-
tastical, mythological thinking of antiquity and the similar thinking of children,
between the lower human races and dreams. This train of thought is not a strange
one for us, but quite familiar through our knowledge of comparative anatomy
and the history of development, which show us how the structure and function of
the human body are the results of a series of embryonic changes which correspond to similar changes in the history of the race. Therefore, the supposition is

justified that ontogenesis corresponds in psychology to phylogenesis. Consequently, it would be true, as well, that the state of infantile thinking in the child's
psychic life, as well as in dreams, is nothing but a re-echo of the prehistoric and
ancient. (1916:27-28)

As the evolution of the embryonic body repeats its prehistory, so the mind
also develops through a series of prehistoric stages. The main task of dreams is to
bring back a sort of "recollection" of the prehistoric, as well as the infantile
world, right down to the level of the most primitive instincts. (1968:89)

Although this idea still survives, many psychoanalysts and psychiatrists in recent years accept it only implicitly, being unaware, it seems,
of its importance to the theories that inform their work. Since,
unfortunately, much of the work of psychoanalysts and psychiatrists has
become divorced from theory, this does not constitute the problem for
them that it should.

G. Stanley Hall, Freud, and Jung are by no means the only important
figures to have been influenced by these early evolutionary ideas. Jean
Piaget, by far the most influential contemporary student of child development, began his remarkable career in the early part of the twentieth century, just at the time psychoanalytic theory was coming into
prominence. There is no doubt that he was influenced by both Freud and
Jung (Ginsberg and Opper 1969:3). Thus, although it is true that Piaget
does attempt to link mental development to actual studies of children
and their physical growth more precisely than do other theorists before
him, he also incorporated the notion of "stages" and "levels" of development which are unfortunately often spoken of as "higher" and "lower."
He also was interested "in relating the increase of knowledge in the individual to the increase of knowledge in a society," a position he refers to
as "genetic epistemology" (Ginsberg and Opper 1969:210). Because of
the great mass of his work, produced over such a long period of time, it
would be difficult to assess just how much this "genetic epistemology"
has influenced his theory of intelligence. But there is no doubt that it is
closely identified with the recapitulation hypothesis and with the evolutionary theory of culture we are discussing. The following quotation
from Piaget makes it clear that he suspects that adults from other cultures
might well not think on the same level that we (western Europeans) do.

Psychology elaborated in our environment, which is characterized by a
certain language, remains essentially conjectural as long as the necessary cross-
cultural material has not been gathered as a control. We would like to see cross-
cultural studies of cognitive functions which do not concern the child only but
development as a whole, including the final adult stages. When Lévy-Bruhl raised

the problem of the "pre-logic" of "primitive mentality," he undoubtedly over-emphasized the opposition, in the same way as his posthumous recantation exaggerates perhaps in the other way the universality of structures. It seems to us that a series of questions remains unanswered by the excellent work of Lévi-Strauss: for example, what is the operational level of adults in a tribal organization, as far as the technical intelligence (completely neglected by Lévy-Bruhl), verbal intelligence, the solution of elementary logico-mathematical problems, are concerned? The developmental data relative to the lower age levels will attain full significance only when we know the situation of the adults themselves. In particular it is quite possible (and it is the impression given by the known ethnographic literature) that in numerous cultures adult thinking does not proceed beyond the level of *concrete operations*, and does not reach that of propositional operations, elaborated between 12 and 15 years of age in our culture. It would thus be of great importance to know whether the preceding stages develop more slowly in the children of such cultures, or if the equilibrium level which will not be exceeded is reached around 7 to 8 years of age, as with our children, or only with a small delay. (1974:309)

Although Piaget apparently denies the recapitulation hypothesis as such (Gould 1977:144), he was clearly influenced by Haeckel and the similarity between his approach and that of the early anthropological evolutionists is quite apparent:

The fundamental hypothesis of genetic epistemology [Piaget's name for his school of thought] is that there is a parallelism between the progress made in the logical and rational organization of knowledge and the corresponding formative psychological processes. With this hypothesis, the most fruitful, most obvious field of study would be the reconstituting of human history—the history of human thinking in prehistoric man. Unfortunately, we are not very well informed in the psychology of primitive man, but there are children all around us, and it is in studying children that we have the best chance of studying the development of logical knowledge, mathematical knowledge, physical knowledge, and so forth. (1969:4)

Thinking in terms of higher and lower stages of thought is characteristic of virtually all students of intelligence and development—even though it is perfectly obvious that such conceptualizations make sense as "higher" or "lower" only in accordance with some arbitrarily imposed standard of measurement. Thus we find ourselves speaking of "concrete" modes of thought which are "lower" than "abstract" modes of thought, prelogical as opposed to logical modes, animistic as opposed to scientific modes, and the like. In fact, little has been accomplished so far in studies of intelligence, especially cross-culturally, and even if it were possible to demonstrate clearly different "styles" of thought it would still be impossible to rank them as higher or lower except in the same arbitrary way we

BUSHMEN, KALAHARI DESERT. The hierarchical outlook in a headline.
(Copyrighted 1929 by American Weekly Incorporated, Great Britain)

have defined and come to believe in "progress." The decision to classify one task as somehow higher than another is fundamentally an arbitrary one, and it is relative to the culture in which the decision is made. Likewise, the ability to perform well on any given task is also strongly influenced by culture.

It is the failure to recognize this relationship that allows people like Arthur R. Jensen (1969) to argue from intelligence-test scores to inherited intellectual inferiority. All such tests are culturally biased, mostly toward literary and verbal skills, reading ability, context, exposure to certain kinds of information, and other like things. Furthermore, they assume that everyone taking them solves problems in precisely the same way, in the same amount of time, and that, indeed, they are all equally interested in solving them in the first place. Memorizing a long list of numerals is deemed more intelligent than memorizing the location of seal breathing holes in the ice, or the migratory habit of caribou, only because our own culture values the one skill more than the other—there is nothing intrinsic about the tasks that makes one fundamentally more intelligent or "higher" than another. Piaget and others have, it appears, established different styles of thought. No one, however, has devised an acceptable standard for rating the styles as higher or lower. This statement is just as true for the thought of children (where a way of thinking is "higher" only because it in general appears later) as it is for cross-cultural differences in thought (where thinking is higher the closer it approximates our own).

The link between IQ testing and the evolutionary paradigm can be seen in the following statement on what has come to be known as "Jensenism":

> One of Jensen's basic assumptions is made explicitly in the comment printed with his approval in the *New York Times Magazine* (Sept. 21, 1969, p. 14). In this he clearly regards "intelligence as the ability to adapt to civilization," adding that "races differ in this ability according to the civilizations in which they live." Building on this, he further assumes that "the Stanford-Binet IQ test measures the ability to adapt to Western civilization," an ability in which he claims American Negroes to be inferior to "Orientals," with the clear implication that, as a blanket category, they are far less well-endowed than American whites. For an educated man to hold such beliefs is regrettable, but for a presumed "scientist" to be allowed to publish them in a popular journal without informed editorial supervision is an example of the unfortunate failure of intellectual responsibility. (Brace and Livingstone 1971:69)

It cannot be entirely coincidental that IQ scores place different groups of people in the same positions on the evolutionary ladder as did the early evolutionists. Indeed, as Kamin (1974) has recently shown, the history of IQ testings and the early use of IQ scores to control immigration reflects all too sadly the belief we have held about other peoples. It would seem that most people, at least most western Europeans, find it virtually impossible to think of intelligence as contextual rather than hierarchical. This incapacity, as we have seen, is an intellectual legacy from as far back as we can remember; but it was these early evolutionists who presented it in its most articulate form. The effects of this way of thinking about development and intelligence are well summarized by George A. Miller:

> Every culture has its myths. One of our most persistent is that nonliterate people in less developed countries possess something we like to call a "primitive mentality" that is both different from and inferior to our own. This myth has it that the "primitive mind" is highly concrete, whereas the "Western mind" is highly abstract; the "primitive mind" connects its concrete ideas by rote association, whereas the "Western mind" connects its abstract ideas by general relations;

the "primitive mind" is illogical and insensitive to contradictions, whereas the "Western mind" is logical and strives to attain consistency; the "primitive mind" is childish and emotional, whereas the "Western mind" is mature and rational; and so on and on. In its most frightening form, this myth includes the claim that these differences are genetically based and derive from this fact that other people are just not as intelligent as Caucasians.

The dangers inherent in this hodgepodge of half-truths do not derive solely from the blunders they inspire in our relations with the Third World. The same stereotype is likely to be applied to ethnic minorities living in the West. Foreign and domestic policies based on such beliefs are paternalistic at best, and at worst can degenerate into frank repression and exploitation. It is of practical importance, therefore, to establish the true facts of the matter. (Miller 1971:vii)

This early evolutionary social-science paradigm, and it is probably fair to describe it as such, influenced many other areas of inquiry besides anthropology and psychology. In the field of criminology, for example, it became part of an exceedingly important movement in so-called "criminal anthropology." Cesare Lombroso, the most important Italian criminologist of the nineteenth century, was the founder of this movement. The influence of the recapitulation hypothesis is easily seen in the following:

In 1870 I was carrying on for several months researches in the prisons and asylums of Pavia upon cadavers and living persons, in order to determine upon substantial differences between the insane and criminals, without succeeding very well. Suddenly, the morning of a gloomy day in December, I found in the skull of a brigand a very long series of atavistic anomalies . . . . The problem of the nature and of the origin of the criminal seemed to me resolved; the characters of primitive men and of inferior animals must be reproduced in our times. (Quoted in Gould 1977:120)

Lombroso separated criminals into two varieties, those who committed crimes because of poverty or other social situations, and "born criminals." Born criminals were, for Lombroso and his followers, "savages," throwbacks to a previous time. They were identifiable through physical stigmata and they shared certain traits such as tattooing and *onomatopoeia* with savage tribes. Similarly, as Gould points out in his fascinating discussion of this (1977), since ontogeny recapitulates phylogeny, a perfectly normal child must pass through a savage phase as well.

Not content to merely link children to savages, Lombroso later went a step further and brought women into his theory:

We also saw that women have many traits in common with children; that their moral sense is deficient; that they are revengeful, jealous, inclined to vengeances of a refined cruelty.

In ordinary cases these defects are neutralized by piety, maternity, want of passion, sexual coldness, by weakness and an undeveloped intelligence. But when a morbid activity of the psychical centres intensifies the bad qualities of women, and induces them to seek relief in evil deeds; when piety and maternal sentiments are wanting, and in their place are strong passions and intensely erotic tendencies, much muscular strength and a superior intelligence for the conception and execution of evil, it is clear that the innocuous semi-criminal present in the normal woman must be transformed into a born criminal more terrible than any man.

What terrific criminals would children be if they had strong passions, muscular strength, and sufficient intelligence; and if, moreover, their evil tendencies were exasperated by a morbid psychical activity! And women are big children; their evil tendencies are more numerous and more varied than men's, but generally remain latent. When they are awakened and excited they produce results proportionately greater.

Moreover, the born female criminal is, so to speak, doubly exceptional, as a woman and as a criminal. For criminals are an exception among civilised people, and women are an exception among criminals, the natural form of retrogression in women being prostitution and not crime. The primitive woman was impure rather than criminal. (Wolfgang 1960:191–192)

Lombroso's views on women were shared by others and were closely linked with the evolutionary paradigm in still another way, the argument from brain size. Paul Broca, the leader of the *craniometry* movement (which preceded IQ testing as a means of comparing individuals and groups) demonstrated that women's brains were smaller than men's:

In general, the brain is larger in mature adults than in the elderly, in men than in women, in eminent men than in men of mediocre talent, in superior races than in inferior races . . . . Other things equal, there is a remarkable relationship between the development of intelligence and the volume of the brain. (Quoted in Gould 1978:44)

Broca did not believe the difference in brain size could be due solely to the difference in size in general between males and females—because he knew *a priori* that women were less intelligent than men! Topinard, one of Broca's disciples, offered an evolutionary explanation for this:

The man who fights for two or more in the struggle for existence, who has all the responsibility and the cares of tomorrow, who is constantly active in combating the environment and human rivals, needs more brain than the woman whom he

must protect and nourish, the sedentary woman, lacking any interior occupa-
tions, whose role is to raise children, love, and be passive. (Quoted in Gould
1978:46)

The link to children and savages was provided by Gustave LeBon in
an article published in one of the best anthropological journals of its
time:

In the most intelligent races, as among the Parisians, there are a large number of
women whose brains are closer in size to those of gorillas than to the most developed male brains. This inferiority is so obvious that no one can contest it for a
moment; only its degree is worth discussion. All psychologists who have studied
the intelligence of women, as well as poets and novelists, recognize today that
they represent the most inferior forms of human evolution and that they are
closer to children and savages than to an adult, civilized man. They excel in
fickleness, inconstancy, absence of thought and logic, and incapacity to reason.
Without doubt there exist some distinguished women, very superior to the average man, but they are as exceptional as the birth of any monstrosity, as, for
example, of a gorilla with two heads; consequently, we may neglect them entirely.
(Quoted in Gould, 1978:46)

As Gould points out, this might not have been totally representative
of Broca's school of thought, but it does make perfectly clear the underlying and ubiquitous evolutionary assumptions and beliefs of the period.
Darwin himself linked women to a past stage of civilization:

It is generally admitted that with women the power of intuition, of rapid
perception, and perhaps of imitation, are more strongly marked than in man; but
some, at least, of these faculties are characteristic of the lower races and therefore
of a past and lower state of civilization. (1875:563–564)

The field of medicine added another element to the equation of savage
= child = women = the mentally retarded. In 1866, J. Langdon H.
Down, M.D., of London, coined the term "mongoloid" to distinguish
what is nowadays much more properly called Down's Syndrome:

I have for some time had my attention directed to the possibility of making a
classification of the feeble-minded by arranging them around various ethnic
standards,—in other words, framing a natural system to supplement the information to be derived by an inquiry into the history of the case.
I have been able to find among the large number of idiots and imbeciles which
come under my observation, both at Earlswood and the out-patient department
of the Hospital, that a considerable portion can be fairly referred to one of the
great divisions of human family other than the class from which they have
sprung. Of course, there are numerous representatives of the great Caucasian

family. Several well-marked examples of the Ethiopian variety have come under my notice, presenting the characteristic malar bones, the prominent eyes, the puffy lips, and retreating chin. The woolly hair has also been present, although not always black, nor has the skin acquired pigmentary deposit. They have been specimens of white negroes, although of European descent.

Some arrange themselves around the Malay variety, and present in their soft, black, curly hair, their prominent upper jaws and capacious mouths, types of the family which people the South Sea Islands.

Nor have there been wanting the analogues of the people who with shortened foreheads, prominent cheeks, deep-set eyes, and slightly apish nose, originally inhabited the American Continent.

The great Mongolian family has numerous representatives, and it is to this division, I wish, in this paper, to call special attention. A very large number of congenital idiots are typical Mongols. So marked is this, that when placed side by side, it is difficult to believe that the specimens compared are not children of the same parents. The number of idiots who arrange themselves around the Mongolian type is so great, and they present such a close resemblance to one another in mental power, that I shall describe an idiot member of this racial division, selected from the large number that have fallen under my observation.

The hair is not black, as in the real Mongol, but of a brownish colour, straight and scanty. The face is flat and broad, and destitute of prominence. The cheeks are roundish, and extended laterally. The eyes are obliquely placed, and the internal canthi more than normally distant from one another. The palpebral fissure is very narrow. The forehead is wrinkled transversely from the constant assistance which the levatores palpebrarum derive from the occipito-frontalis muscle in the opening of the eyes. The lips are large and thick with transverse fissures. The tongue is long, thick, and is much roughened. The nose is small. The skin has a slight dirty yellowish tinge, and is deficient in elasticity, giving the appearance of being too large for the body.

The boy's aspect is such that it is difficult to realize that he is the child of Europeans, but so frequently are these characters presented, that there can be no doubt that these ethnic features are the result of degeneration. (1866:260–261)

Subsequently, another medical doctor, F. G. Crookshank, in his book *The Mongol in Our Midst*, attempted to demonstrate that what Down argued were degenerations to the "Mongol race" in some cases at least had to be seen as even more degenerate types—orangutans! Still another doctor had suggested that "Mongoloid imbeciles are 'unfinished children.'" Crookshank felt that it was important to "enquire how far such data [on the question of "mongolian idiocy"] are reconcilable with anthropological and ethnological dogma" (1909:24). Given the nature of the anthropological dogma we have been discussing, the arguments were not as far fetched as they might otherwise appear.

It was not only with respect to mental retardation that medical science employed the paradigm. A very famous English neurologist, Hughlings

Jackson, in his Croonian Lectures of 1884, argued that the human experience was one which proceeded "from simple to complex, from automatic to voluntary, from well-organized to less well-organized; in short, as an evolution." Health was seen as an evolution, disease as a dissolution. The diseased person is going through evolution in reverse. In this view hallucinations, for example, are seen as "degraded thoughts" and "the mentally diseased person is a sane man who has been pushed down a few steps in evolution" (Van den Berg 1961:64).

It would be quite easy to cite many more examples of just how pervasive this evolutionary paradigm was (or is) but the above will suffice. As Gould points out, the view still survives today even among such well-known authorities as Dr. Benjamin Spock (1977:119). And of course, it permeated English and American literature and is, thus, still a view to be reckoned with. We are just now facing up to the practical realities of a world in which primitives = ethnic minorities = children = women = retarded = mentally ill, and the like. It is commonplace, of course, to hear the mentally retarded referred to as children and children referred to as "little savages." Similarly, with the failure of the Equal Rights Amendment and the arguments over IQ scores continuing, we must sadly conclude that we have not yet established a new and better paradigm.

SUMMARY

The marriage of anthropology to evolutionary theory would seem to have been inevitable. It was a development of great significance, not only to anthropology but to other academic disciplines as well. Although the early view of cultural evolution has been discredited, there are survivals of it even now—in anthropology, psychology, psychoanalysis, and elsewhere. All of the early scholars who dealt with the subject of man employed the same evolutionary perspective, spelled out in its clearest form in Lewis Henry Morgan's *Ancient Society*. Edward B. Tylor gave us one of the earliest English-language definitions of culture. He also made popular the notion of survivals. Before the evolutionists, the prevailing view of "primitive" people held that they had simply fallen from grace and hence were "degenerates." "Progress" came to be seen as possible, not only for western Europeans but for others as well. But even though they held out hopes of progress for all, the scholars of the period remained ethnocentric, racist, and paternalistic. The concept of progress was associated with evolution in such a way as to allow western Europeans to compare themselves, always favorably, with all others. They equated present-day nonliterate people with people of the ancestral past and were led thereby to attempt comparisons of "primitives" with children and even with neurotics and the retarded. This misdirection was made possible, in part, by the misapplication of Haeckel's so-called biogenetic law—"ontogeny recapitulates phylogeny." Although anthropologists themselves quickly gave up this early grandiose evolutionary scheme, its effects linger on, sometimes in an acceptable and useful form as we shall see later, but sometimes sadly, in a most unacceptable and vicious form. Both will become clearer as we proceed.

FURTHER READINGS

Several books dealing with the history of anthropology also deal in part with the issues raised in this chapter. Marvin Harris's *The Rise of Anthropological Theory* is stimulating. For less polemical views there are Fred W. Voget's *A History of Ethnology* and John J. Honigmann's *The Development of Anthropological Ideas*. For the role of the Smithsonian Institution in the formation of American anthropology during the early period, see Curtis M. Hinsley Jr.'s *Savages and Scientists*. George W. Stocking, Jr.'s *Race, Culture, and Evolution* remains probably the best source for seeing the interplay of those concepts as the culture concept developed. Also see his *Observers Observed*.

For information on the earlier period see Margaret Hodgen's *Early Anthropology in the Sixteenth and Seventeenth Centuries* and the volume edited by Novak and Dudley, *The Wild Man Within*. Andrew D. White's detailed account, *A History of the Warfare of Science with Theology in Christendom*, is especially good on the degeneration theory and the resistance to Darwin and other scholars. The best discussions of the recapitulation doctrine can be found in Stephen Jay Gould's *Ontogeny and Phylogeny* and in A. I. Hallowell's *Culture and Experience*. Sidney Pollard's *The Idea of Progress* is a good recent account of that particular idea. The best statements on race can be found in *Race and Intelligence*, edited by Brace, Gamble, and Bond, in Leon J. Kamin's eye-opening, *The Science and Politics of I.Q.*, and in Stephen Jay Gould's discussion of *The Mismeasure of Man*.

To gain a better appreciation of the period discussed in this chapter, try reading some of the originals: Morgan's *Ancient Society*, Tylor's *Primitive Culture*, Frazer's *The Golden Bough*, or perhaps even McLennan's *Studies in Ancient History*. For even more enlightenment, try reading any of the more popular accounts of the time—Mayne Reid's *Odd People: Being a Popular Description of Singular Races of Man*, or Buel's *The Story of Man*, for example.

A very readable popular history of anthropology is Hays, *From Ape to Angel: An Informal History of Social Anthropology*.

CHAPTER II

Historicalism and Diffusion

Here we deal with the reaction to the early evolutionary theory we discussed in the previous chapter. The so-called historical particularists, inspired by the dynamic and forceful Franz Boas, began to systematically undermine the evolutionary argument. They argued that the search for grand laws of evolution or progress was at least premature and perhaps not even possible. Anthropology, they believed, was essentially history; but history and evolution were often confused. Since there were many existing Indian peoples in America it was possible to establish a tradition of actual fieldwork, to get to know "savages" firsthand. This firsthand observation led to the realization that such things as intelligence, morals, progress, and the like were relative rather than absolute. Other anthropologists during this period argued that the proper subject of investigation for anthropology should be diffusion—the process whereby one culture acquires things from another. These people argued that man was by nature uninventive and most things must have been invented only once. Boas, with his relativistic position, was the first to use the term culture in the plural—*cultures.* His students, with Alfred Kroeber in the forefront, began to explore the concept of culture in greater and greater detail. In the preceding chapter we dealt with the early period in the creation of anthropology; here we deal with the formative years of what was to become American anthropology.

The evolutionists had attempted a scheme whereby culture, or civilization, *in general,* had evolved following a uniform pattern. This scheme implied that when an institution, an artifact, or a belief occurred in similar form in more than one place, that fact could be explained by the uniformity of the process involved in bringing it about—that is, by *parallel evolution.* And if different cultures passed through similar stages in roughly uniform ways, the people themselves must also be potentially similar. They must be intellectually able, for example, to cope with the same processes, discoveries, and changes. This notion of intellectual equality was generally referred to as the *psychic unity of mankind.* In addition to being a critical correlate of the concept of parallel evolution, it was also a necessary belief for all monogenists and thus had a long and respectable history.

But how was it possible to reconcile a belief in the psychic unity of mankind with the prevailing beliefs about racial inferiority? This seeming paradox did not really trouble the evolutionists a great deal because they believed that intellectual capacity evolved in tandem with cultural evolution. Indeed, the first chapter of Morgan's *Ancient Society* is entitled "Growth of Intelligence Through Inventions and Discoveries," and we have already commented on the intellectualism of Tylor. An even better example might be seen in the writings of Frazer, who was interested specifically in the evolution of magic, science, and religion essentially as a cognitive phenomenon. (That is, all three of these are seen as human attempts to explain things not otherwise understood, with science, of course, the highest form of explanation.) This culture-intelligence relationship was at least loosely related to the idea of the evolution of brain size. In any case, this view enabled the evolutionary scholars to assume that the psychic capacity of human beings would be fundamentally similar, *provided they were on the same stage of development.* Thus at any given moment in time there could be some people who were intellectually (as well as culturally) inferior to others since they had not yet attained the higher levels of civilization. However inadequate such a view might be, it at least held out hope for those who had not yet attained a civilized mode of life, and it did not simply write them off as genetically or biologically inferior.

Much of this theoretical position can be understood by reminding ourselves that for the most part evolutionists were "armchair" anthropologists. With rare exceptions such as Tylor and Morgan, virtually none of the fathers of anthropology had ever seen any "savages" or "barbarians" and had no firsthand knowledge of such peoples. In any event, they were interested, not in particular peoples or cultures but, rather, in the "grand design," the master scheme whereby the evolution of civilization out of savagery could be comprehended and explained in its entirety.

PROGRESS AND DEGRADATION

But built into the concept of culture itself, as it had been introduced by Tylor and by Arnold (1869), was the idea of "progression." Where later concepts of culture became relativistic, Tylor's was absolutistic. In this way it was similar to Matthew Arnold's view, to what has been referred to in the past as the "humanistic" view of culture, the view that comes to mind when one thinks of etiquette, the fine arts, nobility, and the like. Tylor's great contribution, contrary to what generations of anthropology students have been told in the past, was not to separate the scientific view of culture from the humanistic but, rather, to "fit the notion of culture into the framework of social evolutionism" (Stocking 1968:87). Tylor's work addressed itself most fundamentally to the refutation of the Archbishop of Dublin, Richard Whately, who had argued in 1854: "No community ever did or ever can emerge unassisted by external helps from a state of utter barbarism into anything that can be called civilization" (A. D. White 1955:304).

Tylor was thus a "progressivist," and was responding to the "degradationists." It was absolutely crucial to his argument that he not distinguish between "culture" and "civilization"—"Culture or Civilization, taken in its widest ethnographic sense . . ."—that the whole history of mankind be viewed as progressive and as leading "upward," toward western European civilization. Thus "savages" could be thought of as moral, provided they were not deemed as moral as Europeans, as religious but not of the higher religions, as intelligent but not at the same level as Englishmen. And, inasmuch as the prevailing humanist view was similar to that of the clergy, at least in that it would not accept that savages could be civilized or cultured at all, this view also was challenged by Tylor.

In some ways, however, the humanists were closer to the modern view of culture than was Tylor. They tended to view culture as a "way of life," as something ideational and integrative, something that was internalized and that gave direction and meaning to life, whereas Tylor's view was of something much more materialistic and fragmentary. The great humanists of the time, like Matthew Arnold, were social critics; dissatisfied with their society as it was, they suggested a more "cultured" life in its place. The evolutionists were not interested in a rejection of contemporary values but rather in how the values had come about and how others could attain them. Tylor's work defined new conditions for thinking about culture which helped to bring about the modern view.

In the United States a different situation existed. Large numbers of aborigines were readily available and there was at least some tradition of *fieldwork*. Henry Schoolcraft had worked intensively with American Indians as early as the 1830s (P. P. Mason 1962). Lewis Henry Morgan, as we have already mentioned, was one of the few evolutionists who was not merely an armchair theorist. He had spent considerable time with the Iroquois. Morgan had also greatly influenced Adolph F. Bandelier, who in 1880 began intensive fieldwork in New Mexico (L. White 1940). Frank Hamilton Cushing was conducting his well-known work in Zuñi at about the same time (Green 1979; Gronewold 1972). Erminnie Smith and Alice Cunningham Fletcher had both conducted independent field research as early as 1884 (Lurie 1966). There were others as well. Even so, it is Franz Boas who stands as the significant figure in American anthropology and who is generally credited not only with establishing fieldwork as an integral and necessary part of anthropology but also with establishing anthropology as a legitimate academic subject in the United States.

FRANZ BOAS

Boas, born and educated in Germany, first encountered "savages" in 1883 when he traveled to Baffinland. This was an important encounter for Boas, trained in physics and geography, as the experience helped to convert him to anthropology. How Boas's "relativism" contrasted with the "absolutism" of Tylor is revealed in one of his Baffinland notebooks:

Is it not a beautiful custom that these "savages" suffer all deprivation in common, but in happy times when someone has brought back booty from the hunt, all join in eating and drinking. I often ask myself what advantages our "good society" possesses over that of the "savages." The more I see of their customs, the more I realize that we have no right to look down on them. Where amongst our people would you find such true hospitality? Here, without the least complaint people are willing to perform *every* task demanded of them. We have no right to blame them for their forms and superstitions which may seem ridiculous to us. We "highly educated people" are much worse, relatively speaking. The fear of tradition and old customs is deeply implanted in mankind, and in the same way as it regulates life here, it halts all progress for us. I believe it is a difficult struggle for every individual and every people to give up tradition and follow the path to truth. The Eskimo are sitting around me, their mouths filled with raw seal liver (the spot of blood on the back of the paper shows you how I joined in). As a thinking person, for me the most important result of this trip lies in the strengthening of my point of view that the idea of a "cultured" individual is merely relative and that a person's worth should be judged by his *Herzensbildung* [roughly, "education of the heart"]. This quality is present or absent here among the Eskimo, just as among us. All that man can do for humanity is to further the *truth,* whether it be sweet or bitter. Such a man may truly say that he has not lived in vain. But now I must really get back to the cold Eskimo land. (Boas, quoted in Stocking 1965:61)

After his initial field experience Boas returned to Germany. By 1886 he was again doing fieldwork, this time with the Kwakiutl of the Northwest coast, who were to subsequently occupy much of his time. Three years later he accepted his first job in the United States and went on from that to completely dominate American anthropology (Rohner 1969; Stocking 1974).

To understand what Boas accomplished, it is necessary to understand the uncritical and speculative use of the comparative method and evolutionism by the Americans of his time. It was a period of the most vulgar racism that attempted to make "savages" as close to subhumans as possible, that arranged everything in stages always leading toward western European society and toward democracy, that glorified the wildest speculations with virtually no respect for facts, and that attempted to reduce anthropology to a simpleminded formula explaining everything and nothing at all. Boas's determination to set high standards for fieldwork, to make fieldwork a necessary part of anthropological training, and to collect ethnographic facts diligently and patiently, was a refreshing response to the excesses of others. Remember that anthropology was not yet recognized as a science or, for that matter, even as a university subject. Thus virtually anyone and everyone who wished could submit his or her views on man and culture to whatever audiences would listen. There was often little regard for scientific objectivity. The *American Anthropologist,* the principal anthropological journal then as now, contains many examples of this undisciplined and imaginative procedure:

The cleared spaces . . . in the African Forests . . . are . . . used by the chimpanzees to build immense bonfires of dried wood gathered from the neighborhood. When the pile is completed one of the chimpanzees begins to blow at the pile as if blowing the fire. He is immediately joined by others, and, eventually by the whole company, and the blowing is kept up until their tongues hang from their mouths, when they sit around on their haunches with their elbows on their knees and holding up their hands to the imaginary blaze. (Büttikofer 1893:377)

And again:

It is a remarkable fact that the center of civilization has shifted from near the equator towards the poles. Today the most progressive races inhabit the temperate zone, while the stolid and stationary ones are in the frigid and torrid where there is little variation of temperature. It would almost seem that a diversified

THE ANDAMANS AND ANDAMANESE.—In an article entitled "The Andamans and Andamanese" (*Scottish Geographical Magazine*, Vol. 5, No. 2, Feb., 1889, pp. 57–73) Col. T. Cadell, Chief Commissioner of the Andaman Islands, gives an interesting general account of these very primitive savages. Perhaps the most striking thing in the article is the favorable account he gives of the appearance and disposition of these people, who have generally been presented to the world in a very unfavorable light. He scouts the idea of their ever having been cannibals, and goes on to describe them as "well-made, dapper little fellows," with "smiling, innocent faces," and "pleasant to look upon"—"such jolly, merry little people. * * * You cannot imagine how taking they are. Every one who has to do with them in love with them." By kindness and liberality the English have succeeded in gaining the affections of all the inhabitants of Great Andaman except the Járáwas, who speak a "totally different language" and differ in their customs and weapons, and friendly relations are gradually being established with the people of Little Andaman.

JOHN MURDOCH.

CURIOUS MARRIAGE CUSTOM IN THE ISLAND OF ROTTI.—In this island, one of the Malay Archipelago near Timur, the bride wears a girdle round her waist fastened with nine knots, which, to make them still harder to untie, are covered with wax. Before the bridegroom may enjoy his marital rights he must untie all these knots, using only the thumb and forefinger of his left hand. Two old women are detailed to watch the bridal couple and see that this is done fairly. If the bridegroom should, for instance, try to tear the girdle off, his father-in-law would have the right to claim a heavy penalty from him. It is said that sometimes a month, or even a whole year, is spent in this process. (Mittheilungen der geographischen gesellschaft zu Jena, 1890, p. 168.)

EARLY ANTHROPOLOGICAL REPORTING. The paragraph concerning the Andamans was published in *American Anthropologist*, Vol. III, p. 236, 1980; the note on curious marriage custom appeared in *American Anthropologist*, Vol. IV, p. 160, 1891.

climate, one of sharp contrasts of hot and cold, of rain and snow, was essential to a progressive civilization, and at all events it is in such that the intellect attains its most vigorous growth. In Europe the Germans and English are in advance of the Italians and Spaniards, and in our own country the people of New England claim to be ahead of their fellow-citizens in the south. (Ferree 1890:148)

Boas's respect for facts, more than any other thing, has led people to argue that he was the father of "scientific anthropology" (Mead 1959:35). His revolutionary work in physical anthropology, based upon careful quantitative data, led the way to the destruction of the commonly held beliefs in racial superiority and *racial determinism* that were so much a part of anthropology before him. His early Eskimo experience led him to abandon *geographical determinism* (the idea that geography determines cultural forms) and he brought to American anthropology an eclecticism that enabled his students to develop in a variety of directions—which, as we shall see, they soon did.

In his famous paper on "The Limitations of the Comparative Method of Anthropology" (1896), Boas attacked the uniformity of change as presented by the evolutionists. He argued that even though some aspect of culture—say *shamanism*, the bow and arrow, or masks—could be widely found around the world, this did not have to mean they came into being everywhere for the same causes and were everywhere part of precisely the same evolutionary process:

The fact that many fundamental features of culture are universal, or at least occur in many isolated places, interpreted by the assumption that the same features must always have developed from the same causes, leads to the conclusion that there is one grand system according to which mankind has developed everywhere; that all the occurring variations are no more than minor details in this grand uniform evolution. It is clear that this theory has for its logical basis the assumption that the same phenomena are always due to the same causes. (Boas 1896:275)

The implication of Tylor's and the other evolutionists' view was one of parallel evolution. That is, if a particular pattern existed in two or more places, it could be explained as a parallel development stemming from a common cause and process. Boas wanted to separate *convergent* from parallel evolution. He went on to carefully demonstrate that in a great many cases the assumption of parallel evolutionary stages was incorrect—that it was entirely possible for the same thing to have come about for different reasons. Using specific examples of social organization, art, folktales, and other items of culture, he demonstrated his thesis repeatedly.

The result of this review was not to destroy evolutionism entirely but, rather, to demonstrate that the presumed regularity of history had been grossly exaggerated. Boas felt it was necessary to have detailed historical and ethnographic information on particular cases before any generalization could be permitted, hence the label *historical particularism* is sometimes attached to this school of anthropology. He believed anthropology should be historical, and that it should be *inductive* rather than *deductive*. He felt that individual cases of historical development were valuable and necessary in and of themselves and that, somehow, they would eventually and in normal course lead to generalizations. This belief led Boas and his students into a rather fruitless series of arguments over "what anthropology really was." Was it history or was it science? Should it seek for *laws*—regularities in the way cultures developed over time—or should it seek merely to concentrate on individual cases, that is, specific histories of specific cultures? Should it attempt to generalize, or was generalization pointless? As Marshall Sahlins has since shown, the argument was generated largely because of the failure to see that there is a *specific* as well as a *general* evolution. The individual historical cases, of which Boas was so fond, are examples, in Sahlins's view at least, of specific evolution; the progression of forms through stages of over-all progress is general evolution (Sahlins 1960:43). Later we will discuss the modern evolutionists, of which Sahlins is one of the foremost. And we will also return to the concept of over-all progress. Thus, the anthropology of Boas, as many have observed, was *idiographic* (it dealt with particular or specific cases) as opposed to *nomothetic* (dealing with generalization from a number of cases).

During Boas's time there was also a belief on the part of many that because American Indians (and other "savages") were rapidly disappearing it was crucial to gather as much material as possible. There was a tendency to think there was no time for theory, that theorizing could come later. But Boas's influence on anthropology, in spite of his failure to leave a coherent theory of culture, was direct and profound, since he was almost singlehandedly responsible for the training of the first generation of American anthropologists—Alfred Kroeber, Robert Lowie, Edward Sapir, Fay-Cooper Cole, Alexander Goldenweiser, Melville Herskovits, Ruth Benedict, Leslie Spier, Paul Radin, Clark Wissler, J. Alden Mason, E. Adamson Hoebel, Margaret Mead, Erna Gunther, Ruth Bunzel, Jules Henry, Frank Speck, Alexander Lesser, Melville Jacobs, and others as well.

Although Boas never offered a precise definition of culture, it is clear that his use of the concept was quite different from that of Tylor and led the way for the emergence of modern versions. Tylor consistently used the term only in the singular—*culture*. In this sense there was one single phenomenon, synonymous with civilization, which some people had and some people were somewhere on the way to having. Boas's fieldwork experiences, along with his *relativism*, apparently led him to perceive particular *cultures*, in the plural, and to appreciate that each one had a unity, coherence, and history of its own. Boas attributed this to "the genius of the people," an idea which we will see was developed later by some of his students in a somewhat different form.

INVENTION AND DIFFUSION

If some item of culture is found in two or more places in the world, one explanation for it is that the same thing was *independently invented* in both or all places. The notion of psychic unity, a necessary assumption of parallel evolutionism, is supported by such cases, and for that reason the notion of independent invention was of great importance to the evolutionists. There is, of course, another explanation—namely, that one group received the item from another through a process that came to be designated as *diffusion*. Much of the work of Boas, but more particularly of his students, revolved around the concept of diffusion and these two possibilities.

Although Tylor and others of his general persuasion were perfectly aware that borrowing occurred and was of importance, this awareness was sometimes overlooked by the historicalists in the United States who were eager to destroy the grand speculative evolutionary theories. It was likewise overlooked, or even denied, by the German and English *diffusionists*, although their positions, as we shall see, were not taken seriously for very long.

W. H. R. Rivers, the founder of British diffusionism, seems to have been the first to formally attack the evolutionists. But the extreme diffusionistic position that developed is more usually associated with the names G. Elliot Smith and W. J. Perry. Smith and Perry believed that virtually everything on earth had originated in Egypt and had diffused outward from that point (Smith 1928). Prior to about 6000 years ago, in their scheme, the earth had been inhabited by "natural man" who possessed no clothing, houses, ceremonies, or the like, and more importantly, no agriculture. In approximately 4000 B.C., according to their simpleminded scheme, the residents of the Nile valley adopted an agricultural mode of life and then quickly invented everything. As Egyptian civilization grew and progressed the Egyptians began to travel over increasingly larger distances looking for raw materials, precious metals, and other things they felt they required. This exploration resulted in the spread of the original civilization. The existence of Aztec and Mayan civilizations in the New World, among other things, was offered as evidence for their view. Smith and Perry did not believe that civilization could have been invented more than once because, they argued, man was basically "uninventive."

The work of G. Elliot Smith is another example of the lack of professionalism that characterized anthropology during its formative period. While Smith was a well-known anatomist, he had no training in anthropology, becoming interested in it only because of a trip to Egypt. He was fascinated by the process of mummification and believed it was so complicated it could have been invented only once—which apparently led him to believe that most everything else could also be invented only once. He determined, on the basis of no acceptable evidence whatsoever, that there was a *culture complex*—consisting of sun worship, stone monuments, mummification, the symbol of the swastika, serpent worship, ear piercing, the couvade, and a number of other things—that could be found virtually all around the world. On the basis of his belief, and very little else, he influenced W. J. Perry, who then helped him to spread his "gospel." These two had little actual influence on academic anthropology itself, though their views, as they found a popular audience, may have somewhat embarrassed and inconvenienced the growing number of professional anthropologists. Such things still occasionally happen today, as is attested by the writings of Robert Ardrey, Desmond Morris, and others who decide to become self-appointed anthropological experts or are mysteriously converted to such by overzealous publishers.

The German diffusionists, the *Kulturkreis* (culture circle) school, was a far more sophisticated and scholarly development. F. Ratzel was skeptical of human inventiveness and argued that contact between groups had to be completely ruled out in every case before independent invention could be granted. He was interested in *migration* and other diffusionary processes and sought to understand their general principles (Ratzel 1896). Out of this, primarily through Leo Frobenius (1898), Fritz Graebner (1911), and Wilhelm Schmidt (1939), the major ideas of *diffusionism* developed. It was suggested that not only did similarities exist between individual elements of culture but also between whole *culture complexes* and *culture circles*. It was necessary, they believed, to understand the migration of a number of *traits* simultaneously, traits which were linked as part of a particular culture complex or culture circle. This is clear in the following:

One of the facts which has been established by culture history beyond all peradventure of doubt is that not only discrete culture elements or small groups or elements migrate and exert an influence, but also whole compact culture complexes. If such a culture complex embraces all the essential and necessary categories of human culture, material culture, economic life, social life, custom, religion, then we call it a "culture circle," because returning into itself, like a circle, it is sufficient unto itself and, hence, also assures its independent existence. Should it neglect or fail to satisfy one of the more important human needs, then a substitute for this must be called from another culture—the greater the number of such substitutes that are required, the more it would cease to be an independent culture circle. (Schmidt 1939:176)

The two most basic rules followed by the diffusionists were fairly simple: (1) the "criterion of quality" (or form) holds that when character-istic similarities are found between two culture elements, no matter how far apart they are, if the likeness does not arise from the nature of the object itself, or from the material of which it is made, we must postulate a historical connection (Schmidt 1939:143), (2) the "criterion of quantity" says simply that the greater the number of items shared by two cultures the greater the likelihood that any one item is a result of a historical connection (Schmidt 1939:150).

Graebner and Schmidt, by looking at distributions of contemporary culture traits, reconstructed a small number of original culture circles or *Kreise*. For Schmidt there were four major "grades" of culture —Primitive, Primary, Secondary, and Tertiary—and within each of these were two or three different *Kreise*. These were not always very clear but nonetheless everything was believed to have diffused from these original places. In the process, cultures mixed and changed:

. . . All the American Primitive cultures, the South American (Fuegians, Gez-Tapuya) and the North American (north central Californians, the Algonkins) once formed an old culture together with the Arctic culture (Samoyedes, Koryaks, Ainu, Ancient Eskimo), whose habitat was somewhere in (North) Eastern Asia. To the southwest, the Pygmy culture joined it and it was the first to separate from there and split up into an African and a (South) Asiatic group. On the Southeast, the preparatory stages of the later Southeastern Australian Primitive culture joined, which migrated from there over the present Indonesia and New Guinea to Australia. (Schmidt 1939:223)

Here obviously is speculative historical reconstruction with a vengeance. Also, despite some confusion over this matter in the past, it is basically an evolutionary scheme, for the "grades" can readily be equated with the "stages" of the evolutionists. The diffusionists devel-oped various methods and principles which, they felt, allowed them to establish measures of time and chronology. Very similar ideas and assumptions were employed by H. E. Driver and A. L. Kroeber in their detailed examination of California Indian tribes and their historical relations to each other (1932). They used long trait lists to establish which items of culture were either present or absent and then attempted to define the most important areas of development for certain culture complexes. This was part of the general interest that developed in *culture areas*.

CULTURE AREAS

One of Boas's first arguments, upon his beginning to work in the United States, was with Otis Mason and John Wesley Powell. It had to do with the principles of arrangement in ethnological museums. In brief, Mason and Powell wanted to display *artifacts* according to their presumed position on an evolutionary scale, regardless of where they came from, and also in terms of which particular human "needs" or "wants" they were believed by Mason to be designed to satisfy. Boas insisted that all of the materials from a single tribe or tribal region should simply be grouped together. Classifications, Boas felt, should follow, not precede the study of ethnographic materials. He argued (1) that there was a danger in classifications based upon "analogies of outward appearance" when further investigation might uncover less superficial criteria, and (2) that only in the context of the whole could the individual specimen be understood:

> From a collection of string instruments . . . of "savage" tribes and the modern orchestra, we cannot derive any conclusion but that similar means have been applied by all peoples to make music. The character of their music, the only object worth studying, which determines the form of their instruments, cannot be understood from the single instruments, but requires a complete collection of the single tribe. (Boas 1887:486)

Implicit in the argument among Boas, Mason, and Powell was the idea of culture areas, which came to occupy the attention of American ethnologists throughout the early 1900s. Although Kroeber (1931:249) has suggested that the concept of culture areas was developed by American anthropologists as a "community product," and probably as a result of the greater uniformity of aboriginal culture in the New World and the absence of a documentary history, the term was first employed in 1894 by Otis T. Mason in his presidential address to the Anthropological Society of Washington, "Technogeography, or the Relation of the Earth to the Industries of Mankind" (1894:148). Mason expanded the idea in the following year, and it was also elaborated by Holmes (1914).

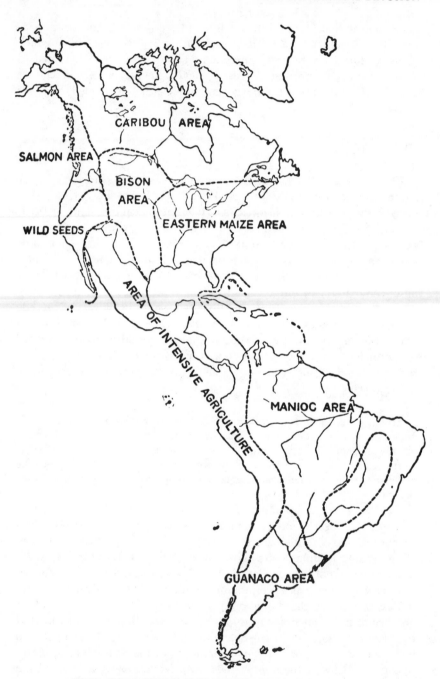

FOOD AREAS OF THE NEW WORLD. (From Wissler, 1938)

SPREAD OF THE HORSE COMPLEX. (From Wissler, 1923)

It is Clark Wissler, however, a psychologist turned anthropologist under the influence of Boas, who is the most strongly identified with the notion of culture areas. In his book *The American Indian* (1917), Wissler named, described, and then formalized culture areas for the entire Western hemisphere. At first he designated eight areas on the basis of the characteristic food available in each; later he elaborated these into fifteen. Thus the Plains culture area was dependent upon the bison, the North Pacific Coast and Plateau areas on the salmon, the California area on wild seeds, and so on.

To arrange groups of people geographically in this way is a simple enough and useful idea for certain purposes, but to also link them to a particular food supply suggests a form of geographical determinism. Neither Boas nor Wissler were geographical determinists. In any case, the thrust of their work at this time was more toward describing trait distributions and *culture centers* than toward explaining them. It remained for later ecologically inclined scholars, as we shall see, to add the dimension of technology to environment and thereby convert this basic idea into one with more explanatory significance.

CULTURE AREAS OF AFRICA. (From Herskovits, 1949)

For Wissler the concern is with the typical culture of the area as defined by the presence of a large number of *culture traits*. Thus in the Plains area a number of tribes possess the traits believed to be characteristic of the area (skin teepee, round shield, sun dance, absence of pottery, absence of agriculture, stone ceremonial pipes, and others). On the periphery of this group of tribes are others which have most but not all of the traits. A culture area is an arbitrary division and contains within it a *culture center* "which coincides with the habitat of the most

TABLE 4

OCCURRENCE OF TRAITS IN SOUTHERN NORTHWEST COAST SUB-AREAS

C, N. W. California; O, S. W. Oregon; L, Lower Columbia; P, Puget Sound
x, trait present; o, absent; –, no data

	C	O	L	P
Body and Dress				
1. Head deformation	o	o	x	x
2. Universal	o	o	x	o
3. General	o	o	x	x
4. Sign of free birth	o	o	x	o
5. Tattooing	x	x	x	x
6. Women on face	x	x	o	o
7. 3 stripes on chin	o	x	o	o
8. Almost solid on chin	x	o	o	o
9. Men, measuring lines on arm	x	x	–	–
10. Women's hair in 2 clubs	x	x	o	–
11. Parted, but flowing	o	o	x	–
12. Dentalium nose ornament	x	x	x	o
13. Women's basketry hat	x	x	x	x
14. Brimless cap	x	x	o	o
15. Brim, peak, and knob	o	o	x	x
16. Flattened cone	o	o	o	x
17. Men's basketry hat	o	o	x	x
18. Brim, peak, and knob	o	o	x	x
19. Flattened cone	o	o	o	x
20. Men's deerskin shirt	o	x	o	o
21. Men's leggings, limited use	x	x	x	–
22. Men's robe	x	x	x	x
23. Of deer fur	x	x	o	o
24. Twined or woven	o	o	x	x
25. Fur strips or mountain goat wool	o	o	x	o
26. Cedar bark or dog hair	o	o	o	x
27. Women's petticoat	x	x	x	x
28. Fringed deerskin	x	o	o	o
29. Fiber	x	x	x	x
30. Fiber for profane use	o	x	x	x
31. Women's deerskin gown	o	x	x	–
Houses				
32. Material redwood	x	o	o	o
33. Sugar pine	o	x	o	o
34. Cedar	o	x	x	x
35. Bark	o	x	x	o
36. Planks vertical	x	x	x	o
37. Breadth 12 feet	o	x	o	o
38. 20 feet	x	o	(x)	o
39. Up to 30 or 40 feet	o	o	x	(x)
40. Up to 60 feet	o	o	o	x

AN EXAMPLE OF A TRAIT LIST. (Portion of a table in Driver and Kroeber, 1932) typical tribes." Culture centers, then, are not precise points but, rather, extensive nuclei. Social units such as *tribes* are different from *culture complexes*, which are "aggregations of culture material" (Kroeber 1931:252).

The concept of a culture area should not be confused with the idea of *age area*. The age area is a concept employed to infer time sequences from space distributions. Whereas *culture area* refers to culture traits as they aggregate, the age-area idea is applicable to separate traits as well as to clusters of traits. The fundamental principles here are that one can infer areas of origin from concentrations of distribution and can infer antiquity from peripheral distributions. That is, the more prevalent a trait is in a given area the greater the probability that it originated there, and the further from the origin point it is found, the older it is likely to be. This statement assumes Wissler's "law of diffusion" (that traits tend to diffuse in all directions from their center of origin) (1926:182).

Despite whatever shortcomings American anthropologists perceived in this general scheme, it was their major focus for a considerable period of time. Perhaps the most important theoretical elaboration of the methods to be employed by diffusionists was an early work of Edward Sapir, *Time Perspectives in Aboriginal American Culture* (1916). Melville J. Herskovits, another of Boas's students, applied it to Africa (1924). As mentioned, A. L. Kroeber began a comprehensive survey of Indian cultures west of the Rocky Mountains using a massive trait list and statistical techniques that he hoped would give him coefficients of similarity—that is, a statistical measure of how alike two different groups were on the basis of how many traits they shared (Driver and Kroeber 1932). He eventually substituted the term *culture climax* for culture center.

PROBLEMS AND IMPLICATIONS

While culture traits, areas, centers, and climaxes may be useful concepts for initial fact-finding and description, they are not very useful for the development of nomothetic explanations. Indeed, Harris refers to diffusion as a "nonprinciple" and argues: (1) that cultural differences and similarities cannot be explained by geographical-historical propinquity; (2) that diffusion cannot account for the origin of traits; (3) that if independent invention has occurred widely, as archaeology now tends to demonstrate, diffusion is a superfluous concept; and (4) that even if independent invention is rare, there is still differential receptivity to cultural influences independent of distance. As diffusion proved to be a sterile

DISTRIBUTION OF THE SINEW BOW. Maps of this kind were often used by diffusionists to show the dispersal of culture traits. (From Wissler, 1923).

notion, it became increasingly apparent that investigators must consider "all the factors of environment, technology, economy, social organization, and ideology" which must be involved in nomothetic explanations (Harris 1968:377-378).

But note that Harris does not mention psychological factors. Thus, while most of this argument is true, diffusion is "superfluous" only if your sole concern is with origins. And surely it is an overreaction to refer to diffusion as "the very incarnation of antiscience" (Harris 1968:378). Likewise, although Harris perceives that "a diffused innovation, no less than an independently invented one, must withstand the selective pressures of the social system if it is to become a part of the cultural repertory," he asserts that there is a single process in the adoption or rejection of an innovation whether the item is invented by the people themselves or borrowed from others (1968:378). Psychologically, this would appear unlikely—the source of an innovation appears to have an influence on whether or not people will accept it; the circumstances in which it is presented can also be influential; so also can the particular values held by the receiving group (Barnett 1953).

It is interesting to note that Schmidt, unlike Harris, thought of culture and cultural processes in psychological terms. Consider this definition of culture:

Culture consists in the inner formation of the human mind and in the external formation of the body and nature in so far as this latter process is directed by the mind. (1939:347)

He defined a culture circle as "a culture complex which embraces all the essential and necessary categories of human nature" (1939:347). This is actually fairly close to Malinowski's "psychological functionalism," which we will discuss in the next chapter. But Schmidt and the diffusionists, like the historical particularists, were more interested in the simple distribution of culture traits than in pursuing detailed explanations, psychological or otherwise. We will return to psychological considerations and the problem of explanations in a later chapter.

Tylor linked the culture concept to evolution; Boas began the separation of the concept of culture from that of civilization; students of Boas began seriously reflecting upon what "culture" means. A. L. Kroeber, one of the first of Boas's students to take his degree, is perhaps the best example of this.

Kroeber had just finished taking his master's degree in literature and was teaching his first classes when in 1896 he met Boas, who had arrived at Columbia, where he had been appointed the first lecturer in anthropology. With only two others, Kroeber enrolled in Boas's first course—in American Indian languages. He became fascinated with the study of language and with Boas. By 1898 he did summer fieldwork with the Arapaho Indians in Wyoming. By 1900 he was hired as a curator for a collection of museum items belonging to the San Francisco Academy of Sciences. Immediately, he began doing ethnographic work among the Klamath Indians of northwest California, being given the sum of $100 to cover all of his costs including collecting further specimens! Kroeber never again left the West Coast except for brief periods in the East to visit relatives or give lectures. He went on to become one of the most significant figures in American anthropology. Although he retained a strong personal attachment to Boas, the two did engage in academic disputes of various kinds from time to time (Kroeber 1970).

SUPERORGANICISM

In spite of several disputes, it appears that Kroeber departed seriously from Boas in only one important respect, but a very important one it was. Whereas Boas had believed the individual, interacting with his environment, was an important unit in the study of culture, Kroeber argued that individuals were entirely subordinate to the culture. It might be suggested that Kroeber, like Tolstoy in *War and Peace*, wanted to destroy the "great man" theory of history. In his famous paper "The Superorganic" (1917), he put forward the following thought-provoking statements:

Here, then, we have to come to our conclusions; and here we rest. The mind and the body are but facets of the same organic material or activity; the social substance—or unsubstantial fabric, if one prefers the phrase,—the existence that we call civilization [culture], transcends them utterly for all its being forever rooted in life. The processes of civilizational activity are almost unknown to us. The self-sufficient factors that govern their workings are unresolved. The forces and principles of mechanistic science can indeed analyze our civilization; but in so doing they destroy its essence, and leave us without understanding of the very thing which we seek. The historian [anthropologist] as yet can do little but picture. He traces and he connects what seems far removed; he balances; he integrates; but he does not really explain, nor does he transmute phenomena into something else. His method is not science; but neither can the scientist deal with historical material and leave it civilization, nor anything resembling civilization, nor convert it wholly into concepts of life and leave nothing else to be done. (1917:212)

Here one sees not only Kroeber's *superorganicism* but also his contention that anthropology is history rather than science. For his antiscience and *reification*, Kroeber has been criticized so regularly that we lose sight of the fact that his was one of the earliest articles that really attempted to understand the meaning of the culture concept, to formally separate cultural from organic evolution, and to suggest the extragenetic or non-biological quality of culture. Kroeber's attitude toward the individual follows from his concept of culture:

The reason why mental heredity has nothing to do with civilization, is that civilization is not mental action but a body or stream of products of mental exercise. Mental activity, as biologists have dealt with it, being organic, any demonstration concerning it consequently proves nothing whatever as to social events. Mentality relates to the individual. The social or cultural, on the other hand, is in its very essence nonindividual. Civilization, as such, begins only where the individual ends. . . . (1917:192)

Kroeber spent much of his life attempting to demonstrate "how patterns of art, religion, philosophy, as well as of technology and science, waxed and waned, acquired their characteristic content and kept rolling majestically along, quite independently of particular individuals" (Harris 1968:328). Perhaps his most famous demonstration of this was his

We may sketch the relation which exists between the evolutions of the organic and of the social (fig. 8). A line, progressing with the flow of time, rises slowly, but ever gatheringly. At a certain point, another line begins to diverge from it, insensibly at first, but ascending ever farther above it on its own course; until, at the moment where the curtain of the present cuts off our view, each is advancing, but far from the other, and uninfluenced by it.

In this illustration, the continuous line denotes the level inorganic; the broken line, the evolution of the organic; the line of dots, the development of civilization. Height above the base is degree of advancement, whether that be complexity, heterogeneity, degree of coördination, or anything else. A is the beginning of time on this earth as revealed to our understandings. B marks the point of the true missing link, of the first human precursor, the first animal that carried and accumulated tradition. C would denote the state reached by what we are accustomed to call primi-

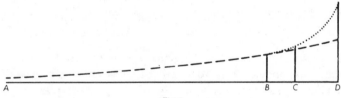

Fig. 8.

tive man, that Neandertal *homo* who was our forefather in culture if not in blood; and D, the present moment.

It is inevitable that if there is any foundation for the contentions that have been set forth, an arguing from one of these lines to the other must be futile. To assert, because the upper line has risen rapidly just before it is cut off, that the one below it must also have ascended proportionally more in this period than in any before, is obviously uncompelling. That our institutions, our knowledge, the exercising of our minds, have advanced dizzyingly in twenty thousand years is no reason that our bodies and brains, our mental equipment and its physiological basis, have advanced in any corresponding measure, as is sometimes argued by scientists and generally taken for granted by men at large.

CULTURE AS SUPERORGANIC. A page from Kroeber, 1917, with his diagram.

comprehensive study of fashion in which he showed how the basic features of style recur periodically, are distinguished from short run "modes," and are largely independent of particular designers. *Patterns* and *configurations* of culture, identified with Kroeber, remain important in the study of culture. He would have delighted in trends such as the spread of "hippie" clothing to the middle class, "Beatles" haircuts, the waxing and waning popularity of Indian jewelry, "punk," and so on.

Kroeber's treatment of the individual as irrelevant to the culture process would seem to place him in the camp of those who would like to believe that psychology is irrelevant to the study of culture. However inconsistent it may appear, Kroeber did not hesitate to employ psychological concepts and assumptions when he needed them, and when he revised his massive and definitive 1923 textbook, *Anthropology,* he provided a thorough chapter on "cultural psychology" (1948).

Not all of Boas's students saw the individual as irrelevant. Alexander Goldenweiser, Edward Sapir, and Paul Radin even more, had deep-seated interests in the relation of the individual to culture. Stanley Diamond says of Radin:

. . . Above all, he stands out among anthropologists of his time for his concern with the individual. Like Boas and Sapir, but more than either, he saw a central task of ethnology as that of understanding the relations of individuals—"specific men and women"—to their own cultures. (1981:67)

This put him in an antithetical position to Kroeber, whose statistical and distributive approach he distrusted:

Intellectually, Kroeber's notion of the superorganic and his consequent lack of interest in the person in history, his sweeping efforts to classify whole civilizations by configurations of traits and qualities, and the eclectic mix of intuitive and quantitative in his methods were opposed to Radin's approach to anthropology. Moreover, Kroeber's insistence—in agreement with Boas—that ethnology was a natural science whose subject matter was composed of discrete, isolable, and objectively determinable elements which could be traced and categorized on their own terms, did violence to Radin's focus on the person as the index and measure of culture. (1981:86)

Radin believed that it was only through a long-standing intimacy with another culture, including a thorough mastery of the language, that an anthropologist could come to truly understand another way of life. Thus he worked with the Winnebago for 50 years and produced one of the most detailed records of another culture ever assembled. This association led him to believe that although "primitive mentality" might differ in degree it did not differ in kind from our own. He certainly did not believe that "primitives" lacked the ability for abstract thought that others had suggested and, indeed, the title of one of his best-known works was *Primitive Man as Philosopher* (1927). *The World of Primitive Man* (1953) is a somewhat neglected but nonetheless brilliant classic of anthropology. Radin, not surprisingly, was the first anthropologist to publish an informant's life history, *The Autobiography of an American Indian* (1920) which later became better known as *Crashing Thunder* (1926).

This early interest in the individual was subsequently, primarily through the efforts of Sapir, to become part of the stimulus for culture-and-personality studies. In some respects Radin was ahead of his time and, because he was a sort of academic gypsy, his work did not have the influence that it might have had. Although he admired Boas he did not entirely agree with him. Although he respected Kroeber, intellectually they were at opposite ends of the theoretical and methodological spectrum.

Although Boas and most of his students often indicated in their work an awareness that cultures had, somehow, a unity or wholeness about them, their concern with traits and elements (and for some of them perhaps, their interest in individuals) kept them from developing this idea of unity to its fullest. There was a tendency to fractionate—to view cultures as made up of bits and pieces—and a corresponding implication of a lack of coherence or integrity. Robert Lowie, another of the most famous of American anthropologists trained by Boas, is usually singled out as being the most guilty of this fragmenting because of the concluding statement in his *Primitive Society:*

> Nor are the facts of culture history without bearing on the adjustment of our own future. To that planless hodgepodge, that thing of shreds and patches called civilization, its historian can no longer yield superstitious reverence. He will realize better than others the obstacles to infusing design into the amorphous product; but in thought at least he will not grovel before it in fatalistic acquiescence but dream of a rational scheme to supplant the chaotic jumble. (1920:331)

However fairly or unfairly, it was to the "shreds and patches" notion that the next important development in anthropology addressed itself. It also spoke increasingly to the related theoretical questions of anthropology as history, as superorganic, and as psychological.

SUMMARY

As is often the case when a new idea comes into being and is promoted for a time, the reaction to it becomes an overreaction. This was the case with the historical particularists' reaction to the early evolutionists. The search for a grand theory that would explain all, they argued, was ill-advised if not useless. Anthropology was history. It was idiographic. If a person wanted understanding it could only come through patient, detailed study of individual cases of cultural growth and change. Boas, the giant of American anthropology, sent his students into the field to gather all the data they could—Indian cultures, like the buffalo and the passenger pigeon, were quickly disappearing; they could theorize later. When they did examine their materials it was mainly in terms of the diffusion and distribution of traits rather than in terms of their invention or discovery. Tylor introduced the term *culture* into English; Boas was the one who perceived that "culture" had a plural form. His students, trained to be eclectic, began their own investigations out of which American anthropology was born and the culture concept came under more and more systematic scrutiny. Alfred Kroeber, Boas's first student, led the way with his claim for the superorganic nature of culture.

FURTHER READINGS

In addition to Harris's very negative account of historicalism and diffusionism, two of the older histories of anthropology have much to say on the subject: Lowie's *The History of Ethnological Theory* and Haddon's *History of Anthropology*. The clearest exposition on the methods of the diffusionists can be found in Schmidt's *The Culture Historical Method of Ethnology*. For a discussion of the confusion over evolutionism see Sahlins and Service, *Evolution and Culture*. Also see Honigmann's *The Development of Anthropological Ideas*, Voget's *A History of Ethnology*, and Leaf's *Man, Mind, and Science: A History of Anthropology*.

For further materials on Boas see Goldschmidt's *The Anthropology of Franz Boas*; Herskovits, *Franz Boas: The Science of Man in the Making*; Rohner's *The Ethnography of Franz Boas*, and Stocking's *The Shaping of American Anthropology 1883-1911*.

For the ambitious, Matthew Arnold's *Culture and Anarchy* might be contrasted with Tylor's *Primitive Culture*, for two quite different treatments of the idea of culture. Some of the books of the time that present discussions of particular instances of diffusion are Wissler's *The American Indian*, Lowie's *Culture and Ethnology*, and Kroeber's *Anthropology*. The extreme and fanciful diffusionism of G. E. Smith and W. J. Perry can be found in their respective books *In the Beginning: The Origin of Civilization* and *Children of the Sun*. Ralph Linton's *The Study of Man* contains a marvelously readable chapter on diffusion, and Wissler's classic paper, "Influence of the Horse in the Development of Plains Culture," is still of interest as well.

Structure and Function

The next period in the history of anthropology is associated with two of the most distinguished figures in the profession: the brilliant Pole Bronislaw Malinowski, trained as an anthropologist in England, and his rival for a following, the Englishman A. R. Radcliffe-Brown. It would appear inevitable that the theoretically limited approach of the historical particularists would have to give way eventually to a more conceptually oriented anthropology. It would seem equally clear that the culture concept itself would be subjected to closer scrutiny as to its meaning and utility. Gathering masses of data over long periods of time is all very well, but eventually it becomes imperative to have some way of ordering and interpreting such data. A theory is needed to generate hypotheses that can then be tested against further data. This theoretical vacuum was filled by what came to be called the *functionalists.* Although we concentrate here mainly on Malinowski and Radcliffe-Brown, it is import to realize that each of them represents an approach in anthropology that was followed by many others.

Radcliffe-Brown, for reasons that are not completely clear, tended to create more ardent disciples than did Malinowski. But the latter certainly did not lack for students and the two of them for a time were the dominant figures in both American and British anthropology. The effect of their work is part of what has been described as a "Copernican revolution" in anthropology. We will discuss the other part of this revolution in the chapter to follow.

It has been remarked that Boas and his students "forged a discipline out of a curiosity" (Murphy 1972:43). Certainly Robert H. Lowie was one of the most significant figures in this accomplishment. Lowie was born in Vienna in 1883 but when he was ten his family emigrated to New York City. His precociousness and ambition can be seen in the fact that he received his B.A. degree from the City College in New York by the time he was eighteen. He then taught for a short time before taking summer courses at Columbia where, like Kroeber, he met Boas and decided on a career in anthropology, insofar as there was such a thing in those days. Clark Wissler, another of the early "greats" of American anthropology, had just been appointed to the chairmanship of the Department of Anthropology at the American Museum of Natural History. He, along with Boas, directed Lowie's career. It was Wissler who arranged for Lowie's first fieldwork with the Shoshone in Idaho in 1906. And it was also Wissler who appointed Lowie as assistant in the American Museum. Their association had lasted for fourteen years when Lowie joined the University of California faculty at Berkeley in 1921, after virtually all of his fieldwork with American Indians was finished (Murphy 1972).

To understand his famous "shreds and patches" statement it is necessary to remember that Lowie, like all of his colleagues, was reacting to the only major anthropological theory of the time—evolutionism. And like Boas, Lowie brought with him to anthropology the same German interest in science, empiricism, and above all to facts and caution. Lowie virtually made his career out of demonstrating over and over again that the stages of evolution postulated by Morgan, Tylor, and others simply would not stand up to the facts. He was a truly unusual and dedicated fact collector. At his death he probably knew more about North American Indians than any other person, and he also had vast quantities of information on other parts of the world. Lowie believed that the demonstrable facts of diffusion completely negated the evolutionists. Thus he argued, with all kinds of ethnographic examples, that the evolutionists were misinformed:

. . . One of Lowie's favorite examples was that of the bow and arrow, which had been diffused throughout the New World and were used by the simplest of hunters and collectors as well as by the armies of great states. This was enough to place even the rudest of the American Indians in the stage of Upper Savagery, one notch above the Polynesians, whose islands had not been reached by the weapon. . . . Yet, the Polynesians were consummate navigators and skilled agriculturalists, possessing stratified societies of remarkable sophistication. Obviously, in this case the progress of the Polynesians had little to do with whether or not they used the bow and arrow. In other technological items, entire stages of evolution were simply bypassed. One common assumption of the evolutionists was that man emerged from the Stone Age to the use of copper, thence to

bronze, and finally to iron. This sequence is borne out by Near Eastern archaeology and undoubtedly represents the actual world-wide sequence of the emergence
of the inventions. But, as Lowie pointed out, the Africans went directly from the
Stone Age to an Iron Age through borrowing. . . . (Murphy 1972:49-50)

This kind of all-out attack completely discredited evolutionism for a
time and earned Lowie a reputation for being destructive but not very
constructive. Like many such accusations, this is a much oversimplified
view. Lowie was well aware that the evolutionists recognized diffusion.
But he felt they had not fitted it adequately into evolutionary theory. He
was also aware there could be multiple origins for things and, in fact,
argued that the *clan* had multiple origins. Lowie was not out to destroy
evolutionism so much as he was to insist that the evidence must always
come first.

Although he can be classified basically as a historical particularist and
a diffusionist, Lowie's views went beyond these points of view to antici-
pate what was to follow, namely, the position known as *functionalism:*

. . . His early work on kinship predated the publications of Malinowski and the
theoretical writings of Radcliffe-Brown, and his criticism of Morgan rested heavily on Morgan's failure to see facts in a contemporary relationship to each other.
And, although it is well remembered that the great British functionalists were
scathing in their denunciation of historical reconstructions, or "conjectural
history," based upon alleged "survivals" of earlier stages of history, Lowie led the
way in his attack upon Morgan's notion that kinship nomenclatures were, in
themselves, survivals. He showed them, instead, to be living and vital parts of
social organisms. But he was a cautious functionalist, whose aims were also
historical. (Murphy 1972:65)

That anthropologists should see cultural facts in their current relationship to each other rather than historically or in evolutionary perspective
became the most basic tenet of functionalism, the development which
followed historical particularism.

Lowie's position on culture, which he expressed early in his first book,
Culture and Ethnology (1917), was similar to Kroeber's view—that
culture was, somehow, a reality of its own, and the causes of culture
would be found only in culture itself. This similarity indicates that
Kroeber was not alone in beginning to question the meaning of the term
culture. Anthropology was expanding and becoming more self-critical
and reflective.

By 1911 eight people had received their anthropological credentials
under Boas: Clark Wissler, Alfred L. Kroeber, William Jones, Albert B.

Lewis, Robert H. Lowie, Edward Sapir, Alexander Goldenweiser, and Paul Radin. As this "first generation" of anthropologists moved out, finding jobs wherever they could, Boas trained others. Soon Columbia ceased to be the only university where anthropological training could be obtained. The University of California, Berkeley, created a department of anthropology, as did others: the University of Chicago, Harvard, Yale, Pennsylvania, Michigan. Still others followed. The number of professional anthropologists kept growing and, encouraged by the eclectic Boas and the similarly eclectic first generation, kept finding new problems and trying new methods and techniques. It was a period of rapid expansion and great activity.

The "second" and subsequent generations of American anthropologists continued their *salvage ethnography* with American Indians in an effort to record these cultures before they were destroyed, but they also began extending their research further afield. Ralph Linton was in the Marquesas by 1920. Margaret Mead did her first fieldwork in Samoa in 1925. Robert Redfield was doing his early work in Mexico in 1926. By the early 1930s many American anthropologists were doing fieldwork overseas. The British, too, were conducting more and more field studies, particularly in Africa. Even so, until the 1930s no dominant orientation or clear-cut theoretical position had emerged to replace historical particularism. And it was still believed by many that to be a successful anthropologist one had to be well versed in all areas of anthropology. Thus the same person was often cultural anthropologist, physical anthropologist, linguist, and archaeologist all joined into one. Linton, in fact, went to the Marquesas as an archaeologist, but changed his interest while in the field and reported on the living Marquesans instead. Several of the anthropologists of this time combined archaeology with their ethnological studies of remnant American Indian groups. Alfred Bowers, who did both archaeological and ethnological work with the Mandan and Hidatsa, is a good example of this combination (Bowers 1950). All of this was soon to change.

In their attempt to show the inadequacies of the early evolutionists the historical particularists did at times tend to overreact. Whereas the evolutionists dealt with the over-all process that had led to civilization (culture), the particularists argued that it was necessary to study individual cultures. Where the evolutionists presented a grand, all-encompassing theory, the particularists became virtually antitheoretical, cautioning always that adequate theory would follow only after the painstaking collection of all the facts. Where the evolutionists reconstructed history the particularists demanded accurate, detailed, historical data. It was a relatively simple matter for the particularists to demonstrate, in case after case as Lowie and others did, that the evolutionary paradigm was incorrect. They produced cases where, in the evolutionists' view, people who should have been matrilineal were in fact patrilineal. They found people who should have been polytheistic but who were monotheistic. They also produced cases demonstrating that the same custom could arise in two different places for quite different reasons, thus destroying the notion that similarities were necessarily the result of parallel evolution. But in all this criticism they failed to come up with a coherent body of theory of their own. The world we observe being exceedingly complex, it can be comprehended only through adequate concepts that fit together and give it meaning. But this conceptualization was precisely what was missing in the work of Boas and the first generation of particularists. Melford Spiro had put it very well:

That the method of radical empiricism (historical particularism) should have led, too, to scientific agnosticism, is not at all surprising. Cultural phenomena are indeed complex, as Boas rightly cautioned; but this method could hardly have decreased the impression of their complexity. The fact is, of course, that the phenomenal world—the physical no less than the cultural—is always complex; it is, as William James put it, a "booming, buzzing confusion." Hence, it is at least arguable that the order and simplicity now perceived to characterize the physical world are conceptual rather than phenomenal. For we anthropologists are no exception to a universal law of perception: viz., that any stimulus field becomes a perceptually meaningful field only when it is structured. But having decided to collect all the ethnographic facts, and to collect them as objectively as possible—that is, without explicit theory—anthropology was confronted with an enormous corpus of unstructured ethnographic material. And, as in any other unstructured situation, the resultant perception was one of enormous complexity. (Spiro 1972:577)

Two of the developments to emerge out of this background, at virtually the same time—the 1920s—were *functionalism* and British (as opposed to French) *structuralism*. More precisely we should term these *psychological functionalism* and *structural functionalism*. The first of these is associated with Bronislaw Malinowski and the second with A. R. Radcliffe-Brown. It is strange, perhaps, that the two major influences on American anthropology at this time both came from British-trained anthropologists. But however strange, the impact of these two scholars was by far the most important and exciting development in anthropology since Tylor and changed the Boasian tradition into a more dynamic enterprise.

BRONISLAW MALINOWSKI

What Radcliffe-Brown was attempting to do can be better understood when we first consider his "competitor," Bronislaw Malinowski. Born in Krakow (then in Austria though now in Poland), Malinowski received a Ph.D. in physics and mathematics but shortly thereafter was threatened with tuberculosis. He is reported to have walked from his university with Frazer's *The Golden Bough* under his arm, determined to read it in the original English to take his mind off his problem. As quoted by H. R. Hays, Malinowski later commented:

No sooner had I read this great work than I became immersed in it and enslaved by it. I realized then that anthropology, as presented by Sir James Frazer, is a great science, worthy of as much devotion as any of her elder and more exact sister studies and I became bound to the service of Frazerian anthropology. (Hays 1958:314)

In 1910 Malinowski, whose health had improved, entered the London School of Economics, where he met Sir James Frazer and studied anthropology under A. C. Haddon, C. G. Seligman, and Edward Westermarck. In 1914 he was traveling in the Pacific. With the outbreak of the World War he became technically an "enemy alien" because of his place of birth. He was allowed by a sympathetic Australian government to stay in the Trobriand Islands, provided some modest financial assistance, and between 1915 and 1918 spent approximately two full years in ethnographic research. This was a development of great significance for the growing science of anthropology, for out of it Malinowski fashioned not only a number of now classic books but also a stimulating theory of cultures.

Although Malinowski did not cut himself off from other Europeans entirely he did pitch his tent in a Trobriands village and spent his time in much more intensive day-to-day contact with his subjects than had any previous anthropologist. Within six months he understood their language well enough to dispense with an interpreter. He could thus later speak with an authority previously unknown on matters of native culture and, as he was also a gifted writer, he emerged for a time as the unchallenged leader of anthropology in Britain. The standard he set for ethnographic fieldwork has rarely been surpassed to this day.

Malinowski's functionalism included many of Radcliffe-Brown's principles but went far beyond them. Beyond the *sociological functionalism* that both scholars took from Durkheim and their previous somewhat

SYNOPTIC SURVEY OF BIOLOGICAL AND DERIVED NEEDS AND THEIR SATISFACTION IN CULTURE

A Basic Needs (Individual)	B Direct Responses (Organized, i.e., Collective)	C Instrumental Needs	D Responses to Instrumental Needs	E Symbolic and Integrative Needs	F Systems of Thought and Faith
Nutrition (metabolism).....	Commissariat	Renewal of cultural apparatus	Economics	Transmission of experience by means of precise, consistent principles	Knowledge
Reproduction...	Marriage and family				
Bodily comforts.	Domicile and dress	Charters of behavior and their sanctions	Social control		
Safety.........	Protection and defense			Means of intellectual, emotional, and pragmatic control of destiny and chance	Magic Religion
Relaxation.....	Systems of play and repose	Renewal of personnel	Education		
Movement.....	Set activities and systems of communication				
Growth........	Training and apprenticeship	Organization of force and compulsion	Political organization	Communal rhythm of recreation, exercise, and rest	Art Sports Games Ceremonial

MALINOWSKI'S BASIC HUMAN NEEDS. This table presents essentials of his "pure functionalism." (1939a:938–964)

similar training, Malinowski's theory went on to build on what he felt were seven basic human "needs." Culture was seen as the instrument through which these needs were met. Malinowski, however, insisted that there were individual as well as group needs, and it was here that the greatest rift occurred between structural functionalism and Malinowski's more comprehensive psychological functionalism, which he referred to as "pure functionalism." The differences are well expressed in the following:

> Professor Radcliffe-Brown is, as far as I can see, still developing and deepening the views of the French sociological school. He thus has to neglect the individual and disregard biology.
>
> Functionalism differs from other sociological theories more definitely, perhaps, in its conception and definition of the individual than in any other respect. The functionalist includes in his analysis not merely the emotional as well as intellectual side of mental processes, but also insists that man in his full biological reality has to be drawn into our analysis of culture. The bodily needs and environmental influences, and the cultural relation to them, have thus to be studied side by side. (Malinowski 1939a:939)

The emphasis on the individual and on biological and psychological factors in addition to purely social facts was one that was being promoted by others at the same time, as we shall see. The main thrust of Malinowski's functionalism, however, consisted of showing how the various elements of culture contributed to the culture as a unified, consistent whole. This outlook entailed always attempting to correlate one set of activities with the whole. In this work he was doing what Radcliffe-Brown was attempting to do with social systems. But Malinowski was much more ambitious. In *Coral Gardens and Their Magic* (1935), for example, Malinowski focused on horticultural activities and attempted to relate them to the cultural whole—which included such things as the family, the kinship system, political organization, land tenure, technical processes, religion, and magic. He demonstrated how important it was to see customs, beliefs, and institutions in their cultural context, and he continually railed at those who attempted to pull out "traits" or artifacts and study them in isolation—thus dissenting from the "shreds and patches" notion of Lowie (Lowie 1920:331). Nor did he believe one could readily compare items cross-culturally, not because each culture had a unique history, but because of the dangers of violating their proper context and hence changing them into something they were not.

At the same time that institutions or customs had to be shown as contributing to the culture as a whole, they also had to be shown as meeting specific human needs—for, after all, what was culture but a "vast instrumental reality," created precisely for that purpose? However we may look back on it today, it was at the time an ambitious and exciting scheme. Malinowski shared with Radcliffe-Brown the use of the concept "function," the belief that people were organized in "systems," that these constituted "wholes" of some kind, and that the parts therefore contributed something to their wholeness. They both believed in the importance of fieldwork and they also shared the belief that anthropology should be a science, not a pseudohistory. Above all, they both believed anthropology should be theoretical and not merely an exercise in random fact gathering. Since they wrote and taught during precisely the same period, the combination produced an electrifying effect on anthropology. The late Audrey Richards gives us some idea of this when speaking of Malinowski:

> The idea that rites, beliefs, and customs, however extraordinary they appear to an observer, actually fill "needs," biological, psychological, and social, became commonplace in anthropological teaching. It is difficult now to believe that Malinowski's teaching on this point could ever have struck his students as being brilliantly new. The changed outlook was probably due to the fact that discussions of the function of aspects or institutions of tribal life led directly into fieldwork material, either Malinowski's own extraordinarily rich collection of field notes or those of his first students. Those who listened to his lectures on the Trobriand Islanders will remember his intense absorption in the activities of the people he described and his stress on what actually happened as distinct from what anthropologists had guessed had happened in the past. This gave the work a vividness which the existing textbooks, and even the best contemporary missionary or anthropological monographs, lacked. Were kinship terms a survival of past stages in history? The answer lay, Malinowski would tell us, in the empirical material. How were the terms used? What was the index of emotional content? Or again, what was the function of myth or folk tale? The answer lay in a description of how these stories were actually recited; the occasions on which they were recited, and the manner of those who spoke, whether it was bragging, serious or lighthearted. In comparison with works such as those of Frazer, Crawley, Westermarck, or Durkheim which we read at the time, or with the ethnographic work produced by observers paying short visits to different tribes, such as that of Rivers or Seligman, the work seemed lively and stimulating, and we began actually to visualize ourselves "in the field." (1957:18-19)

It appears that one reason many of the British anthropologists entered the camp of Radcliffe-Brown rather than follow Malinowski lay in the sheer bulk and richness of the ethnographic materials that had to be presented as a description of a culture. They felt it was unmanageable and thus they chose to abstract one important feature, social structure, and attempted to make it the prevailing and only legitimate anthropological interest:

> The complexity of primitive institutions that was revealed by such methods [Malinowski's] and their wide limits of variation began to strike with alarm those who were optimistic enough to believe that social typologies could be immediately constructed, and by those who hoped to reduce their material to a few simple abstract postulates. Malinowski and his pupils were considered to have collected

BRONISLAW MALINOWSKI (1884–1942). (London School of Economics and Political Science)

too many facts of too many kinds to make simple comparative work possible. Gluckman described Malinowski's data as "too complex for comparative work" and he and Evans-Pritchard have constantly criticized it as being "overloaded with (cultural) reality" . . .

. . . They did not come to the conclusion that the comparisons they had in mind were too ambitious for the existing state of our knowledge, but decided instead that it would be better to have fewer facts, so as to make the comparisons easier. (Richards 1957:28)

Thus it was Malinowski and his followers who carried on and added to the study of culture in Great Britain. Although Malinowski did not improve much on Tylor's definition of 1871, his influence was overwhelming with respect to demonstrating the crucial significance of the concept. He was selected to write the article on "culture" in the American *Encyclopedia of the Social Sciences* in 1931. In this article he wrote, "The social heritage (culture) is the key concept of cultural anthropology" (1931:621), and thus set forth a way of thinking about anthropology and culture that remains a key ingredient in our notions of culture today.

In the culture concept of Malinowski, and to a somewhat lesser extent in the structural functionalism of Radcliffe-Brown, we see clearly the influence of Matthew Arnold's view of culture as it contrasted with that of Tylor:

. . . Although Tylor thought rather more in terms of evolutionary product and Arnold of individual process, both men conceived culture in normative humanist terms as a conscious "cultivation" of the capacities which are most characteristically human. But while Tylor took humanistic culture and fragmented it for purposes of analysis, Arnold's culture . . . was, both for the individual and for society, an organic, integrative, holistic phenomenon. Tylor's analytic evolutionary purpose forced him to place great emphasis on the artifactual manifestations of culture, on those objects of "material culture" which were easily and convincingly arranged in hierarchical sequence; Arnold's culture, like that of most modern anthropologists, was an inward ideational phenomenon. For Arnold much more than for Tylor culture was a "way of life." (Stocking 1963:795)

A. R. RADCLIFFE-BROWN

At the same time that Boas was turning out the first generation of his students in America, A. R. Radcliffe-Brown was studying anthropology at Cambridge under W. H. R. Rivers. He also trained with A. C. Haddon, said to be "the father of scientific fieldwork in British anthropology" (Fortes 1949:viii). In 1906 he began the fieldwork in the Andaman Islands that was to become the basis for his book *The Andaman Islanders*. His preliminary account of this work was accepted as his Ph.D. dissertation; but partly because of the first World War it was not published in book form until 1922. Radcliffe-Brown spent the years 1910-1912 in western Australia doing further fieldwork. From 1916 to 1919 he was director of education in Tonga. From there he went to South Africa and thence to Australia. During most of this time he wrote and lectured profusely. Some of his most important papers were published between 1922 and 1926. Thus when he arrived as professor of anthropology at the University of Chicago in 1931 he brought with him an impressive, semilegendary background. Being handsome, urbane, and sociable, he quickly attached to himself a wide following. Ralph Linton was teaching at the University of Wisconsin and establishing his own

A. R. RADCLIFFE-BROWN (1881–1955). (National Anthropological Archives, Smithsonian Institution)

reputation at the time. Being somewhat isolated in Madison, Linton spent much of his time with colleagues at the University of Chicago and there encountered Radcliffe-Brown. Some idea of that time can be gathered from the following:

Personal animosity did not prevent the two men from offering a joint seminar session at the University of Wisconsin in 1936. Radcliffe-Brown came to Wisconsin University accompanied by a collection of his devoted followers, and the session turned into a confrontation and was one of the most stimulating events that Wisconsin social sciences had produced. The two men provided quite a contrast on the rostrum: Radcliffe-Brown, tall and arrogant in beautifully tailored English clothes, a monocle, and a long cigarette holder; Linton, big and burly in rumpled unmatched tweeds and smoking a pipe. Linton did not attack Radcliffe-Brown's functional theories in total, but he did reject his rather arbitrary formulations of so-called structural-functional laws as not being based upon empirical fact but upon intuitive speculation. Furthermore, Linton, both by training and personal inclination, disliked the imposition of any elaborate theoretical system such as that Radcliffe-Brown was trying to achieve. He also felt that Radcliffe-Brown in his sociological search of "laws" was ignoring the biological and psychological reality of man. . . . (A. Linton and Wagley 1971:39-40)

Even so, Linton, like many other American scholars of the period, accepted the basic tenets of functionalism. *Social anthropology* (Radcliffe-Brown's label for his type of anthropology) became firmly established in the United States with the University of Chicago as its headquarters.

Although its proponents tried to dismiss the concept of culture as irrelevant to the mainstream of anthropology, structural functionalism is of importance to us here because of the effect it had on developments to come. Radcliffe-Brown, following a tradition established by the great French sociologist Emile Durkheim, believed that anthropology should study *social systems* rather than culture:

This brings us to a fundamental axiom of the science of society, as I see it. Is a science of culture possible? Boas says it is not. I agree. You cannot have a science of culture. You can study culture only as a characteristic of a social system. Therefore, if you are going to have a science, it must be a science of social systems. (Radcliffe-Brown 1957:106)

But Boas's belief that a science of culture was not possible grew from his beliefs about the historical processes involved in the formation of culture, not from his objection to the concept as such. Not so Radcliffe-Brown, who attempted to demonstrate that the culture concept was less meaningful than the concept of social systems. The simplest way to understand what Radcliffe-Brown had in mind is to consider his organic analogy.

. . . it is convenient to use the analogy between social life and organic life. An animal organism is an agglomeration of cells and interstitial fluids arranged in relation to one another not as an aggregate but as an integrated system of complex molecules. The system of relations by which these units are related is the organic structure. As the terms are here used the organism is *not* itself the structure; it is a collection of units (cells or molecules) arranged in a structure, i.e., in a set of relations; the organism *has* a structure. Two mature animals of the same species and sex consist of similar units combined in a similar structure. The structure is thus to be defined as a set of relations between entities.

As the word function is here being used the life of an organism is conceived as the *functioning* of its structure. It is through and by the continuity of the functioning that the continuity of the structure is preserved. If we consider any recurrent part of the life-process, such as respiration, digestion, etc., its *function* is the part it plays in, the contribution it makes to, the life of the organism as a whole. (Radcliffe-Brown 1952:178–179)

In somewhat simpler terms: just as an individual human being constitutes a finite system with a distinctive structure—each organ performing a particular activity, the function of which is to contribute to the maintenance of the system as a whole (the secretion of gastric fluid is an activity of the stomach, the function of which is to change protein into a form in which it can be absorbed and distributed by the blood to the tissues) (Radcliffe-Brown 1952:179)—so a human society constitutes a similar system with its distinctive structure and functions. A "natural science of society" must recognize the natural system, discover its structure, and perceive how each part functions in relation to the system. Radcliffe-Brown was able to explicate, using this analogy, a number of previously less well-understood facts about kinship and social structure.

In spite of his rejection of a science of culture, and although it is by no means completely clear what he meant by *culture*, Radcliffe-Brown did employ a concept of culture. For him, culture was considered (1) a set of rules for "fitting human beings together into a social system," (2) "common symbols and common meanings attached to them" (1957:99), and (3) "a certain common set of ways of feeling and a certain common set of ways of thinking" (1957:102). But, he argued, as these rules, symbols, and common ways could not exist independently of real living and interacting human beings, all an investigator could do was study specific acts of behavior. Language was used by Radcliffe-Brown as an example of this proposition:

Culture cannot exist of itself even for a moment; certainly it cannot continue. What, for example, is the basis of the continuity of language? . . . A language you recognize as a body of speech usages, and you can describe it in terms of a set of rules. It is quite clear that a set of speech usages does not remain unchanged, even for a comparatively short period. But English today is still English, though not that spoken in the eighteenth century. We recognize a certain fundamental continuity. What is the basis of it? It is that at any moment of time between the eighteenth century and the present day we could have put our finger on a certain body of human beings who constituted the English-speaking community of that time *and had a structural continuity as a group.* The continuity of the language depends on continuity of the social structure. Just so does the existence and continuity of the whole of culture as a characteristic of the group. You cannot have coaptation without culture and you cannot have the continuity of culture without continuity of social structure. The social structure consists of the social behavior of actual individual human beings, who are *a priori* to the existence of culture. Therefore, if you study culture, you are always studying the acts of behavior of a specific set of persons who are linked together in a social structure.

On that basis I would say no science of culture is possible, that even a science of language is part of the total science of which I am speaking. (Radcliffe-Brown 1957:107–108)

But the social structure—which is not the actual behavior of human beings in Radcliffe-Brown's theory but, rather, an abstraction from behavior—could also exist only if there were individuals *a priori* to the behavior. Radcliffe-Brown, like many creative scholars, was not always completely consistent in his views. In any case, the fact that rules, symbols, and common ways, including languages, exist only if people exist does not mean they do not exist at all. And if they exist, presumably they can be studied. Surely Radcliffe-Brown did not mean to tell us we cannot study dreams, thoughts, stories, religion, and their likes, all existing only if people exist *a priori*? That the implications of this rejection were not completely clear in Radcliffe-Brown's own mind can be seen if we continue the quotation above:

. . . I can qualify that statement a little in this way: while no complete science of culture is possible by itself, you can have an independent scientific treatment of certain aspects, of certain portions of culture. They will not give you the final scientific conclusions, but they will give you a certain number of quite important provisional ones. (1957:108)

Unfortunately, Radcliffe-Brown never told us what an incomplete science might be as distinguished from a "complete science," or precisely what "portions of culture" might be amenable to scientific treatment, or what "final scientific conclusions" may be, or what he meant by "important provisional ones." The above qualification is all the more confusing when one finds Radcliffe-Brown elsewhere arguing that it is permissible to use "logical fictions":

Force is a logical fiction, a convenient concept by which we can describe a certain type of physical phenomena. *Interest* is a similar logical fiction for describing biological phenomena; it is a shorthand description of a series of acts of behavior—not itself a real entity, but valuable in describing phenomenal reality. (1957:44)

Apparently one can study and use logical fictions—"not themselves real entities"—but one cannot study culture or language because "it cannot exist of itself." But both language and culture, and social structure as well, are precisely what Radcliffe-Brown meant by a "a logical fiction"—"a shorthand description of a series of acts of behavior." As has been noted above, Radcliffe-Brown was given at times to grandiose pronouncements that are often as incomprehensible as they are ambitious. Consider Lowie's remark on Radcliffe-Brown:

The grandiloquent use of the term "law" is most regrettable and in some circumstances leads to absurdity, as when Radcliffe-Brown writes of "a universal sociological law though it is not yet possible to formulate precisely its scope, namely that in certain specific conditions a society has need to provide itself with a segmentary [clan] organization." Whoever heard of a universal law with an as yet undefinable scope, of a law that works in certain specific *but unspecified* conditions? Is it a law that some societies have clans, and others have not? Newton did not tell us that bodies either fall or rise. (Lowie 1937:225)

But even Lowie admitted, somewhat grudgingly, that when Radcliffe-Brown set aside his theoretical pronouncements and set to work on data he did bring order to what had previously appeared chaotic. Thus he wrote insightful articles on such topics as joking relationships, taboo, totemism, law, the relationship of mother's brother to sister's son, and many other customs of interest to anthropologists. Although not all of his work has survived the test of time, it was always stimulating and exciting. It would appear that Radcliffe-Brown was at his worst when he came to the subject of either culture or psychology.

In retrospect it seems, as Audrey Richards stated, whatever Radcliffe-Brown and his colleagues were not interested in they subsumed under the term culture and thus arbitrarily eliminated from anthropology:

It was argued that social structure should be clearly separated from the other aspects of man's social heritage. These came to be subsumed under the title "culture," a word which has often been used in the post-war years almost in a pejorative sense to describe a sort of rag-bag of odds and ends in which to thrust all facts and ideas in which the social anthropologist was not at the moment interested. (Richards 1957:29)

These particular obfuscations, however, were probably less misleading in the further development of anthropology than were Radcliffe-Brown's well-known pronouncements on the relationship of anthropology to psychology:

How do I meet the criticism that social science and psychology both observe the same entities, acts of behavior of the individuals? If the subject matter, the data, constituted the only difference between two sciences, then there would be no difference between the sciences of the psychologist and the sociologist. You can, however, take an act of behavior and observe it in two totally different systems. The social scientist and the psychologist are not concerned with the same system and its set of relations. The social scientist is concerned with relations he can discover between acts of diverse individuals; the psychologist with relations between acts of behavior of one and the same individual.

Psychology deals with the system we call *mind*. Mind . . . is the name of the system of mental relations, a system of which the units, individual acts of inner and outer behavior, are connected with one another by relations of inter-dependence. You do not have to bring in the body, which I believe exists always with the mind. . . . The physiologist studies the body; the psychologist, the mind; the physiological-psychologist, the system mind-and-body. (1957: 45–46)

Aside from arbitrarily excluding much of what most anthropologists, psychologists, social psychologists, psychiatrists, and psychoanalysts are interested in, the above statement has to stand as one of the best examples of what Ernest Becker has called the "fetishist reaction":

It is the "fetishist" reaction to the protean problem of a science of man that has lasted up to the present day and continues to trouble us. I call it "fetishist" because it is just that: an attempt to cope with an overwhelming problem of conceptualization by biting off very tiny pieces of it and concentrating on them alone, even, to push the analogy, deriving all one's sense of self, all one's delight in life and work, from the feverish contemplation of a ludicrously limited area of reality. Of course, this does not characterize all the disciplinarians, and especially not those we are going to talk about, but it does characterize the discipline as a whole. (1971:81–82)

It certainly characterizes Radcliffe-Brown who, in his attempt to define the boundaries of social anthropology, went so far as to claim:

No relationship *between two persons* can by my definition be a psychological relation. The only psychological relations are those which exist within one mind —unless you admit telepathy. (1957:47)

Anyone is free to define psychology or culture as they wish. But Radcliffe-Brown did more—he specifically outlawed the study of psy-chology and culture for those who would follow his social anthropology. Both Radcliffe-Brown's antipsychological and anticultural orientation are doubtless related to his competition with Bronislaw Malinowski to dominate anthropology. Malinowski, as we shall see, depended heavily upon psychology and the concept of culture for his version of function-alism. Likewise, there was an increasing interest in psychology and in the individual by many American anthropologists who, although not in the camp of Malinowski, had not been convinced by Radcliffe-Brown. It is difficult to reconcile Radcliffe-Brown's public pronouncements on the subject of anthropology and psychology with his background and training in psychology under W. R. Rivers, a psychologist famous for his Torres Straits expedition of 1898 (Fortes 1949:viii). It is also difficult to reconcile them with this excerpt from his angry (unmailed) letter to Robert Lowie in May of 1938, protesting Lowie's treatment of him in *The History of Ethnological Theory* (1937):

2. page 227. "R.B. *now* overtly recognizes study of the individual" page 230. "R.B.'s recent inclusion of the individual as a legitimate object of enquiry." In the Andamans in 1906-8, as many people know, I carried out systematic investigations on individuals, having taken with me a full equipment for experimental psychology. It is true that I have not published and shall never publish my observations. They were part of a systematic investigation of variability, in physical characters (anthropometric measurements, hair etc.) in physiological characters and in mental character (sense-acuity, illusions, reaction-time, pain, colour vision, emotional type, etc.). I do not think that any anthropologist had at that date ever done what I did, namely collect and record the dreams of a number of individuals with the aim of determining variability of type. I gave a paper at Cambridge before I went to the Andamans on the study of individual variability in communities of different type, and presented a sketch of my results in 1909. This particular part of my work was not relevant to the subject of my book and so was not included.

From 1901 when I began my four years work in a psychological laboratory and in a psychiatric clinic to 1934 when I was President of the Chicago Society for Individual Psychology, I have never ceased to be a psychologist. As such I think that a good deal of the work at present being done on individuals in non-European communities is thoroughly unscientific.

Moreover my students know that I have always taught (1) that the function of social institution can only be seen in its effect in *individuals* (2) that the only data of social anthropology are observations of acts of behavior (including speech) of *individuals* or products of such acts and (3) that culture is something that exists only *in an individual.* One of my criticisms of those who belong to the Boas tradition is that they talk about culture acting on individuals and individuals acting on culture, which seems to me pure nonsense. Individuals act on individuals and on materials. If anthropologists would only come down out of that cloud-cuckoo land where "culture-traits" and "culture-complexes" and "patterns" and "configurations" diffuse, move about, spread (whether on wings or feet I know not) act and interact, and realize that what they ought to deal with are actual human individuals and their relations I should hail that revolution with joy. It is one I have been working for all my life, but I fear it will not come about. (Radcliffe-Brown 1938)

Radcliffe-Brown's abandonment of the culture concept, which he used in his famous early book *The Andaman Islanders* (1922), is perhaps not so difficult to understand, since he did attempt to include some of its content, however inadequately, in his subsequent definitions of social structure (Richards 1957:15). But, in any case, it was certainly not Radcliffe-Brown's intention to be a "fetishist," inasmuch as he firmly believed in a *science* of human beings that would solve the increasingly pressing problems of his day:

. . . Ever since his student days Radcliffe-Brown had held unwaveringly to the belief that the only road to the solution of the ills of human society is the long and arduous one of first building up the scientific knowledge upon which effective remedies can be based with some hope of success. This was the theme of all his extramural activities. He wrote for the press, gave public lectures, addressed many conferences of bodies concerned with education and social welfare, and most successfully of all, organized vacation courses in applied anthropology. (Fortes 1949:x)

This belief he shared with Boas. He also shared with Boas a distaste for the evolutionists who had preceded them both. He did not share Boas's historical orientation; history, he asserted, was *idiographic* whereas anthropology should be *nomothetic*. That is, it should search for "acceptable generalizations," universal laws that would be the equivalent of laws of physics and would apply to human social behavior. But realize that he objected not to history as such but rather to the "reconstructed history" of the evolutionists—which he thought of contemptuously as pseudohistory. Radcliffe-Brown pointed out, rightly, that most of the societies of interest to anthropology did not have any written history. Unfortunately, his lack of interest here led him not to utilize historical records even when they were available.

Radcliffe-Brown made his greatest contribution, not by actually discovering any general laws of human social behavior, but by helping to set anthropology in an entirely new direction and by insisting on higher standards of fieldwork and analysis. He insisted that anthropology use the standard scientific procedure of starting from a hypothesis, testing it by intensive fieldwork, modifying it if necessary, and continuing the process. This insistence meant that anthropology had to have a theory from which to derive testable hypotheses—precisely what was so conspicuously absent in the work of Boas and his followers.

Following Radcliffe-Brown's lead, a host of able fieldworkers produced a wealth of permanently valuable contributions to anthropology. Because Radcliffe-Brown taught at the major English universities (including Oxford where he held the first chair in anthropology), founded a chair of social anthropology at the University of Cape Town, founded the chair of social anthropology at the University of Sydney, went to the

University of Chicago as professor of anthropology, and shortly before his death was appointed the first professor of sociology at Farouk I University in Alexandria, he had, like Boas, a profound influence on the profession of anthropology. In the tradition of British social anthropology stimulated and promoted by Radcliffe-Brown are such distinguished figures as E. E. Evans-Pritchard, Meyer Fortes, Raymond Firth, Lucy Mair, S. F. Nadel, Max Gluckman, Edmund R. Leach, Audrey Richards, and many more. The collective contributions of these British anthropologists are so monumental, and their work of such a high standard that the early arguments between Malinowski and Radcliffe-Brown must be seen as inconsequential.

Radcliffe-Brown took the concept of "function" from Durkheim. But he defined it in such a way that it could be applied only to "social structure"—hence structural functionalism. The idea was, as we have seen, that one could study social structure—the relations between the members of groups—and one could then determine the function of any given behavior in terms of how well it promoted the well-being of the group. This was usually stated in terms of "unity," "harmony," "consistency," or "solidarity"—"a condition in which all parts of the social system work together with a sufficient degree of harmony or internal consistency" (Radcliffe-Brown 1952:181). The idea of the functional unity of a social system, Radcliffe-Brown felt, was a hypothesis worthy of testing by the systematic observation of facts. Although Radcliffe-Brown did have an idea of culture—really "ideology"—as did most of his followers, neither he nor his followers can be said to have contributed much to further development of the culture concept.

Neither Malinowski nor Radcliffe-Brown were antievolutionary in their views in spite of their railings against pseudohistory and historical reconstructions. Radcliffe-Brown clearly accepted a type of evolutionism which he traced to Herbert Spencer; and Malinowski, having been influenced by Frazer and Westermarck, was even more heavily committed to an evolutionary view, but neither Radcliffe-Brown nor Malinowski can be said to have contributed to the further development of such theory.

Not only did both believe in evolutionism but both also failed to overcome the basic paradigm involved with all its trappings of superiority-inferiority. In spite of their good intentions it is hard to take exception to Marvin Harris's view of this:

> . . . The judgment of history lies heavy on those anthropologists who believed themselves free of ethical involvement because they were advocates of the "Native" cause before the tribunals of the European racists while at the same time preaching moderation to the exploited and underprivileged.

Were it constructive in this context to plunge into a discussion of ethics, I should raise the question, never entertained by Malinowski, of why the Africans who had been invaded, conquered, enslaved, and exploited owed the Europeans anything else in return. The basic premise of Malinowski's position involved him in the assumption that the Europeans had a right to be governing the Africans and that every future adjustment rightfully demanded that the European interests be given their legal and customary due. Despite the admonitions to the Europeans that they had better be nice to the natives or the natives would go on misbehaving, there *is* a sanctimonious note in Malinowski's theory [of culture change] which helps to explain why anthropology is still a dirty word among many African nationalists . . . . (1968:557)

As for Radcliffe-Brown:

As late as 1950, Radcliffe-Brown's "Introduction" to *African Systems of Kinship and Marriage* included an opening quote from Gobineau advising Europeans who wish their civilization to spread, of the importance of knowing and comprehending those who were to be benefited. This is followed by the author's wish that "this book will be read not only by anthropologists, but by some of those who are responsible for formulating or carrying out policies of colonial government in the African continent." (Harris 1968:517)

And, as one of other major flaws in the functionalists' approach was the inability to accommodate change in social systems or cultures, they have also been charged with complicity in maintaining the colonial status:

. . . Between 1930 and 1955 the overwhelming bulk of the contributions of the structural-functionalist school was based upon fieldwork in African tribal societies located in European, especially British, territories. Under such circumstances it is impossible not to draw a connection between the proposal to study social systems *as if* they were solitary and *as if* they were timeless, with sponsorship, employment, and indirect association of the members of this school by and with a now defunct colonial system. (Harris 1968:516)

Here, however, is a good place to observe that there is a great difference between motives and functions. Even if it can be clearly demonstrated that the consequence (function) of twenty-five years of functionalism was to help perpetuate an unchanging colonial situation, it still does not follow that the functionalists' intention (motive) was that their approach should have that consequence. Perhaps for a few it was. But that most anthropologists had no such intentions is quite clear. Let us take an example of this from Malinowski:

There is a moral obligation to every calling, even to that of a scientific specialist. The duty of the anthropologist is to be a fair and true interpreter of the Native . . . .

He ought to be able to make clear to traders, missionaries, and exploiters what the Natives really need and where they suffer most under the pressure of European interference. There is no doubt that the destiny of indigenous races has been tragic in the process of contact with European invasion . . . .

Shall we, therefore, mix politics with science? In one way, decidedly "yes" . . . . (1945:3–4)

And from the Trobrianders he made so famous:

I would point to the political nature of anthropology, in that it has been concerned with data that is collected from studies of "primitive" societies and therefore carries a biased picture to those who read it. For instance, I have many times felt very embarrassed and awkward when I meet new people and they ask me, "Where are you from?" and I say, "Oh, I am from the Trobriand Islands," and they reply excitedly, "Ohhh, Malinowski, free love!!" What I am pointing out is that if we are going to depend on anthropological studies to define our history and our culture and our "future," then we are *lost.* (Kasaipwalova 1973:454)

As Michael Young points out in his fine collection of Malinowski's work, in spite of the great ethnographer's intentions:

There is a painful echo of Malinowski's own words in the [above] quotation from John Kasaipwalova, one of the most articulate and influential Trobrianders of the present generation, who still smarts with resentment at the indignities of colonialism and the spurious identity ascribed to him by "anthropology" . . . . The modern Trobriander, in short, is asserting the right to be a "fair and true interpreter" of his own culture. (Young 1979:17)

There can be no apology for the indignities of colonialism and imperialism, but anthropologists, like others, are people of their own times and circumstances. To attempt to blame anthropologists, of all people, for the ills of colonialism and *modernization*, which seems to be a now common practice in Third World countries, is simply far-fetched. In any case, the functionalists were avowedly ahistorical if not antihistorical. This outlook led them to deal with societies and cultures as if they were timeless, and they were accordingly unable to deal adequately with culture change. To argue that their failure to deal with change came from their being colonialists rather than from their being anthropologists, or vice versa, would take us far beyond the scope of this volume.

Interestingly, although an interest in motives is implied in Malinowski's need theory of culture, neither he nor Radcliffe-Brown attempted to clearly distinguish motives from functions, one of the major shortcomings of this tradition of anthropology, and one of the sources for much unnecessary confusion in anthropological work. To observe, for example, that the function of marriage in tribal societies is to create political ties between two groups of people does not demonstrate that it was the intention of the people to do that. That the performance of the rain dance promotes social solidarity among the participants says nothing about the motives of the actors. Most certainly one is not justified in saying that people engage in religious rituals of various kinds because they wish to promote social solidarity even if, in fact, such rituals do have that function.

One final matter in this discussion: Malinowski shared with Radcliffe-Brown the firm conviction that the science of anthropology should be related to practical human affairs—to the moral crisis of which Ernest Becker speaks:

> He looked upon his subject as a science, its role being "first handmaiden to a general theory of human society"; but he saw it also in its bearings upon human affairs—"a theory trying to achieve a deeper grasp of human nature and human history," perhaps capable of being used to influence the makers of policy but above all "useful in creating a saner attitude, finer and wider ideals in the minds of men." (Firth 1957:7)

But unlike Radcliffe-Brown, Malinowski cannot be said to have been a disciplinary "fetishist." Indeed, he might well be considered one of the forerunners of what we now conceive of as an "interdisciplinarian," an early practitioner of a further development in anthropology often called "culture-and-personality," to which we will turn in the next chapter. Malinowski was a colorful and most influential scholar as well as a gifted teacher. He left an indelible mark on his students, many of whom were also students of Radcliffe-Brown. He was also, unlike most anthropologists, a gifted writer. That he was aware of having this skill, or at least was aware of his attempt to achieve it, is illustrated by a remark attributed to him by Mrs. B. Z. Seligman: "Rivers is the Rider Haggard of anthropology; I shall be the Conrad" (Firth 1957:6). Malinowski was one of those strong personalities who inevitably make enemies as well as friends. While he was intelligent and sensitive in most things, his enthusiasm often overcame him and aroused hostility in others. He is reported, for example, to have referred to the distinguished Fritz Graebner as "a museum mole" (Hays 1958:325) and he tended always to ignore or minimize the importance of the contributions of other functionalists including, of course, Radcliffe-Brown. His accomplishments, however, must not be undervalued because of his personality characteristics. Some idea of the complexity of Malinowski the man, his very ambivalent feelings about the Trobrianders and his fieldwork, as well as what the fieldwork experience was like, can be gained from perusing his controversial *A Diary in the Strict Sense of the Term*, published after his death (1967).

SUMMARY

The period from roughly 1915 to the early 1930s was one of intense growth and activity in anthropology. American and British anthropologists began doing fieldwork all over the globe. There was considerable innovation both in methods and in theory. The greatest intellectual stimulus came at this time from Radcliffe-Brown and Malinowski, who offered competing brands of an anthropological theory known as functionalism. Whereas Radcliffe-Brown's version came to be known as structural functionalism, Malinowski claimed to have a "pure" functionalism. Malinowski's theory of culture was much nearer to all-encompassing than was Radcliffe-Brown's "natural science of society." Malinowski emphasized psychological and biological needs as well as social needs; Radcliffe-Brown argued that there was no place for psychology or biology in anthropology. But both of these men felt that anthropology should be a science, that it should not be history, that it should not be primarily concerned with evolution, and that the parts of any whole, whether a social system or a culture, had to function for the maintenance of that whole. Since both of these figures were intelligent, dynamic, colorful personalities, and since they tended to compete vigorously with each other to dominate the field, it was an exciting time in the history of anthropology. Radcliffe-Brown attempted to ignore the culture concept as much as possible, with only limited success. Malinowski retained and promoted it and further clarified its meaning.

FURTHER READINGS

Marvin Harris's *The Rise of Anthropological Theory* has a detailed chapter on "British Social Anthropology" which discusses both Radcliffe-Brown and Malinowski. For a very different interpretation and point of view see the two books by I. C. Jarvie, *The Revolution in Anthropology* and *The Story of Social Anthropology*. A more recent history, specifically on British anthropology, is Adam Kuper's *Anthropologists and Anthropology: The British School; 1922–1972*. See also Ian Langham's *The Building of British Social Anthropology* and George Stocking's *Functionalism Historicized*.

Detailed articles on various aspects of Malinowski's work can be found in the collection edited by Raymond Firth, *Man and Culture* (1957). Michael Young has edited a collection of Malinowski's work with an interesting introduction entitled, *The Ethnography of Malinowski: The Trobriand Islands 1915–18*. For more details on Radcliffe-Brown see his *Festschrift* edited by Fortes, *Social Structure Studies Presented to A. R. Radcliffe-Brown* (1949), and also Radcliffe-Brown's posthumously published statement of his position, *A Natural Science of Society*.

For a different, more sympathetic, and more detailed view of Radcliffe-Brown than that presented here see the volume edited by Adam Kuper, *The Social Anthropology of Radcliffe-Brown.*

Malinowski's major books, *Sex and Repression in Savage Society, The Sexual Life of Savages in Northwestern Melanesia, Coral Gardens and Their Magic,* and *Crime and Custom in Savage Society,* remain as worthwhile and fascinating anthropological studies. Radcliffe-Brown's works were primarily theoretical. *The Andaman Islanders,* while not completely representative, is still of interest.

A few representative works in the tradition of British social anthropology, all worth reading, are Fred Eggan, *Social Organization of the Western Pueblos;* E. E. Evans-Pritchard, *The Nuer;* Raymond Firth, *We, the Tikopia;* Meyer Fortes, *The Dynamics of Clanship among the Tallensi;* Reo Fortune, *Sorcerers of Dobu;* Max Gluckman, *Order and Rebellion in Tribal Africa;* Ian Hogbin, *Law and Order in Polynesia;* Edmund Leach, *Political Systems of Highland Burma;* Lucy Mair, *An African People in the Twentieth Century;* Mervyn Meggitt, *The Lineage of the Mae Enga of New Guinea;* S. F. Nadel, *A Black Byzantium;* Audrey Richards, *Economic Development and Tribal Change;* and M. G. Smith, *Government in Zazzau: 1800–1950.*

CHAPTER IV

American Developments

In spite of their influence, not all anthropologists, particularly those in the United States, followed the functionalism of either Malinowski or Radcliffe-Brown. American developments did, however, follow a course more similar to that of Malinowski in that they continued the concern with psychology and the concept of culture. A number of investigators, stimulated primarily by the brilliant linguistic anthropologist Edward Sapir, became increasingly interested in individual human beings, in personality, and in the question of how individuals acquired and were related to the culture of which they were a part. Ruth Benedict and Margaret Mead were also in the forefront of this new "culture-and-personality" movement, which for a time occupied the attention of many of the major figures in American anthropology.

Some scholars rejected both social anthropology and culture-and-personality studies in favor of a newer, more scientific brand of evolutionism with a basis in *technoenvironmental determinism.* One of these scholars, Leslie White, met with a great deal of resistance because of his identification with the thought of Karl Marx at a time when such identification was politically undesirable. Julian Steward, on the other hand, found a ready acceptance for his ideas, which were similar in their fundamentals to those of White. A current version of this tradition is found in Marvin Harris's cultural materialism. Still other American anthropologists followed their own interests, eschewing these theoretical developments.

During the period when Radcliffe-Brown and Malinowski were reacting against evolutionary and historical reconstructions, demanding that
anthropology become a science and developing their structural-
functional approach, other important developments were taking place.
One of these was labeled *culture-and-personality* and has more recently
been termed *psychological anthropology*. Remember that both Linton
and Malinowski criticized Radcliffe-Brown for omitting psychological
and biological phenomena in his attempt to create a science of society.
They were not alone in expressing such reservations and there was a
growing interest in how the individual was related to culture. This interest produced the second half of the so-called "Copernican revolution" in
anthropology, mentioned previously.

. . . Despite the important differences that divided these schools [culture-and-
personality and social anthropology], it should be observed that they also had
much in common. First, in contrast to the earlier historical schools, both displayed almost systematic indifference to problems of a historical nature. This is
not to say, as is sometimes charged, that they dismissed historical variables as
irrelevant, but rather that they viewed the task of anthropology as something
other than historical reconstruction. Second, in contrast to an older trait-list
approach, both emphasized the primacy of context, pattern, configuration, and
structure. Third, instead of a descriptivist approach, both were theoretically
oriented. Primitive societies were to be studied for the light they could shed on
theoretical issues: in one case—and here they differed—sociological, and in the
other, psychological (Spiro 1972:579).

The description does not refer merely to the difference between
Radcliffe-Brown and Malinowski but rather to a newer and much more
actively psychological point of view. Like structural functionalism, these
new culture-and-personality studies attempted to be scientific and nomothetic as opposed to historical and idiographic. They also attempted to
consider wholes rather than merely parts. And they were avowedly
theoretical.

CULTURE-AND-PERSONALITY

Various writers have expressed different ideas as to where the beginnings of culture-and-personality are to be found. Milton Singer, in a
survey of culture-and-personality theory and research, says that it was
the encounter of anthropology with psychoanalysis that brought about
the new development:

. . . It was in fact the encounter of anthropology, and to a lesser extent sociology
and political science, with psychoanalysis, that gave rise to culture and personality studies. (Singer 1961:10)

The early importance of psychoanalysis is evident by 1920 when Kroeber reviewed Freud's book *Totem and Taboo* (1918) in the *American Anthropologist*. Although the review was not entirely critical it was, in general, much more negative than positive. Kroeber spent the bulk of the review demolishing Freud's attempt to find the origins of culture in the *Oedipus complex*. Nonetheless, Kroeber had been sufficiently taken by psychoanalytic theory to undergo analysis in 1917 and to practice as a lay analyst in San Francisco during 1918–1919 (Theodora Kroeber 1970:105). Furthermore, when twenty years later Kroeber wrote another review of the same book he had somewhat changed his tone:

> He now thinks Freud's explanation of culture would deserve at least "serious consideration as a scientific hypothesis," if it were restated as a proposition about the constant operation of certain psychic processes—for example, the incest drive, incest repression, and filial ambivalence—in widespread human institutions. He still finds that psychoanalysis refuses to undertake such a restatement, because of its indifference to history and to accepted scientific attitudes, and this dogmatic all-or-nothing attitude which resists influences from without. (Singer 1961:10).

C. G. Seligman, one of the important influences on Malinowski, took as his theme for his presidential address to the Royal Anthropological Institute of Great Britain and Ireland in 1924 the subject, "Anthropology and Psychology: A Study of Some Points of Contact." He discussed primarily Carl Gustav Jung's recently conceived types of personalities —introvert and extrovert—in relation to the study of anthropology. Europeans, he felt, were predominantly extrovert whereas Hindus were introvert. He also suggested the unconscious should be investigated among "non-European races" through the study of dreams. Seligman returned to the psychoanalytic theory of Freud and Jung, which he regarded as of importance to anthropology, in a later paper as well (1932).

The influence of psychoanalysis was also felt in early fieldwork. Thus while Malinowski was in the Trobriands (1914–1918) he received information and literature from Seligman that stimulated him to pursue topics which were to have great impact on psychoanalytic theory and on anthropology. In his subsequent books, *Sex and Repression in Savage Society* (1927) and *The Sexual Life of Savages* (1929), he argued against a universal Oedipus complex as Freud had described it on the grounds that in matrilineal societies (like the Trobriands) the expression of Oedipal feelings and conflict would differ from that in Europe. Malinowski argued that in the Trobriand family it was the mother's brother who held authority and not the father—hence a boy's antagonism would be directed not toward his father but toward his mother's brother, a situation not considered by Freud. The issue of Oedipal conflict in the Trobriands has been taken up more recently by Melford E. Spiro, who has argued most convincingly in his book *Oedipus in the Trobriands* (1982) that Malinowski's interpretation was quite incorrect.

Still another figure of importance with regard to the relationship of psychoanalytic theory to anthropology was the Hungarian-born scholar Geza Roheim. Roheim, a psychoanalyst, was as close to a psychoanalytic purist as it was possible to be. He had also done fieldwork of his own as early as 1927 in Africa and Australia. He argued that if anthropologists (like Malinowski) could not find Oedipal feelings as Freud conceived of them, they, themselves, must be suffering from unresolved Oedipus complexes! Needless to say Roheim did not endear himself to other anthropologists with this approach. And, because much of his own work depended upon an unquestioning belief in a theory of universal symbols which he got from Freud, his analyses of various myths and customs were not generally accepted by other anthropologists. Nonetheless, in spite of his excesses, Roheim did make a contribution to culture-and-personality studies. He suggested, for example, that *Homo sapiens* as a species has certain universal characteristics that could account for some kind of universal sexual complex. And he also suggested that such constant features of human life as these had to do with *"the origin and function of culture"*; the expression became the title of one of his most important works (1943). Thus, although he infuriated many of his colleagues, he was instrumental in laying the groundwork for the contemporary view of culture that assumes a number of psychobiological constants that give rise to and make inevitable a cultural mode of life for *Homo sapiens*. But even so, the more or less classical psychoanalytic approach of Roheim has generated little enthusiasm and has few practitioners, the most notable being perhaps George Devereux and Weston LaBarre.

Basic unsolved questions about human nature have also been suggested as the starting point for culture-and-personality studies, and they are obviously related to the impact of psychoanalytic theory on anthropology and vice versa. Melford E. Spiro has suggested that culture-and-personality studies could have come about only when certain time-honored traditions of thought broke down. Modern science, Spiro argued (1951), is the heir to a tradition which has always elaborated dichotomies — real-ideal, means-ends, theory-practice, mind-body, matter-spirit, and many others. The clear separation between the individual and his society or culture, Spiro said, is another example of this dichotomizing. And this, he went on, was probably inevitable, given the belief in an inherent human nature which unfolded itself by a maturational process that was regarded as natural. However much people may have disagreed about what this human nature really was, they all agreed that for the most part society and/or culture were not involved in it. This notion is in evidence in psychoanalytic theory. It is found in G. Stanley Hall. And it clearly stimulated much of the work in culture-and-personality in the 1920s and 1930s. Margaret Mead, in the preface to the 1939 reissue of her book *From the South Seas*, graphically described the situation:

> It was the simple—a very simple—point to which our materials were organized in the 1920s, merely the documentation over and over of the fact that human nature is not rigid and unyielding, not an unadaptable plant which insists on flowering or becoming stunted after its own fashion, responding only quantitatively to the social environment, but that it is extraordinarily adaptable, that cultural rhythms are stronger and more compelling than the physiological rhythms which they overlay and distort, that the failure to satisfy an artificial, culturally stimulated need—for outdistancing one's neighbor's in our society, for instance, or for wearing the requisite number of dog's teeth among the Manus— may produce more unhappiness and frustration in the human breast than the most rigorous cultural curtailments of the physiological demands of sex or hunger. We had to present evidence that human character is built upon a biological base which is capable of enormous diversification in terms of social standards. (1939:x)

Mead, however, just like a great many other anthropologists, although disavowing Freud's biological and ethnocentric point of view, in her later work took over and used much of psychoanalytic theory. This influence is perhaps most clear in her work with Gregory Bateson on *Balinese Character* (1942).

A third suggestion as the beginnings of culture-and-personality studies has been offered by John Honigmann:

> Culture and personality studies began among North American Indians with the collection of personal documents, a category in which I include autobiographies, and psychological analyses . . . . (1961:96)

This is a reasonable enough point of view given the nature of American anthropology at the time. There was the interest in "salvage" anthropology, with its inevitable dependence on a few older informants. This led to more intimate contact between anthropologist and informant, to more and more in-depth interviewing, and doubtless to a greater interest in the person being interviewed. Although there had been numerous biographies and autobiographies of American Indians prior to the 1920s, there was, at this time, a more deliberate attempt to use such materials in anthropology. Paul Radin and Edward Sapir, both students of Boas's, were the most important figures in this respect. But it should be made clear that Radin's attempt to use this kind of material, most notably in his well-known *Crashing Thunder* (1926), can be deemed in the culture-and-personality tradition only in that he emphasized the individual as an important source for information—information which he ultimately would use to describe and understand culture—not psychology, personality, or even the "individual-in-culture." This was the dominant orientation of most life histories until about 1945 (Langness and Frank 1981).

In Honigmann's revision of the article just quoted (1972) he stresses that culture-and-personality fieldwork actually began in 1928 with the publication of Mead's famous and now quite controversial book, *Coming of Age in Samoa*. Again, a reasonable enough view given the prevailing ideas of the time about the inevitable biological process that presumably shaped maturation.

Raymond Fogelson (1977) suggests that culture-and-personality studies arose as a reaction to two trends in the anthropology of the 1920s—first against the trend toward reification of cultural phenomena (Kroeber's superorganic) that tended to obscure the individual locus of culture; second, against the methodological trend of ethnographers toward atomizing culture into ever more discrete particles (Lowie's shreds and patches).

Kluckhohn, Murray, and Schneider in their massive reader, *Personality in Nature, Society, and Culture* (1955) suggest that the roots of the culture-and-personality tradition can be most importantly traced to a seminar in culture-and-personality conducted at Yale University in 1932–1933 by Edward Sapir and John Dollard and also to work done by W. I. Thomas, who was surveying the field at the same time for the Social Science Research Council (1955:xvi). Robert A. LeVine, in his textbook on the subject, concurs and goes on to add the names of Ralph Linton and A. Irving Hallowell, suggesting at the same time that the work of these men was overshadowed in the public eye by the less scholarly publications of Ruth Benedict, Geoffrey Gorer, and some of their colleagues (1973:viii).

While opinions on the origin of culture-and-personality studies vary, all agree on the key role played by Sapir. As was previously noted, Sapir was one of the earliest of Boas's students. It has also been said that he was the most brilliant of all of them. Primarily a linguist, like so many of his contemporaries, he was well-versed in other aspects of anthropology as well. He was remarkably talented in general, being a poet, pianist, and composer of sorts, in addition to writing for a variety of sophisticated magazines. As early as 1917 Sapir reviewed a book on psychoanalytic method. In 1921 he reviewed, favorably, Rivers's *Instinct and the Unconscious* (1920). In 1923 he reviewed Jung's *Psychological Types* (1923). Both he and Radin were well-informed on Jung's work. He was also acquainted with the great psychiatrist Harry Stack Sullivan, a relationship of mutual intellectual stimulation which was instrumental in the rapprochement of anthropology and psychiatry. Although Sapir did not really write extensively on psychology, there is no doubt of his powerful influence on Ruth Benedict and Margaret Mead, who helped develop the new field of culture-and-personality.

To fully understand Sapir's significance in the development of culture-and-personality, and hence in the further development of the culture concept itself, one must understand his reaction to Kroeber's attempt to establish culture as a "superorganic." In retrospect, and in view of Becker's thesis, it might be suggested that Kroeber's attempt to define culture as a superorganic, as an entity existing independently in its own right and independently of individual men and women, was not only an attempt to define culture more precisely but was also an attempt to establish a distinctively anthropological subject matter as opposed to psychology, sociology, or some other discipline. David Bidney has commented on this point also:

> . . . The older generation of anthropologists, whether evolutionists, diffusionists, functionalists, or culturologists, all agreed [implicitly] to maintain the independence and distinctness of anthropology as a science. They thought that if they could demonstrate the autonomy and reality of culture as a reality *sui generis,* then this would justify and validate their claim for an autonomous science of cultural anthropology. (1967:xvii)

Be this as it may, Kroeber's insistence on the unimportance of individuals represented a sharp break with Boas, who had always had an interest in the individual and in the individual's relationship to his or her culture. Although Boas had not pursued this interest himself, he had encouraged his students to do so.

Boas had also, as we have seen, converted the early notion of culture (civilization) from singular to plural. But he had not actually added or changed substantially the definition of culture that had come from Tylor and Arnold. Nor had anyone else, it appears, until Kroeber's ideas on the superorganic nature of culture appeared in 1917. This departure seems to have had the effect of stimulating others—most notably Sapir—to consider more carefully the meaning of the concept of culture. Sapir responded immediately in an article entitled "Do We Need a Superorganic?" (1917). He took Kroeber to task and accused him of using overly selective examples to make his point. He suggested that had Kroeber dealt with religion, aesthetics, philosophy, and things of that sort as well as with the realm of sciences and invention, he would not have been able so easily to denigrate the importance of the individual in history. What, he asked, of figures like Jesus? Mohammed? Were they, as individuals, unimportant to the further course of history? Would events have followed the same path had these particular individuals not existed? Sapir did not think so, and this opinion led him to define culture in a way importantly different from any that had previously been suggested. John Honigmann, following Sapir, has commented on this point:

> Cultural anthropology, he [Sapir] said, emphasized the group and its traditions but pays little regard to the individuals who make up the group and who actualize its traditions in individual variations of behavior. Anthropology might also focus on persons and see culture in its "true locus," namely, "in the interactions of specific individuals and, on the subjective side, in the world of meanings which each one of these individuals may unconsciously abstract for himself from his participation in these interactions—in much the same way as psychiatry focuses on a whole individual and observes him in his world of social relationships." (1972:125)

By suggesting that culture might be something internalized by individual human beings as a "world of meanings," Sapir set the stage for more recent concepts of culture. What he had in mind here might be best illustrated by what later become known as the Sapir-Whorf hypothesis— basically, that the language a person internalizes affects the way he perceives the world around him. Language, of course, is a part of culture; hence it is possible to assume that one can internalize other aspects of culture as well as language. Sapir also forged a strong link between anthropology and psychiatry that is still developing. We now have, for example, a "cultural psychiatry" (Kennedy 1973), a *Transcultural Psychiatric Research Review,* and so on, all ultimately resulting from the stimulating early work of Sapir and those he influenced.

Sapir had also suggested two years previously in a well-known 1924 paper, "Culture, Genuine and Spurious," that it was possible to distinguish between culture as man's entire material and social heritage, and culture as "those general attitudes, views of life, and specific manifestations of civilization that give a particular people its distinctive place in the world" (1924:405). This latter, as Honigmann points out (1972:124), was a new version of what had interested certain historians—particularly in Germany—the notion of "national genius." It was an idea Boas subscribed to as well. Sapir's close friend Ruth Benedict was to carry this idea to its extreme anthropological fruition in her famous book, *Patterns of Culture* (1934).

Ruth Benedict, like Sapir, was a gifted poet. A student at Vassar, her background was in English and literature. After her graduation from Vassar in 1909, she taught English for a time and then married in 1914. She came to anthropology rather late in life, conducting her first field-work with California Indians in 1922 at the age of thirty-five. Benedict received her Ph.D. from Columbia in 1923 and began teaching at Columbia in the same year. She worked during the summers with the Zuñi (1924–1925), the Cochiti (1925), and the Pima Indians (1926). She was extremely close to Boas, her mentor, and, as mentioned, to Edward Sapir. Margaret Mead, her first student, also had a great influence on her (Bateson 1984; Howard 1984; Kardiner and Preble 1961; Mead 1959; Modell 1983). Benedict was roundly criticized by many of the anthropologists of her time for her overly humanistic and literary approach. Nonetheless, *Patterns of Culture* remains probably the most widely read book of anthropology, and Benedict made a significant impact on the discipline.

The core of *Patterns of Culture* is the contention that culture is patterned—that each culture selects from infinite possibilities only a few and that these, which must be congruent with each other, constitute a configuration. This configuration is, then, an "integrated whole" that has consistency and is reflected, Benedict believed, in all of the various parts of the culture.

A culture, like an individual, is a more or less consistent pattern of thought and action. Within each culture there come into being characteristic purposes, not necessarily shared by other types of society. In obedience to these purposes, each people further and further consolidates its experience, and in proportion to the urgency of these drives the heterogeneous items of behavior take more and more congruous shape. (Benedict 1934:46)

Borrowing terms from the philosopher Friedrich Nietzsche, Benedict attempted to characterize the Zuñi Indians of the southwest as "Apollonian," the Apollonian character being restrained, relatively unemotional, not given to excesses, emphasizing perfection, and so on. The Kwakiutl of the Pacific northwest coast, by contrast, were "Dionysian" to an extreme degree—they were violent, warlike, given to wild dancing and extremes of behavior, as in the cannibal-society dance in which the dancers were said to bite off pieces of living flesh. They were, in general, quite the opposite of the placid Zuñi. Benedict characterized the Dobuans of Melanesia, who had been studied and described by the British anthropologist Reo Fortune (1932), as being near to what we define as paranoid—because they were so suspicious and distrustful of each other, attempted to destroy each other's gardens through magic, and were remarkably sour and disapproving types in general. Although it has been subsequently shown that Benedict was far too selective in the materials she picked to demonstrate her thesis, she did in this way manage to introduce the notion of "national genius" into anthropology. This was the German tradition of Kant, Hegel, Dilthey, and Spengler that was transmitted to her in part from her own reading and in part from Boas.

While there is more to Benedict's work than is suggested above, its significance here lies in her contention that a culture is somehow the personality of its members "writ large" (Honigmann 1972:121) but at the same time determines the personality of its members by selecting for those "temperament types" that are congruent with it. This contention does not imply, however, that there are no deviants at all and that every-one shares the same temperament:

. . . no anthropologist with a background of experience in other cultures has ever believed that individuals were automatons, mechanically carrying out the decrees of their civilization. No culture yet observed has been able to eradicate the differ-ences in the temperament of the persons who compose it. It is always a give-and-take. (1934:220)

Even so, the notion of culture as a determinant of personality became the dominant orientation in culture-and-personality studies, albeit in increasingly sophisticated versions. It is also largely because of Benedict's work, following Boas, that the notion of cultures (plural) became increasingly important and the equation of culture (singular) with civili-zation became untenable. Benedict's *cultural relativism*, her respect for other ways of life, left no room for judging one culture as "higher" than another. There were no "stages" of development but, rather, merely different styles of life which demanded to be judged as equal. Her famous quotation from the Digger Indians at the beginning of *Patterns of Culture* makes her attitude very clear:

God gave to every people a cup, a cup of clay, and from this cup they drank their life. . . . They all dipped in the water but their cups were different. (1934:33)

Benedict's work was stimulating and led to further work on *themes of culture* by Morris Opler (1945) and others who believed that her idea of a single overriding theme or configuration was too simple to be very useful. It also led, eventually, especially during the years of World War II when it became important to know as much as possible about enemies and allies, to studies of *modal personality* and *national character* (the type of personality or character most frequently found in a society or nation) (Inkeles and Levinson 1954).

Margaret Mead's pioneering work in the field of culture-and-personality is by now even better known than that of her mentor Benedict. She almost singlehandedly created the field of cross-cultural *socialization* studies (Langness 1975). Her study of adolescents in Samoa (1928) did much to promote the culture concept, however much it may have subsequently become increasingly controversial (Freeman 1983). Her work in New Guinea, *Growing Up in New Guinea* (1930), helped to establish her as one of the significant figures in American anthropology, particularly in the new subdiscipline that was emerging. *Sex and Temperament in Three Primitive Societies* (1935), her stimulating argument about sex and gender, likewise received much attention and helped to establish her even more prominently in the public eye. Mead, of course, remained a dominant figure in American anthropology for over half a century and her name became a household word virtually worldwide. We need not go into her subsequent work here as we are interested only in this particular period in the history of the study of culture. But LeVine is surely correct when he suggests that the work of Benedict (and by implication at least, Mead) so overshadowed the work of other anthropologists that the latter have been neglected (1973:viii). There is no doubt that Mead knew what she was about when it came to writing for a wide audience and thereby attracting attention. In the preface to the 1973 edition of *Coming of Age in Samoa* she writes:

> I can emphasize that this was the first piece of anthropological fieldwork which was written without the paraphernalia of scholarship designed to mystify the lay reader and confound one's colleagues. It seemed to me then—and it still does—that if our studies of the way of life of other peoples are to be meaningful to the peoples of the industralized world, they must be written for them and not wrapped up in technical jargon for specialists. As this book was about adolescents, I tried to couch it in language that would be communicative to those who had most to do with adolescents—teachers, parents, and soon-to-be parents. I did not write it as a popular book, but only with the hope that it would be intelligible to those who might make the best use of its theme, that adolescence need not be the time of stress and strain which Western society made it; that growing up could be freer and easier and less complicated. (Mead 1973)

Mead, although she was influenced by Radcliffe-Brown, as her monograph *Kinship in the Admiralty Islands* (1934) shows, was not led astray by the simplicities of Radcliffe-Brown's version of structuralism. She retained and used the concept of culture in spite of his insistence (1957) that there could be no science of culture. Likewise, she was not intimidated

because of the lack of an operational definition of culture and she continued to demonstrate in her vast output of articles, books, and public lectures just what completely cultural animals we really are. If her early
work *Sex and Temperament in Three Primitive Societies* (1935) is a
dubious but plausible account, *Male and Female* (1949) is a more mature
and convincing one. Even more convincing is the work on Balinese
character (Bateson and Mead 1942; Mead and MacGregor 1951) and the
work she conducted during and just after World War II. *And Keep Your
Powder Dry* (1942), Mead's analysis of American character, is another
example, along with *Soviet Attitudes toward Authority* (1951).

Theory is often more implicit than explicit in Mead's work but it was
always informed by a clearly formulated, consistent, and strongly held
view of the nature of human culture (Webb 1968). Her theoretical position is probably best seen in such works as "The Concept of Culture and
the Psychosomatic Approach" (1947), *The Study of Culture at a
Distance* (Mead and Metraux 1953), "The Cross-Cultural Approach to
the Study of Personality" (1956), "Cultural Determinants of Behavior"
(1958) and *Continuities in Cultural Evolution* (1964).

Mead's emphasis on culture comes through perhaps most clearly in
her discussion of *enculturation* as contrasted with socialization:

> So it is important to reaffirm the difference between the study of enculturation
> —the process of learning a culture in all its uniqueness and particularity—and the
> study of socialization—the set of species-wide requirements and exactions made
> on human beings by human societies. Unless, in each case, the full details of
> enculturation are recorded and, later, are examined as meticulously as are tech-
> niques of drumming or singing, and are analyzed, in context, in many systematic-
> ally chosen cultures, the probability of our developing a cross-culturally viable
> theory of socialization is negligible.
>
> Each time a member of some other discipline arrives at a generalization about
> socialization based on an indiscriminate use of anthropological materials, each
> time an anthropologist applies to his own work the treatment of socialization
> currently in vogue in the behavioral sciences, which has not passed through the
> refining crucible of comparative study of enculturation, the confusion is further
> compounded. Controversies arise in which the anthropologist, or someone with a
> genuine knowledge of enculturation, objects that the particular generalization
> made by a behavioral scientist does not take culture (by which he means *cultures*)
> into account; in reply, the behavioral scientist insists that he has taken as a basic
> premise the idea that man is a cultural animal, that all culture is learned, and so
> forth. But to the extent that they are talking past each other, the controversy
> remains unresolved. (Mead 1963:187)

This was a period of extraordinary activity, particularly directed
toward the untangling of culture from personality and, more generally,

the relationship of anthropology to psychology. It appears that Leslie White may have authored the first published paper on culture and personality in 1925 although he later, as we will see, turned his attention in a very different direction.

Ralph Linton, who had argued the personality issue with Radcliffe-Brown, was another of the pioneers of this tradition. The clearest expression of his position can be found in his book *The Cultural Background of Personality* (1947) where he attempts to carefully define the various terms and their relationships to each other. Kluckhohn, in addition to editing *Personality in Nature, Society and Culture*, also wrote on "The Influence of Psychiatry on Anthropology in America During the Past 100 Years" (1944), and, with O. H. Mowrer, "Culture and Personality: A Conceptual Scheme" (1944).

Alexander Goldenweiser, a neglected although gifted scholar, wrote carefully on the subject in his fine book, *History, Psychology and Culture* (1933). Gregory Bateson expressed himself on the issue in a number of papers in the early 1940s (1942, 1942a, 1944) and John W. M. Whiting published his attempt to utilize learning theory in the study of a New Guinea culture, *Becoming a Kwoma* (1941).

One of the more sophisticated versions of culture-and-personality studies was the creation of the psychoanalyst Abram Kardiner. In collaboration with Edward Sapir, Ruth Benedict, Ruth Bunzel, Ralph Linton, Cora DuBois, and Carl Withers, Kardiner developed in the late 1930s and early 1940s a new and important approach to the question of culture-and-personality differences. He postulated a *basic personality structure* which he believed would be typical of the members of any given culture. To show how this basic structure occurred, he divided *institutions* into two types, primary and secondary. *Primary institutions* —mostly those having to do with the treatment of very young children and based more or less on the Freudian model—were considered to be the most important in the formation of basic personality. *Secondary institutions* were those which came into play to satisfy the basic personality needs created by primary institutions. These included such things as rituals, religion, folktales, and other so-called *"projective systems."* This idea was a powerful innovation, allowing Kardiner and his associates to demonstrate the effects of one cultural system on another, mediated by basic personality structure.

The best example of this interaction between personality and institutions, which in fact stimulated Kardiner to construct his scheme, can be found in Freud's *The Future of an Illusion* (1928). In this book Freud suggests that the experiences of early childhood determine later religious beliefs. That is, if parents in a given culture are nurturant and benevolent

PRIMARY INSTITUTION	EGO STRUCTURE (SON)	PRIMARY INSTITUTION	CHECKS
Patriarchal Family			
Absolute to power of father	Hatred—repressed	Fear of ghosts —cause illness	Propitiation by food sacrifice
Impose discipline	Submission	Immobility of lineage cult	
Exploit	Ingratiation	Loyalty to dead	Reward for repression of hatred
Frustrate needs (subsistence		Concept of illness due to sin (displeasing a god)	
Basic Disciplines			
Oral—Nursed long			
Anal—Continent at 6 months	Obedience to discipline rewarded	Cleanliness	
		Insistence on compulsive act as part of cure	
Sexual—Object and aim taboos	Denial of importance of sex	Oedipus Tales —repressed female hatred	One intercourse keeps woman pregnant
Sibling Inequality			
	Sibling hatred	Fear of magic	Taboo against use in lineage
	Aggression repressed	Blood brotherhood —homosexuality	
	Aggression expressed	*Ombiasy:* warrior	Can control fate Can control property
	Crime	Law	Severity of punishment
	Acquiescence	Belief in fate	Fate can be controlled
		Tromba— mpamosavy	Neurosis-psychosis
Subsistence			
Economy	Work for reward of love and subsistence	Smooth working of economy. Submission rewarded	
Plenty	No food anxiety	No rituals for rice	
Communal land	No differentiation of labor	Emphasis on diligence	
Prestige Economy			
Social Immobility	Uselessness of strife	Deification and control over others	Many checks on ostentation
	Jealousy	*Tromba*—fate Rage of gods	Illness and absence of support
Property Laws	Property as means of enlarging ego	Law	Punishment
	Deification— Lineage cult		Malevolent magic

KARDINER'S OUTLINE FOR LINKING PRIMARY AND SECONDARY
INSTITUTIONS IN TANALA SOCIETY (After Kardiner, 1939).

to infants and children, the character of the supernaturals in that culture will reflect "projections" of such experiences. This suggestion gave Kardiner the clue to how culture, in general, could affect personality development, in general. Thus, benevolent, kindly, attentive parents do not produce, directly, images of benevolent, kindly supernaturals but, rather, a personality type that is satisfied and gratified by the belief that supernaturals are of that character. The ritual, then, by its very performance, is believed to bring about a desired gratification because, after all, is that not the way gratification has been obtained from parents (as opposed to gratification obtained by begging or beseeching the supernaturals to intervene on one's behalf)? It is basically a simple idea:

$$\text{primary institutions} \rightarrow \text{personality type} \rightarrow \text{secondary institutions}$$

The most fundamental problem with this scheme, which Kardiner himself realized, was how to explain the existence of the primary institutions (which, it should be observed, are arbitrarily defined as primary in the first place). Without such an explanation, the scheme does no more than attempt to explain one aspect of culture and/or personality by another in a strangely circular manner—precisely the same problem encountered in Ruth Benedict's more simple-minded scheme. Nonetheless, the ideas set forth by Kardiner and his associates were, and are, of potentially great value. It may eventually prove possible in this way to explain religious practices as we explain anything else—that is, in terms of actual causes and effects. For a long time it was believed that religion was not a proper subject for anthropological investigation because it simply did not lend itself to this kind of study. Note, however, that if a completely satisfactory explanation is forthcoming from this tradition it will be a result of the merger of psychology and anthropology.

A contemporary, more sophisticated, and more productive version of Kardiner's approach has been mostly associated with John W. M. Whiting of Harvard. This work combines statistical cross-cultural investigations and learning theory along with the approach mapped out by Kardiner. It also opens up possibilities for overcoming the major objection to Kardiner's scheme—the arbitrariness and inexplicability of the primary institutions. Whiting's scheme is as follows (Whiting and Child 1953:310):

$$\begin{pmatrix} \text{maintenance} \\ \text{systems} \end{pmatrix} \rightarrow \begin{pmatrix} \text{child-training} \\ \text{practices} \end{pmatrix} \rightarrow \begin{pmatrix} \text{personality} \\ \text{variables} \end{pmatrix} \rightarrow \begin{pmatrix} \text{projective} \\ \text{systems} \end{pmatrix}$$

Thus, where Kardiner and his associates had arbitrarily lumped together as primary institutions such diverse things as child-rearing, property, economy, and so on, Whiting and his co-workers have separated child-rearing practices from *maintenance systems*, the latter being defined as:

> By maintenance systems we mean the economic, political, and social organizations of a society — the basic customs surrounding the nourishment, sheltering, and protection of its members, which seem a likely source of influence on child training practices. (Whiting and Child 1953:310)

While this might appear a simple modification it is, in fact, as Harris (1968:45) has pointed out, a modification of great significance. It offers a solution to the problem of the origins of child-rearing practices, precisely the weak point in the Kardiner scheme; and it also promises to bridge the gap between psychological anthropologists and those of a more materialist persuasion. Maintenance systems, in this scheme, can be taken as those fundamental technoenvironmental features that are the most primary and basic of all—for example, temperature, type of soil, amount of moisture, kinds of crops that can be grown or types of animals present, tools available for exploiting these, and the like. The belief that these technoenvironmental features are primary and causal in explanations of cultural phenomena constitutes the core, as we shall see, of the materialist position. Thus Whiting's position, although considered here under the rubric of culture-and-personality, has a footing in other less explicitly psychological positions such as cultural ecology and cultural materialism. And he can, then, for example, attempt to show a relationship between a harsh environment in which women must work hard (maintenance system), the amount and kind of care they can give their infants (child-rearing), the resulting personality type (personality variable), and the character of their supernaturals (projective system); indeed, such a relationship has been found in studies already done. Or one might link average temperature to sleeping arrangements, to care of infants, to personality, and to the projective system; this too has been done. While these studies are not as yet definitive, they are remarkably promising attempts (Whiting, Kluckhohn, and Anthony 1958; Whiting 1964). They demonstrate, again, the utility of using personality variables in the study of culture.

Notice that this approach violates the basic argument of the functionalists in that it deals with various aspects of culture, which Whiting and associates call "customs," and it takes them out of context in order to compare them. In this respect it tends to go back to the era of "shreds and patches." Whiting deliberately chose the term *custom* rather than "culture trait" or "culture pattern," "because the latter have been used to include nonbehavior items [items of *material culture*] of 'culture' " (Whiting and Child 1953:17). Thus he defines culture as behavior and clearly separates it from artifacts:

For our purpose a canoe and a technique of paddling are events of quite different order. The building of a canoe and the technique of paddling are both behavior phenomena, but the canoe itself is not, and we need a cultural concept which will clearly exclude artifacts from its meaning. (Whiting and Child 1953:17)

This is a departure from the definition Malinowski employed which, following Tylor in this respect, did not make this distinction:

It [culture] obviously is the integral whole consisting of implements and consumers' goods, of constitutional charters for the various social groupings, of human ideas and crafts, beliefs and customs. (Malinowski 1944:36)

Or again:

This social heritage is the key concept of cultural anthropology. It is usually called culture. . . . Culture comprises inherited artifacts, goods, technical processes, ideas, habits, and values. (Malinowski 1931:621)

Although Whiting shares with the cultural materialists a definition of culture which emphasizes behavior, he is nonetheless more of an idealist than a materialist. He does not insist that anthropologists should study only overt, observable behavior, he employs psychological constructs such as personality and projective systems, and he is, in general, interested in mental as well as material phenomena. For Whiting, cognitive factors are, in principle at least, as legitimate and as amenable for study as are the more overt behavior patterns insisted upon by the materialists. Thus he occupies a kind of middle ground between two widely differing contemporary points of view.

Two other definitions are of special interest because they have come to be associated with major theoretical approaches in anthropology. These are the behavioral and cognitive definitions of culture. The *behavioral definition* focuses upon observable patterns of behavior within some social group. For this approach, "the culture concept comes down to behavior patterns associated with particular groups of peoples, that is to 'customs,' or to a people's 'way of life' " (Harris 1968:16). The *cognitive definition*, on the other hand, excludes behavior and restricts the culture concept to ideas, beliefs, and knowledge. While most early definitions *included* the cognitive dimensions, they were not restricted to them. (Spradley 1972:6)

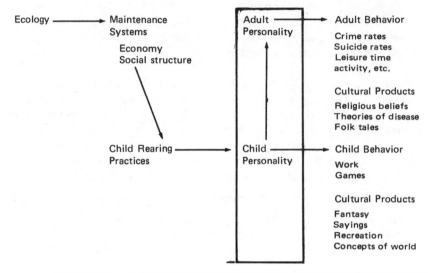

WHITING'S 1963 CULTURE-PERSONALITY-BEHAVIOR SCHEME. (B. Whiting, 1963:5)

The Whiting definition of culture embraces both cognitive and overt behavioral factors. It eliminates material things—tools, houses, clothing, and other artifacts and possessions. The materialists, especially Harris (1964:22), would include material things but exclude cognition. As both materialists and idealists would agree that cognition is, indeed, behavior, their argument on this score is methodological rather than theoretical. But to insist that definitions of culture should exclude artifacts, however, is an important theoretical innovation. We shall return to it in the following chapter. The concept of culture itself remains central, of course, no matter which part of the argument one accepts.

A revision of Whiting's scheme in 1963 introduces another important consideration—ecology—and opens up still further possibilities (see the diagram). This scheme is more in line with Whiting's recent work on values (Whiting, Chasdi, Antonovsky, and Ayres 1966) but is still not without problems, as Beatrice Whiting points out:

> To summarize the conceptual background in another way, the researchers viewed ecology, economics, and social and political organizations as setting the parameters for the behavior of the agents of child rearing. They viewed child behavior as an index of child personality and adult behavior and beliefs and values as indices of adult personality. The causal relationships implied in this scheme are open to discussion, and such discussions, with present available knowledge, ultimately end with a problem similar to that of the priority of the chicken or the egg. (B. Whiting 1963:5).

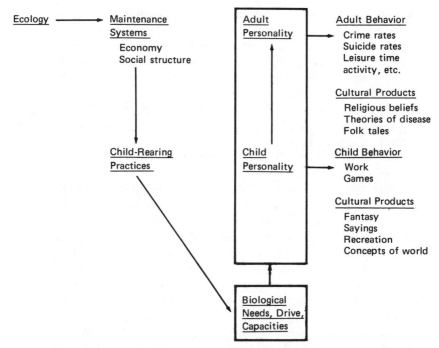

THE LEVINE EXPANSION (LEVINE AND LEVINE, 1966) OF THE WHITING CULTURE-PERSONALITY-BEHAVIOR SCHEME, AS PRESENTED IN LEVINE (1973).

Robert and Barbara LeVine have added a still further dimension (see their diagram) to the Whiting model, and a useful one, but it does not resolve the problem of causality mentioned above. This general scheme, and LeVine's later elaboration of it in his book *Culture, Behavior, and Personality* (1973) holds great promise for further studies of religious belief and ritual, as well as for other cultural phenomena. It also promises to strengthen the relationship between anthropology and psychoanalytic theory.

Anthony F. C. Wallace, another scholar who engages in culture-and-personality studies, has concentrated much more on cognitive processes than most others. His definition of culture, although stressing behavior as Whiting's does, more explicitly refers to cognitive factors also:

Those ways of behavior or techniques of solving problems which, being more frequently and more closely approximated than other ways, can be said to have a high probability of use by individual members of society. (1970:7)

It is this problem-solving character of culture that has occupied Wallace's attention mostly, but he has also done extensive work on the questions of culture and mental illness and the distribution of personality characteristics.

This tradition of culture-and-personality studies owes a great deal to the work of A. Irving Hallowell, whose brilliant work in this tradition spanned forty years and remains as stimulating today as it was when written (Hallowell 1955, 1976; Spiro 1965). This tradition also, as we shall see later, attempts a broad evolutionary approach to problems of culture and the individual, one which emphasizes the importance of biology as well as psychology.

The majority of all culture-and-personality studies to date, from Benedict right down to the present time, have used culture as an *independent variable* (the one that is manipulated in an experiment) to explain one or more *dependent* (in this case personality) *variables* (the one whose behavior is assumed to follow from the manipulation of the other). This procedure is perfectly acceptable and we now have much information on how culture influences personality. But it is unfortunate that the reverse has so rarely been attempted—that is, using personality variables as independent variables and studying different aspects of culture as dependent variables. Melford E. Spiro suggested such a reorientation of culture-and-personality studies in 1961 and in another paper published in the same year, "Social Systems, Personality, and Functional Analysis," attempted to develop a theoretical scheme that would permit us to "translate the acts of individuals into the regularities of social process," the problem that Raymond Firth had defined as central to the anthropological concern (1954:11). Spiro's position in its simplest form is similar to Malinowski's functionalism:

. . . since man is a generalized, fetalized, and plastic animal and since everywhere he is necessarily social, a typically human existence depends on the existence of socially shared behavior patterns which satisfy his (1) biological needs, (2) those group needs that are an invariant concomitant of social life (Aberle 1950) and (3) those emotional needs that develop in the interaction between biology and society. (1961b:96)

But Spiro's theoretical position goes beyond Malinowski as it has been subsequently developed and offers what is now perhaps the most sophisticated means we have in psychological anthropology for attempting to actually relate the acts of individuals to culture (Spiro n.d.).

The attempt to bridge the culture-and-personality gap led to a great deal of extremely interesting research from the 1920s through the early 1960s. Many scholars were influenced, not the least of which were Gregory Bateson, whose innovative study *Naven* introduced to the literature the concepts of *ethos* and *eidos* (1936) and Cora DuBois, whose

The People of Alor (1944) has become an anthropological classic. Other well-known studies of the period include Gorer and Rickman's *The People of Great Russia* (1949), Hsu's *Under the Ancestor's Shadow: Chinese Culture and Personality* (1948), Spiro's *Children of the Kibbutz* (1958), G. Spindler's *Sociocultural and Psychological Processes in Menomini Acculturation* (1955), and Wallace's *The Modal Personality Structure of the Tuscarora Indians, as Revealed by the Rorschach Test* (1952). There were many others, of course, and hundreds of articles dealing with both methodological and theoretical questions.

OTHER AMERICAN DEVELOPMENTS

Not all anthropologists of this period jumped on the bandwagons of either culture-and-personality studies or social anthropology. Many, including some of the most productive and notable, followed their own designs and made important and enduring contributions. One of the most notable of these was Robert Redfield. Although he received a degree in law in 1921 he subsequently became interested in anthropology and took graduate work at the University of Chicago. He was the first anthropologist to study a peasant community and during the 1930s, with his associates, carried out a comparative study of four communities on the Yucatan penninsula. This led him to formulate his idea of the *folk-urban continuum*, one that became extremely useful and influential in virtually all social science.

Redfield set for himself the task of describing "What can be said that is general and true about the condition of mankind before civilization?" (1953:1). He believed that we could do this by generalizing from surviving primitive peoples as "surviving primitive peoples have remained substantially unaffected by civilization" (1953:2). The characteristics that he felt were important were that such folk societies were small — every adult could know everyone else. They were isolated and illiterate. Such communities were also homogeneous — their people had the same ways of behaving. They also, according to Redfield, had a strong sense of group solidarity — they naturally felt that they all belonged together. There were no full-time specialists — what one person did was pretty much what everyone else did. The relationships among people were based on personal status — there were few or no strangers. Even nature was regarded as personal and humanlike. The groupings that existed in such communities depended upon *status* and *role* and not on practical utility or legal contracts. Relationships were also essentially familial, based upon the extension outward of primary kinship roles in the *nuclear family*—everyone was a father, brother, mother, sister, or the like to many others. The incentives for work in such communities were mostly noneconomic and arose from tradition and obligation rather than from the desire for material reward as such—the economy is submerged in social relations. These communities, Redfield argued, were held together "by common understandings as to the ultimate nature and purpose of life" (1953:12). The controls for action were informal. Political institutions, if not absent entirely, were few and simple. The principles of rightness that inform action were tacit and understood by all, not being subject either to criticism or to reflexive thought. Finally, what held people together was a shared sense of the moral, "by largely undeclared but continually realized ethical conceptions" (1953:15).

This characterization of Redfield's has been of great importance in social science. It is still influential even though there are those who believe it is a terribly oversimplified and in some respects erroneous view of such societies (Edgerton 1976). Although Redfield did not intend to imply that folk societies were either better or worse than others the tendency is very strong to conclude that as you move from folk to urban things get worse and worse. Redfield, who was influenced by Radcliffe-Brown, believed that these characteristics were so functionally related that a change in one would necessarily affect one or more of the others. Redfield also wanted to be able to say "this is what they did; this is how they felt; this is the way the world looked to them" (1953:1-2); but obviously, as he was generalizing from archaeology and from existing "primitives," he could not really have known how any individuals actually felt or how the world looked to them. Whereas we tend, perhaps even like to think, that the price we pay for civilization is anomie and alienation leading to mental illness, drugs, a breakdown of the family and moral order, and like ills, hard evidence for this idea is difficult to come by. But once one has this idea, then just as was the original evolutionary paradigm it is hard to abandon.

Redfield was influenced by Radcliffe-Brown during the latter's presence at the University of Chicago during 1931–1937. In his book *The Folk Culture of Yucatan* (1941) Redfield attempted to more explicitly define culture as contrasted with *society* and *community*. The definitions of society and community were similar to those of Radcliffe-Brown, who, as we have previously noted, had only a very ambiguous view of culture (Singer 1978:208). Redfield was only one of a number of scholars who wanted to clarify and distinguish these concepts so as to eliminate the previous competition between them. Singer reports that this period marked ". . . a public and professional recognition of the shift from the global and intellectually imperialistic concepts of culture and social systems to an analytical distinction between the two concepts as quasi-independent" (1978:206).

Another important and influential scholar of the period was Melville J. Herskovits. Herskovits was an early user of psychological tests, he pioneered in cross-cultural studies of perception, and he believed that culture was a determinant of personality (Campbell 1973:vii). Even so, he is not generally identified primarily with the culture-and-personality school. Herskovits wrote on African influences on Black American culture when many had assumed or argued there were none. He worked in Africa and the Caribbean as well as in Brazil. He was a pioneer in economic anthropology. Along with Benedict, Herskovits was a vociferous proponent of cultural relativism and of the culture concept in general. He is also said to have introduced the concept of enculturation (Titiev 1964). Among other works, he authored *Dahomey, an Ancient West African Kingdom* (1938) and *The Myth of the Negro Past* (1941). His wife and collaborator brought out a collection of his statements and articles on cultural relativism in 1973, *Cultural Relativism.*

Still another influential voice of the period, with decidedly psychological interests but not usually identified as a culture-and-personality scholar, was Homer G. Barnett. His work on invention and culture change in the 1940s, and his book *Innovation: The Basis of Cultural Change* (1953) remain useful and stimulating to this day. In his work Barnett attempted to explicate the motives for accepting inventions and discoveries as well as what kinds of individuals might be the most amenable to change. He also produced a fine work on religion, *Indian Shakers: A Messianic Cult of the Pacific Northwest* (1957).

One of the truly dominant figures in American anthropology, George Peter Murdock, defied categorization by being one of the pioneers in *behavioral science*, although it had not yet been so labeled when he began his participation. As behavioral science has become so prominent in recent years, Murdock's description is worth quoting:

The past decade [the 1940s] has witnessed a revolutionary development in the psychological and social sciences. A number of disciplines that had previously pursued independent courses in the analysis of particular facets of man's individual and social behavior have been discovered to dovetail into one another so neatly that they are well on the road to being fused into a single integrated science. The first major steps in achieving this integration were made at the Institute of Human Relations at Yale University, but the movement has spread to other institutions and is being pressed forward with especial vigor by the Department of Social Relations at Harvard University.

This development has been widely misunderstood as a mere pooling of separate scientific skills and techniques on cooperative research programs. The significant fact, however, is that the integration has taken place at the level of theory. At least four previously distinct systems of theory have been found to interdigitate so that each supports the others and is in turn illuminated by them. These four are the theory of learning and behavior developed by experimental psychologists, the theory of social relationships and social structure developed by sociologists and social anthropologists, the theory of culture and cultural change developed by anthropologists with significant assistance from sociologists, and the theory of personality and its formation developed by psychoanalysts and psychiatrists. (1949a:377)

Although Murdock wrote on a wide variety of subjects during his long career and like Herskovits was a champion of the culture concept, he is probably best known for his work on social structure. *Social Structure* ". . . represents a synthesis of five distinct products of social science — one research technique and four systems of theory":

The research technique upon which the volume depends, and without which it would not have been undertaken, is that of the Cross-Cultural Survey. Initiated in 1937 as part of the integrated program of research in the social sciences conducted by the Institute of Human Relations at Yale University, the Cross-Cultural Survey has built up a complete file of geographical, social, and cultural information, extracted in full from the sources and classified by subject, on some 150 human societies, historical and contemporary as well as primitive. From these files it is possible to secure practically all the existing information on particular topics in any of the societies covered in an insignificant fraction of the time required for comparable library research. (1949b:vii)

This project resulted in what we now know as the Human Relations Area Files, the monumental achievement of Murdock and his colleagues which provides readily available coded information on more than 1200 of the world's cultures (see *Outline of Cultural Materials*, Murdock, et al. [1971] for categories and locations of the files).

Social Structure was Murdock's attempt to clarify and explain the various forms of family, kin, and clan that had long fascinated anthropologists and occupied so much of their attention. He was interested in the evolution of these forms as well as their variation and, although the book was not well received by British anthropologists, there is no doubt that it is an American classic and did much to clarify and bring order to what had previously been much more confused. As Alexander Spoehr has commented, "When Murdock entered the academic field, scholars were still writing about 'mother-right' and 'father-right,' " which gives some idea not only of Murdock's achievement but also his durability. In

1981 he published his *Atlas of World Cultures!* A sampling of Murdock's other writings can be found in *Culture and Society* (1965). Although Murdock was interested in the evolution of social structures he cannot be classified along with those few anthropologists who can be considered "modern evolutionists" to distinguish them from the early evolutionists we have already considered.

MODERN EVOLUTIONISTS

One of these, Julian Steward, was among the first anthropologists to emphasize ecology as a determining influence on culture and on the evolution of culture. His work with *"primitive bands"* was of great significance to anthropology in that he established the band as a meaningful unit of social organization for cross-cultural work and demonstrated causal explanations for the existence of various types of such bands. He did this by showing how, despite different technologies and environments associated with different primitive bands, there were underlying ecological conditions that produced similar types and subtypes. He made a similarly important discovery linking population density and agricultural techniques with Pueblo social organization. He also identified parallel evolutionary developments in five different regions of the world—Peru, Mexico, Mesopotamia, Egypt, and North China—a finding of great theoretical importance. Steward's work has had a profound impact on archeology and has, in fact, been instrumental in bringing about the so-called "new archeology."

Steward's *cultural ecology*, as described by himself, imposes these procedures:

First, the interrelationship of exploitive or productive technology and environment must be analyzed. . . . Second, the behavior patterns involved in the exploitation of a particular area by means of a particular technology must be analyzed. . . . The third procedure is to ascertain the extent to which the behavior patterns entailed in exploiting the environment affect other aspects of culture. (Steward 1955:40–41)

This scheme allowed him, with considerable success, to link techno-environmental factors to certain kinds of associated behavior patterns and thence to other aspects of culture. Since these things are linked in precisely this way, change—evolution if you will—can occur only in a certain way, which depends most fundamentally on the technoenvironmental features.

Although more recent work has questioned the validity of the concept of *patrilocal* bands (Lee and DeVore 1968:7), Steward's work remains one of the most challenging influences on present-day cultural anthropology. The emphasis on ecology or technoenvironmental features as basic is also the crucial element in both Leslie White's culturology and Marvin Harris's cultural materialism.

Leslie White, like both Malinowski and Radcliffe-Brown, was determined to make anthropology a science. Like Malinowski, he wanted a science of culture, not of society. He was adamantly opposed to biological or psychological *reductionism*. He refused to give up the concept of culture and took a position, similar to Kroeber's superorganicism, which came to be known as *culturology*. As we have already noted in the case of Kroeber, this position holds that culture has an existence independent of human beings. Thus, those who may wish to explain some aspect of culture must explain it in terms of some other aspect of culture. They must not, whatever they do, according to White, attempt to explain it in terms of psychology, biology, sociology, or anything other than culture:

. . . Culture is a continuum of interacting elements [traits], and this process of interaction has its own principles and its own laws. To introduce the human organism into a consideration of cultural variations is therefore not only irrelevant but wrong; it involves a premise that is false. Culture must be explained in terms of culture. Thus, paradoxical though it may seem, "the proper study of mankind" turns out to be not Man, after all, but Culture. The most realistic and scientifically adequate interpretation of culture is one that proceeds as if human beings did not exist. (L. White 1969:141)

White does concede that human beings are necessary as "carriers of cultural traditions" (White with Dillingham 1973:37) even though they need not be taken into account to explain changes in that tradition. Like Kroeber, White refuses to concede that human beings—no matter what their genius—have anything at all to do with the cultural process:

. . . Francis Galton and William James espoused the theory that periods of great cultural development are due to genius. But this theory leaves wholly unexplained why geniuses should be abundant at certain times. In short, the genius theory provides no valid explanation at all. It explains culture change in terms of genius, but it leaves genius unexplained. It explains the known facts of culture in terms of the unknown (or unascertained) facts of biology. The reason for simultaneous inventions is perfectly simple and clear from a culturological point of view. . . . Human beings are necessary as carriers of cultural traditions; they are not necessary for an explanation of changes in these cultural traditions. This of course cannot be emphasized too greatly. If we look at a process of evolving culture and think of cultural growth, we find that when cultural evolution reaches a certain point, a certain threshold, certain syntheses of cultural traits become possible; and by becoming possible they become inevitable. (White with Dillingham 1973:36–37)

This view is obviously so extreme that not everyone has been willing to accept it completely. Both Kroeber and White have been accused of the *reification* of culture—that is, of making a material thing out of something that is in reality only a mental thing.

Leslie White's commitment to cultural evolution expressed itself in his so-called "basic law of cultural evolution":

Other factors remaining constant, culture evolves as the amount of energy harnessed per capita per year is increased, or as the efficiency of the instrumental means of putting the energy to work is increased. Both factors may increase simultaneously of course. (1969:368)

White viewed himself as being in the direct line of evolutionary theory from Morgan to Tylor. He was also in the direct line of Frederick Engels and Karl Marx, a fact that was used in an unprincipled and unscientific attack on him during the period of national paranoia in which he did most of his productive work. His link to Marx can be seen very clearly in the following:

Technology is the hero of our piece. This is a world of rocks and rivers, sticks and steel, of sun, air and starlight, of galaxies, atoms and molecules. Man is but a particular kind of material body who must do certain things to maintain his status in a cosmic material system. The means of adjustment and control, of security and survival, are of course technological. Culture thus becomes primarily a mechanism for harnessing energy and of putting it to work in the service of man, and secondarily, of channelling and regulating his behavior not directly concerned with subsistence and offense and defense. Social systems are therefore determined by technological systems, and philosophies and the arts express experience as it is defined by technology and refracted by social systems. Cultural systems like those of the biological level are capable of growth. That is, the power to capture any energy is also the ability to harness more and still more of it. Thus cultural systems, like biological organisms, develop, multiply, and extend themselves. (L. White 1969:390–391)

The most fundamental assumption of Marxist philosophers is that nonideological factors determine social organization and ideology. One of the clearest statements of this proposition can be seen in the following by Marvin Harris, the most important and vociferous contemporary proponent of this general point of view:

We are led inexorably to conclude that thoughts about institutions are constrained by the institutions under which men do their thinking. Now there arises the question, whence come the institutions? Marx attempted to answer this question by giving separate consideration to different varieties of institutions. He split the nonideological aspects of sociocultural life into two parts: the economic structure ("the real foundation") and the "legal and political superstructure." He came to distinguish, therefore, three major sociocultural segments: (1) the economic base; (2) the legal-political arrangements, which in modern terms correspond to social structure, or social organization; and (3) "social consciousness" or ideology. Marx and Engels then boldly proclaimed that it was in the economic base that the explanation for both parts of the superstructure—social organization and ideology—were to be found.

Why was it not the other way round? Why not the dominance of social organization over economics? The answer there is contained in the phrase which associates "relations of production" with "a definite stage of development" or man's "material powers of production." It is the stage of development of the material powers of production which renders the "relations of production" *independent* of man's will. For no group of men can will into existence whenever and wherever they choose, the apparatus of production—*coup de poing*, plows, or Bessemer converters—except in a *definite order of progression*. That order of progression corresponds precisely to what the combined efforts of archaeologists and ethnographers have revealed it to be. The unbroken chain of technological innovations which connects digital computers with Oldowan choppers does not admit of deviations or leaps (although the rate of change might conceivably vary rather widely). Stone tools *had* to come before metal tools; spears *had* to come before bows and arrows; hunting and gathering *had* to precede the plow; the flint strike-a-light *had* to be invented before the safety match; oars and sails *had* to precede the steamboat; and handicrafts *had* to precede industrial manufacture. Indeed, none of the major opponents of cultural materialism has ever seriously questioned these facts.

The Boasians, for example, frequently pointed out that technology is cumulative and that objective measures of progress are possible in this realm. Thus, the only point at issue (aside from details concerning the order of emergence of certain innovations) is whether "the mode of production in material life determines the general character of the social, political and spiritual" aspects of sociocultural life. This, it will be seen at once, is an eminently empirical issue, not to be answered by logic alone. (Harris 1968:231-232)

The Marxist idea, then, in its most basic form is as follows:

economic base (technoenvironmental)	→	legal-political arrangements (social organization)	→	social consciousness (ideology)

The influence of Marx on Leslie White is not mere conjecture; neither is the neglect of Marx by social scientists in the United States. It is a most interesting, if unpleasant and shortsighted chapter in the history of American anthropology. White attended the New School in New York, where he took courses in anthropology from one of Boas's early students, Alexander Goldenweiser. He then moved to the University of Chicago where he studied with Edward Sapir and Fay-Cooper Cole, taking his Ph.D. degree in 1927. His first job was at the University of Buffalo, where he read Lewis Henry Morgan for the first time. He was profoundly impressed by Morgan, in spite of having been told by his Boasian professors that evolutionism was defunct, and he soon went on to read Marx and Engels. This study led him, in turn, to make a trip to the Soviet Union in 1929. Upon his return he took a position at the University of Michigan, where he eventually created a strong department of anthropology and trained a number of brilliant students.

White's discussion of culture emphasized its dependence upon the ability of human beings to *symbolize*. He argued that it was the ability to create and use symbols that set human beings apart from other animals and enabled them to carry on their elaborate cultural way of life. A symbol, White said:

> . . . may be defined as a thing the value or meaning of which is bestowed upon it by those who use it. I say "thing" because a symbol may have any kind of physical form; it may have the form of a material object, a color, a sound, an odor, a motion of an object, a taste. The meaning, or value, of a symbol is in no instance derived from or determined by properties intrinsic in its physical form: the color appropriate to mourning may be yellow, green or any other color; purple need not be the color of royalty; among the Manchu rulers of China it was yellow. The meaning of the word "see" is not intrinsic in its phonetic (or pictorial) properties. . . . The meanings of symbols are derived from and determined by the organisms who use them; meaning is bestowed by human organisms upon physical things or events which thereupon become symbols. Symbols "have their signification," to use John Locke's phrase, "from the arbitrary imposition of men." (L. White 1969:25)

This point was, and is, of great significance, as many people had argued up to White's time that there was no essential difference between the minds of animals and people except one of degree. Although this issue remains not completely understood, recent research into the symbolic and language competence of chimpanzees indicates that man is, indeed, very different in this respect (Gardner and Gardner 1971; Premack and Premack 1972; Premack 1971). White's insistence upon this point stimulated a great deal of thought on the matter and helped to further refine our views about the nature of culture.

Julian Steward and Leslie White were virtually the only proponents of evolution during the period when most other anthropologists were turning to structural functionalism and psychological anthropology.

Steward's ideas were rather quickly accepted and incorporated into the mainstream of anthropology. White, on the other hand, did not have such an easy time of it, in large part owing to his obvious identification with Marx, a stigma that Julian Steward managed to avoid. Marx was simply not acceptable to most American scholars during this period of time for reasons that had nothing whatever to do with his intellectual or scholarly work—another example of the relationship of government to social-science research. The denial of more general acceptance to White must be traced in part, however, to the extremity of his position and also, perhaps, to his abrasive and dogmatic style of writing. Most anthropologists are not so willing as are Leslie White and others of his general persuasion to dismiss human beings and their beliefs and ideas as irrelevant to the processes of change and evolution.

Some of the practitioners of White's culturology, mostly his students, believe not only in material determinism and evolution, but also, like the earlier evolutionists, in "progress." Progress is defined by them, or at least by some of them, as "increase in organization, higher energy concentration, and with a qualification . . . towards increasing heterogeneity" (Sahlins and Service 1960:8). However reasonable this definition may sound, and however much it appears that change actually has been in this general direction over time, it still remains no more than an article of personal or national faith that it is "progress." It is progress by definition, as can be seen more clearly, perhaps, when the more specific statements of these modern-day evolutionists are considered. For example:

> Culture, continuing the life process, appropriates free energy and builds it into an organization for survival, and like life, culture moves to maximize the amount of energy exploitation. (Sahlins and Service 1960:9)

One might well ask why the minimization of energy exploitation should not be progress? Or why not simplicity of organization? To argue that some change constitutes progress because it seems to have, in fact, occurred over time is to sadly ignore what might have happened in the past or what could happen in the future.

Marvin Harris shares many of the fundamental assumptions of culturology and cultural ecology, but does not share the belief in progress. According to Harris, as we have noted, the major shortcoming of all the approaches to culture we have so far examined, except those of White and Steward, is that they are *idealistic* as opposed to *materialistic*. They attempt to explain culture, or some particular aspect of culture, in terms of thought or ideas, rather than in terms of the (presumably) prior and more fundamental environmental or technoenvironmental (material) features:

. . . If there had been an orderliness in human history, it cannot, as the Enlightenment philosophers supposed, have originated from the orderliness of men's
thoughts. Men do not think their way into matrilineality, the couvade, or
Iroquois cousin terminology. In the abstract, can a good reason be found why
anyone should bother to think such apparently improbable thoughts? And if one
man had thought of them, whence arose the compulsion and the power to con-
vince others of their propriety? For surely it could not be that these improbable
ideas construed as mere spontaneous products of fancy occur simultaneously to
dozens of people at a time. Obviously, therefore, thoughts must be subject to
constraints; that is, they have causes and are made more or less probable in
individuals and groups of individuals by prior conditions. (Harris 1968:231)

Harris believes there are a number of important issues in anthropology in which his position of *cultural materialism* is vindicated and the
idealist position is shown to be in error. The question of India's sacred
cattle is perhaps the best example. It has long been held by students of
India that if the Indians did not hold cattle to be sacred, and did not
allow them, therefore, to compete with humans for food and space, there
would be less hardship and starvation in the country than there is. That
is, if it were not for their religious beliefs (ideology), the Indians would
be better off economically (materially). Harris attempted to show in an
article entitled "The Cultural Ecology of India's Sacred Cattle" (1966),
that, in fact, if the topic was approached from a technoenvironmental
framework, it was possible to demonstrate that Hindu ideology had little
or nothing to do with it. The presence of large numbers of cattle could be
adequately explained in purely ecological or technoenvironmental terms
—the cattle, he argued, provided energy to till the fields, milk, hides,
dung for fuel, and the like, did not really compete with humans for food,
and thus had an over-all positive rather than a negative function in the
Indian ecosystem. If Harris is right, the instance would be a demonstration of his position discussed above, and the prior causal significance of
technoenvironmental factors and the relative insignificance of ideology.
Although the issue has not been settled, there are many who are not convinced and who still subscribe to the original view that the Hindu beliefs
are in this case dysfunctional (Bennett 1967; Heston 1971; Freed and
Freed 1972, 1981; Vaidyanathan, Nair, and Harris 1982). There are similar kinds of arguments that have to do with the explanation for the
potlatches of the northwest coast of America (Codere 1950), "primitive"
warfare (Vayda 1961), communal hunting territories (Leacock 1954;

Knight 1965), and, more recently, Aztec cannibalism (Harner 1977; Harris 1977).

The most ambitious of these attempts at ecological/materialist explanations, and perhaps the most compelling as well, is Roy A. Rappaport's attempt to explain a New Guinea religious ritual in ecological terms, *Pigs for the Ancestors: Ritual in the Ecology of a New Guinea People* (1967). Rappaport starts out "by regarding culture, in some of its aspects, as part of the means by which animals of the human species maintain themselves in their environments" (1967:5). He attempts to demonstrate that Maring religious ritual is a mechanism that "regulates some of the relationships of the Tsembaga [a subgroup of the Maring] with components of their environment" and it does this, he maintains, in essentially the same way a thermostat works:

> The systematic relationships described in this study are more than regulated; they are self-regulated. The term *self-regulation* may be applied to systems in which a change in the value of a variable itself initiates a process that either limits further change or returns the value to a former level. This process, sometimes referred to as "negative feedback," may involve special mechanisms that change the values of some variables in response to changes in the values of others. Thermostats, for instance, may be regarded as mechanical regulating mechanisms in systems in which measurable quantities of heat emanating intermittently from a controlled source and the temperature of a surrounding medium are variables. It will be argued here that Tsembaga ritual, particularly in the context of a ritual cycle, operates as a regulating mechanism in a system, or set of interlocking systems, in which such variables as the area of available land, necessary lengths of fallow periods, size and composition of both human and pig populations, trophic requirements of pigs and people, energy expended in various activities, and the frequency of misfortunes are included. There are numerous additional variables to be considered as well. (1967:4)

Although Rappaport has been criticized with respect to various details of his analysis and measurements (McArthur 1974), *Pigs for the Ancestors* is a stimulating and important work which made clear, contrary to much previous functional theory on religion, that ritual actions have an effect on the external world as well as merely on the internal world of the participants. That is, not only does religious ritual function to dispel fear and anxiety, but it also in this case at least, regulates relationships of groups of people to each other, to their livestock, and to their flora and fauna. The most difficult problem in ecological and materialist approaches is how to deal with the ideas or ideology of the people involved and, similarly, with their motives. In a recent revision of *Pigs For the Ancestors* (1984) Rappaport has attempted to answer his critics.

For example, it is not completely clear in Harris's work just what role he ascribes to ideas. At times he appears to be insisting that ideas have no place at all in how humans relate to their technoenvironments. For example, in his otherwise encyclopedic work, *The Rise of Anthropological Theory* (1968), he simply dismisses Max Weber's monumental study, *The Protestant Ethic and the Spirit of Capitalism* (1930), on the grounds that it deals with only a single case (1968:285). Indeed, he does not even include Weber in the bibliography. Inasmuch as Weber's thesis was that capitalism could not have arisen in Europe without the ideology of Protestantism, a clear example of power ascribed to ideas, Harris's treatment of this work is open to question.

Surely there has to be a feedback of some kind between people, their ideas, and their environment. To argue that human thoughts have no causal significance at all—that is, to say "stone tools *had* to come before metal tools; spears *had* to come before bows and arrows . . ." (1968:232), is rather like saying the cause of the bow and arrow was simply the prior existence of trees. Spears, if indeed they came before the bow and arrow as it now appears they did, were converted into arrows and applied to bows through the mental acts (ideas) of people—and the same mental ability that enabled someone to make the conversion also permitted others to grasp the utility of the idea and to use the bow and arrow themselves. Harris's view that culture must be defined simply as behavior, and that human behavior is determined solely by technoenvironmental factors, like all such behaviorist views, tends to reduce human beings to the status of mere pawns in some great mysterious game, the rules of which can be determined by factors totally unrelated to the pieces themselves.

For those unwilling to accept *a priori* the absolute primacy of technoenvironmental factors, the claim that they alone determine both social organization and ideology is not well substantiated as yet. The study of culture involves recognizing that the thoughts, as well as the acts, of human beings are important variables in the invention, transmission, and further evolution of mankind and culture. That they are important can be seen in the fact that at least since Turgot, through Arnold, Tylor, Boas, Malinowski, Benedict, Steward, White, Harris, and the untold diverse others, investigators have found it necessary to cling to the culture concept in one form or another. Why, for example, does Steward find it necessary to speak of *cultural* ecology? Why, if ecology is the study of an organism's relation to its total environment, need there be one ecology for others but a different one—*cultural ecology*—for humans? Why is it necessary to specify *human* ecology as contrasted with any other? Why speak, as we have in recent years, of *human* geography or its synonym, *cultural* geography? Why does Marvin Harris specify that it is *cultural* materialism rather than some other kind?

The answer, it would appear, is that humans possess an awesome ability to act upon the environment as well as be acted upon by it. At least part of this ability does seem to be the result of man's ability to symbolize, which if shared at all by other animals is shared in a most rudimentary form. Symbolization is fundamentally a psychological phenomenon, not a technoenvironmental feature. While one who so wishes may attempt to study cultural phenomena without considering the symbolic processes associated with culture, the study inevitably must be limited to a passing glance rather than a full view.

It is much to Rappaport's credit that he has attempted to deal with this issue rather than either simply denying the importance of human thought or ignoring it. He does this by insisting that two different models of the environment are significant in ecological studies, the "operational" and the "cognized." It is well worth noting what he has said of this:

Although this study had been primarily concerned with the role ritual plays in the material relations of the Tsembaga, it is nevertheless the case that the Tsembaga say that they perform their rituals to rearrange their relations with spirits. It would be possible in an analysis of the empirical consequences of ritual acts to ignore such rationalizations, but anthropology is concerned with elucidating causes, as well as consequences, of behavior, and proximate causes are often to be found in the understandings of the actors. It seems to me, therefore, that in ecological studies of human groups we must take these understandings into account.

I have suggested elsewhere (Rappaport 1963:159; 1967:22) that two models of the environment are significant in ecological studies, and I have termed these the "operational" and the "cognized." The operational model is that which the anthropologist constructs through observation and measurement of empirical entities, events, and material relationships. He takes this model to represent, for analytic purposes, the physical work of the group he is studying. The Tsembaga environment has been represented as a complex system of material relationships composed of two subsystems distinguished from each other by differences in the materials exchanged in each, but affecting each other through mechanisms amenable to direct observation.

The cognized model is the model of the environment conceived by the people who act in it. The two models are overlapping, but not identical. While many components of the physical world will be represented in both, the operational model is likely to include material elements, such as disease germs and nitrogen-fixing bacteria, that affect the actors but of which they may not be aware. Conversely, the cognized model may include elements that cannot be shown by empirical means to exist, such as spirits and other supernatural beings.

Some elements peculiar to the cognized model may be isomorphic with elements peculiar to the operational model. The Tsembaga say, for instance, that they are loath to build houses below 3,500 feet because certain spirits that are abroad at night in low areas give one fever. The behavior of these spirits—and the consequences of their behavior—corresponds closely to that of anopheles mosquitoes, which the Tsembaga do not recognize to be carriers of malaria. But elements, and relationships among elements, in the two models need not always be isomorphic or identical. The cognized and operational models may differ in some aspects of their structure as well as in the elements included in each.

This is not to say, of course, that the cognized model is merely a less adequate representation of reality than the operational model. The operational model is an observer's description of selected aspects of the material world. It has a purpose only for the anthropologist. As far as the actors are concerned it has no function. Indeed, it does not exist. The cognized model, while it must be understood by those who entertain it to be a representation of the material and nonmaterial world, has a function for the actors: it guides their action. Since this is the case, we are particularly concerned to discover what the people under study believe to be the functional relationships among the entities that they think are part of their environment, and what they take to be "signs," indicating changes in these entities or relationships, which demand action on their part; but *the important question concerning the cognized model, since it serves as a guide to action, is not the extent to which it conforms to "reality" (i.e. is identical with or isomorphic with the operational model), but the extent to which it elicits behavior that is appropriate to the material situation of the actors, and it is against this functional and adaptive criterion that we may assess it.* Maring notions of disease etiology are certainly inaccurate, but the slaughter and consumption of pigs during illness is just as effective when undertaken to strengthen or mollify spirits as it would be if it were specifically undertaken to alleviate stress symptoms. (Rappaport 1967:237–239)

I have quoted this at such length because it is terribly important and it is related to one of the issues which appears to trouble Harris so much.

Just as Harris's materialism allies him with Steward and White, so his views oppose him dramatically to many others in the anthropological profession. Part of the reason is simply his materialism, but another part lies in his views on psychologizing. The issues are seen most clearly in the current controversy over *emic* rather than *etic* approaches.

The terms *emic* and *etic*, as well as the distinction between them, were the creation of the distinguished linguist Kenneth Pike (1954). In brief, emic statements, in Harris's usage, refer to distinctions or meanings as they are perceived by the actors themselves—the people themselves, if the reporter is an anthropologist or linguist studying them. Etic statements are those whose meanings can be verified by independent investigators using similar operations—what the people being observed may personally believe about them is simply not relevant to their truth or falsity.

Harris believes that virtually all ethnographic reports suffer from the failure to distinguish clearly between emic and etic statements. That is, the monographs contain some etic statements and some emic statements, indiscrimininantly mixed so that the reader cannot know which is which. There is little doubt that this confusion does, in fact, occur. Indeed, the goal of the "new ethnography," to which we will shortly return, is to eliminate this problem by focusing strictly on emic categories until they are clearly understood, and only then begin speaking about etics. Harris conceded that emics are not necessarily less empirical or subject to scientific study than are etics. But he also believes that all past ethnographic work has been biased towards emics (1968:576). This bias could be largely eliminated if anthropologists would clearly distinguish between operational and cognized models.

But what is most unfortunate about this bias, from Harris's point of view, is that emic statements get hopelessly confused at times with what he regards as improper psychological statements and categories. Because this confusion then encourages explanations based upon mental states it is, in Harris's view, to be avoided at all costs. Harris goes on to show, with several examples, that even "structural" anthropologists—like Radcliffe-Brown, his followers, and Leslie White—depend heavily upon psychologically derived terms. They speak constantly of such things as "fear," "evasion," "feelings," "sentiments," "jealousy," "shame," and an infinite variety of others, in spite of their antipsychological theories. It is entirely possible to argue that since this vocabularly has characterized anthropology from its very beginning, and still continues, as Harris himself admits, it might be fundamental to ethnographic description. One might still object to it, not on the grounds that it should not be done at all, but, rather, that it should be done better than it has been. Harris apparently thinks it should not be done at all.

It is not clear what an anthropological monograph completely devoid of psychological terms and assumptions would look like. Although Harris's *The Nature of Cultural Things* (1964) attempts to demonstrate a method of investigation that would presumably yield such a monograph, no one has as yet actually produced one.

ETHNOSCIENCE AND FOLK MODELS

Beginning in the mid 1950s, stimulated by the work of such people as Conklin (1955), Frake (1961), French (1956), Goodenough (1956), Lenneberg and Roberts (1956), Lounsbury (1956), Metzger and Williams (1963), and others, the field of linguistics began what came to be known as the "new ethnography" (Sturtevant 1964; Cunningham et al. 1981).

This development had to do primarily with the controversy mentioned earlier over "emic" as opposed to "etic" approaches.

The most important claim of the "new ethnographers" is that they will be able to give more precise descriptions of cultural phenomena than heretofore possible—cultural descriptions that will be modeled on linguistic ones. Just as the linguist works with standard units—in terms of *phonemes, morphemes, phonology* and *grammar*—so will the ethnographer, they claim, be able to find the proper units for comparison. Thus, rather than imposing our own units and classifications on other cultures, arbitrarily forcing them, as it were, to have such things as economics, politics, or religion as we have done since the very beginning of anthropology, we will be able to elicit their meaningful units and classifications. Perceiving these will give us the "inside" view, the subject's own view of the world and things as opposed to our own ethnocentric and egocentric views. In terms of aims this approach is not fundamentally very different from those of Boas, Malinowski, and most other fieldworkers (Berreman 1966). The claim for a new ethnography is based primarily on the availability of new linguistic methods; the approach is most often termed *ethnoscience*. Using this method, we have already found that other people do not always classify things around them as we do. Where we, for example, have general categories like "plants" and "animals," for some people there are only certain kinds of plants and animals. Where we have color terms like *scarlet, maroon,* and *pink,* many people would lump all of them under a single term. Likewise, where we lump a number of relatives together under the term *uncle* or *aunt,* many people would distinguish terminologically between father's sister and mother's sister. We distinguish between natural and supernatural, between magic and science, between logical and illogical, and between other pairs, whereas other people do not. But although ethnoscientists argue that only by first ascertaining the categories other people use will we eventually (perhaps) be able to derive universal categories, the opponents of ethnoscience argue that, carried to its logical extreme, ethnoscience would result in purely relativistic descriptions of particular cases. Insofar as the units and categories of one culture are found to be relative to that culture and no other, there would be no basis for comparison and hence no science. Spiro, in his *Burmese Supernaturalism*, has stated such a point of view:

As between the "emic and" "etic" approaches, then, my approach is unabashedly etic. The former approach leads to a descriptive and relativistic inquiry whose interest begins and ends with the parochial. The latter approach leads to a theoretical and comparative inquiry in which the parochial is of interest as an instance of the universal. If the former issues in ethnography, the latter (although based on ethnography) issues in science. Since I am interested in science, the explanations offered in this study use concepts which are analytic rather than substantive; their reference is usually to a theoretical construct rather than to an ethnographic category; and their domain is usually the class "supernaturalism" and not merely Burmese supernaturalism. (1967:6)

Harris, as we have noted, although hostile to what he sees as an emic bias in anthropology, does not believe that emic studies need, necessarily, be more subjective or unscientific than etic studies. Many have noted that to date most ethnoscientific studies have concerned themselves with exceedingly small domains which some regard as basically trivial—local classifications of colors, plants, insects, disease, and the like. Furthermore, they have been mostly unconcerned with whether or not any new scientific insights can be derived from such studies. In this respect they are like the purely descriptive ethnographic efforts of the historical particularist. This limited character may be a result of the difficulties of actually doing ethnoscientific research in the field, for such work is extremely time-consuming and demanding. However, the late James Spradley demonstrated in his book on urban nomads, *You Owe Yourself a Drunk* (1970), that this method gives positive insights for the investigation of other cultures or subcultures. Michael Agar's work on heroin addiction, *Running and Ripping: A Formal Ethnography of Urban Heroin Addicts* (1973), is similar in this respect. Another book which used ethnoscience and is a transition between that and the current work on folk models is Michelle Z. Rosaldo's *Knowledge and Passion: Ilogot Notions of Self and Social Life* (1980).

It would be of great importance for the study of culture to have thorough emic data from as many cultures as possible. With such data it would then be possible to see to what extent there are real similarities and differences in the ways people classify, attach meanings to things around them, and communicate with one another. It would also be of great benefit to know how people in various cultures express their innermost thoughts, feelings, and states of mind. Ethnoscience has developed into studies of *folk models* with precisely this in mind, an endeavor of much promise and significance. Following D'Andrade, let us say that "A folk model is a cognitive schema which is intersubjectively shared by a social group" (1983), a "schema" being a system of interrelated concepts which represent a mental model of something. Folk models that have been studied range from the definition of the notion of a "lie" (Sweetser 1983), to labels for the opposite sex (Holland, 1983), to notions of illness (Price-McGough 1983), to local theories of emotion (Lutz 1983), to color terms

(Conklin 1955; Berlin and Kay 1969), navigational systems (Gladwin 1970), folk conceptions of time (Givens 1977), and increasing numbers of other such folk models as well.

SUMMARY

There developed in the United States during the 1920s and 1930s an interest in how personality might be subject to the demands of culture. Many of the most important anthropologists of the time were drawn into this attempt, including such notables as Edward Sapir, Margaret Mead, Ruth Benedict, and Gregory Bateson. Like social anthropology, this was an attempt also to make anthropology more scientific. One result of this interest was the growth of a closer relationship between anthropology, psychiatry, and psychoanalytic theory. In the hands of such people as A. Irving Hallowell, Anthony Wallace, John W. M. Whiting, Robert LeVine, Melford E. Spiro, and others this has developed into a most significant means of trying to understand the long-standing issue of the relationship of the individual to his or her society and culture. Some anthropologists remained independent of this movement as such and went on to develop other schemes such as the folk-urban continuum and the notion of enculturation; they were also involved in the development of behavioral science. Some modern versions of evolutionism and materialism also became influential. Similarly, there have been significant developments in ethnoscience and folk models.

FURTHER READINGS

There are several good general collections and books on culture-and-personality: Kaplan's *Studying Personality Cross-Culturally;* Hsu's *Psychological Anthropology;* Honigmann's *Personality in Culture;* Wallace's *Culture and Personality;* the volume edited by Kluckhohn, Murray, and Schneider, *Personality in Nature, Society and Culture;* and LeVine's recent *Culture, Behavior and Personality.* Two recent textbooks have appeared: Bock's *Continuities in Psychological Anthropology* and Bourguignon's *Psychological Anthropology.* For detailed personal accounts of the work of twenty of the most distinguished practitioners of psychological anthropology see *The Making of Psychological Anthropology,* edited by George D. Spindler.

For works dealing with child rearing, personality, and culture see Kardiner's *The Individual and His Society,* Whiting and Child's *Child Training and Personality,* Beatrice Whiting's collection *Six Cultures: Studies of Child Rearing,* Spiro's *Children of the Kibbutz,* Bateson and Mead's *Balinese Character: A Photographic*

Analysis, and Williams's *Introduction to Socialization.* Also *Cross-Cultural Human Development* by Munroe and Munroe and the massive new *Handbook of Cross-Cultural Human Development* edited by Munroe, Munroe, and Whiting.

Cultural materialism is the main theme of Marvin Harris's *The Rise of Anthropological Theory* although it is also a history of anthropology. Harris also presents his position in *The Nature of Cultural Things* and, more importantly, in *Cultural Materialism.* Leslie White's position is ably presented in his famous work *The Science of Culture* and, more recently, in *The Concept of Cultural Systems.* Julian Steward, in addition to his *Theory of Culture Change,* speaks to his position in *Evolution and Ecology: Essays on Social Transformation by Julian H. Steward,* recently edited by Jane C. Steward and Robert F. Murphy. For the views of George Peter Murdock see *Social Structure* and *Culture and Society.* Biographical materials on eight of the great anthropologists, including Redfield, White, and Steward, are in *Totems and Teachers,* edited by Sydel Silverman. There is a recent biography of Mead by Jane Howard, *Margaret Mead: A Life* as well as a memoir by her daughter Mary Catherine Bateson, *With a Daughter's Eye: A Memoir of Margaret Mead and Gregory Bateson.* There is also a recent biography of Ruth Benedict, *Ruth Benedict: Patterns of a Life,* by Judith Schachter Modell, and a biographical study of Gregory Bateson as well, *Gregory Bateson: The Legacy of a Scientist,* by David Lipset.

Two special issues of the *American Ethnologist* deal with ethnoscience, cognition, and folk models: *Folk Biology (American Ethnologist* 1976) and *Symbolism and Cognition (American Ethnologist* 1981).

CHAPTER V

The Ethnographic Present

Although it is obvious that cultures are constantly changing and that human lives are lived in a state of constant and ongoing flux, when an anthropologist returns from fieldwork and writes a monograph or book describing the people he or she studied it must be understood as frozen in time, in what is termed the *ethnographic present.* In extreme cases the ethnographic present is in part a reconstruction of how such and such a culture was just prior to or at the point of contact with Europeans. Similarly, when discussing the history of anthropological theory, it is obvious that ideas from the earlier periods do not totally disappear when new developments occur but, rather, remain viable and useful along with the new developments themselves. Thus I have resisted the temptation to head this chapter "contemporary developments" or "recent trends." I wish to emphasize that the culture of anthropology, if you will, like all culture, is an ongoing process subject to fads, breakthroughs, flashbacks, and constant change and thus this description must, too, be frozen in time.

STRUCTURALISM

One influential development in anthropology as it is currently being practiced is associated with what is now termed structuralism and with the name of its most visible practitioner, Claude Lévi-Strauss.

Claude Lévi-Strauss, by far the greatest French anthropologist ever, was born in Belgium in 1908. He was a student at the University of Paris, where he took a degree in philosophy. From 1934 to 1937 he was professor of sociology at the University of São Paulo, Brazil. During this time he read Robert Lowie's *Primitive Society* (1920), his first introduction to anthropology. In 1938–1939 Lévi-Strauss undertook an expedition into central Brazil. Little is known of this except that it formed the basis for his writings on the Nambikwara and Tupi-Kawahib Indians. After a short tour of military service in France, Lévi-Strauss arrived in 1941 at the New School for Social Research in New York. During 1946–1947 he served as French cultural attaché in the United States. From 1948 to 1958 he was at the University of Paris and he was also, during most of this time and until 1960, secretary general of the International Council of Social Sciences. In 1958 he was appointed to the newly created chair of social anthropology at the Collège de France. In 1968 he was awarded the highest scientific distinction in France, the gold medal of the Centre National de la Recherche Scientifique (Leach 1970). He was named a foreign associate of the United States National Academy of Sciences in 1967 and, in 1973, was elected to the French Academy, an organization founded in 1635 and limited to only forty members. His influence is so great that he has become one of the best-known anthropologists in the history of the discipline.

Historically, Lévi-Strauss is in the same tradition of anthropology as Emile Durkheim, Marcel Mauss, and Radcliffe-Brown. But he has extended the tradition into the very realm that Durkheim and Radcliffe-Brown claimed to have abhorred, the psychological. This, among other things, places him in the cultural idealist tradition and thereby opposes his position to that of the materialists. To understand this difference let us use as an example, following Harris, the contrasting explanations for the division of labor in society.

Adam Smith (1776) had explained the existence of a *division of labor* in purely economic terms—greater specialization of labor provides a more efficient means of production and hence cheaper goods for all— hence, it was believed, greater "happiness" for all. Durkheim (1893) challenged this purely materialistic view by demonstrating that the division of labor was not, in fact, associated with greater "happiness." He then substituted for the efficiency in Smith's original explanation the functional importance of social solidarity and the reduction of competition:

The division of labor thus emerges as a social arrangement not for increasing productivity, but for reducing competition. Its principal effect is to increase the amount of heterogeneity among the parts of the social organism, thereby multiplying and intensifying their mutual dependence. In other words, the *function* of the division of labor is to preserve social solidarity. (Harris 1968:476)

Marx, too, had given prominence to rivalry and competition. But for him this social problem could not be resolved merely through the division of labor but, instead, only through the struggle between *social classes*. Durkheim, who shared the interest in rivalry and competition, took an entirely opposite view—one that in Harris's opinion was most unfortunate as it put him directly into the idealist camp. Durkheim rejected the idea of class struggle and in doing so he also rejected economic explanations. Thus he began a mode of explanation completely independent of technoeconomic factors:

Durkheim's unique contribution was thus the founding of a science of culture which could explain sociocultural phenomena without getting involved in techno-economic causation. Henceforth it would suffice merely to investigate the manner by which a given trait or institution contributed to the maintenance of solidarity among the members of the social organism. (Harris 1968:476)

Here we see, if Harris is correct, the origins of the French sociological tradition that was later to result in both Radcliffe-Brown's functionalism and Lévi-Strauss's structuralism, sharing at the very least the idealism to which Harris is so adamantly opposed. But to understand the idealism of Lévi-Strauss we must also understand his psychological bent, which he does not share with Radcliffe-Brown.

Durkheim, like Radcliffe-Brown, wanted a science of society devoid of psychology. Indeed, the thrust of one of his major works, *Suicide* (1897), was to prove that suicide could be explained purely sociologically, with no recourse to the individual or psychology. Yet, as Alex Inkeles has shown, Durkheim did employ an implicit psychological theory:

. . . despite his intention to go "directly" to the causes of suicide, "disregarding the individual as such, his motives and his ideas," Durkheim was in the end forced to introduce a general theory of personality as the intervening variable between, on the one hand, the state of integration of social structures and, on the other hand, the varying rates of suicide he sought to explain. To the question of how the origin of suicide could lie in the degree of integration of a social structure, he replied by referring to man's "psychological constitution," which, he said, "needs an object transcending it." This object is lacking in the weakly integrated society, and consequently "the individual, having too keen a feeling for himself and his own value . . . wishes to be his own only goal, and as such an objective cannot satisfy him, drags out languidly and indifferently an existence which henceforth seems meaningless to him." (Inkeles 1959:252)

In fact, as Bender pointed out in his dissertation on the development of ethnology in France:

Actually, Durkheim was not categorically opposed to psychology. Sociology, in fact, may be considered a part of psychology, he went so far to say, though not individual psychology (1897:312 and 1912:xviii). The *conscience collective* and the *conscience individuelle* are psychic in nature. While the organic and the mental form two distinct orders of reality, the *conscience individuelle* and the *conscience collective* form two sub-species of the same order, the psychic order of reality. Durkheim never attempted to describe the exact nature of the *conscience individuelle*. Sometimes it is treated as a residual category, including everything not found in the *conscience collective*. It is clear, however, that he meant the *collective* [sic: *conscience*?] *individuelle* to include both idiosyncratic and collective elements. The laws of the *conscience collective* can only be understood on the collective level, he emphasized. (1964:22)

This is the same kind of psychologizing that Harris has noted. In this case the object "transcending" the "psychological constitution" is no more or less than the social order itself. And the social order transcending individual people is the result of the *"collective conscience,"* defined by Durkheim in *The Division of Labor in Society* (1893) as follows:

The totality of beliefs and sentiments common to average citizens of the same society forms a determinate system which has its own life; one may call it the *collective* or *common conscience*. No doubt, it has not a specific organ as a substratum; it is, by definition, diffuse in every reach of society. Nevertheless, it has specific characteristics which make it a distinct reality. It is, in effect, independent of the particular conditions in which individuals are placed; they pass on and it remains. It is the same in the North and in the South, in great cities and in small, in different professions. Moreover, it does not change with each generation, but, on the contrary, it connects successive generations with one another. It is, thus, an entirely different thing from particular consciences, although it can be realized only through them. (1893:79–80)

However ambiguous the concept of the "collective conscience" may appear, it has been an extremely influential idea. It can, of course, be substituted for culture. "The totality of beliefs and sentiments common to average citizens of the same society" is, in fact, a commonly understood definition of culture. It is necessary to understand the idea of the collective conscience if one is to attempt to understand Lévi-Strauss. But there is also one further figure in the French sociological tradition we much mention because of his influence on Lévi-Strauss.

Marcel Mauss was Durkheim's nephew, but he was also a professional associate of Durkheim's and, after Durkheim's death, became the most prominent scholar in this particular tradition. In his most famous work, *The Gift* (1954/1924), Mauss attempted to explain much of sociocultural life through what he called "collective representations," a notion with obvious ties to the collective conscience. But Mauss was also interested in bringing psychological studies more into line with sociological ones, a position which, of course, Durkheim would not have considered. Mauss was interested in such things as obligation, motive, and in general the meaning of gift-giving to the participants themselves. Mauss believed he had uncovered one of the fundamental bases of social life in the universal process of gift-giving. Out of his interest in this, particularly his interest in the "inside" view, Mauss came to realize that there may be absolutely fundamental "structures" of some kind in the mind that would be prior to the collective representations and would determine them. It is here that we find the most important link with the contemporary work of Lévi-Strauss.

Mauss attempted in *The Gift* to reduce all varieties of gift-giving to one "elementary form," the principle of reciprocity. That this principle has psychological as well as sociological importance can be seen in Mauss's use of terms like "obligation," "motive," "generosity," "morals," and the like. He wished to show that the gift exchange of primitive societies could not be explained in terms of the purely economic motives of "civilized" society but was motivated rather by the more basic principle of reciprocity. Upon this principle, he believed, ultimately depended all social solidarity. He further held, following the early evolutionists, that contemporary "primitive" societies were representative of archaic or past forms of life and thus could tell us about our own history and development.

Lévi-Strauss, in his first famous work, *Les Structures Elémentaires de la Parenté* (1949) (*The Elementary Structures of Kinship*), extended Mauss's notion of reciprocity to one further commodity that could be exchanged—women. He argues that the purpose of *incest taboos*, a universal feature of all human societies that has long puzzled anthropologists, was simply to bring about an exchange of women. Kinship systems, then, also a universal feature of human life, can be studied from the point of view of how they represent different systems of exchanging women and what implications follow from different modes of exchange. For instance, there are societies in which it is permissible, and indeed even preferred, to marry a *cross cousin*, but in which at the same time *parallel cousins* are taboo as marriage partners—one cannot marry the opposite-sex child of one's father's brother or mother's sister (children of siblings of the same sex being parallel cousins), but can marry the opposite-sex child of father's sister or mother's brother (children born to siblings of different sex are cross cousins). In our own system of kinship (except in rare cases) all of these cousins would be prohibited as marriage partners. Thus the exchange of women between groups following different rules would result in different networks of kin and in different forms of social organization.

But not only were sociological advantages to be derived from reciprocity but there was also, Lévi-Strauss argued, a fundamental human psychological "need" for it. And the only way to properly understand this need, he continued, was to appeal to the "fundamental structures of the mind." In order to learn about these fundamental structures of the mind, Lévi-Strauss turned to studies of child development, particularly to studies of the development of thought. He found what he believed to be an important clue in the duality established by the fact that we all must experience the difference between "self" and "other." This experience, he thought, made reciprocity a part of the search for psychological security. Harris has objected that Lévi-Strauss's search for elementary mental structures is merely the same procedure as positing "instincts" whenever an explanation is needed (1968:491). But while it is true that if there are indeed such things as elementary structures of the mind we are not very close to understanding them, nevertheless in all fairness to Lévi-Strauss we must observe that the search for such elementary structures is very different from simply making up a new instinct whenever one is required. There is now a rapidly growing anthropological tradition of studying how both children and adults think, and how they think must surely have something to do with how they experience each other and the world around them. (See, for example, Berland 1982; Biersak 1982; Cole and Means 1981; Cole and Scribner 1974; Cole et al. 1971; Gladwin 1970; Hiatt 1978; Hutchins 1980; Price-Williams 1975). There is also a relationship between Lévi-Strauss's search for elementary structures of the mind and the concept of the "unconscious" as formulated by Freud and Jung, although Lévi-Strauss has creatively reinterpreted the Freudian notion of the unconscious:

According to Lévi-Strauss, then, one must distinguish the subconscious, which is individualistic and can be considered as full of recollections and images collected over the course of a lifetime, from the unconscious, properly speaking, which imposes structural laws upon unarticulated elements that come from elsewhere — drives, emotions, representations, memories. The subconscious is the individual lexicon containing an accumulated vocabulary of one's personal history: that vocabulary only becomes significant to the extent that it is structured according to the laws of the unconscious and, thus, is fashioned into a discourse. What is significant is that these laws are the same for all individuals, under all circumstances. The structure is the important part, the vocabulary the unimportant. (Shalvey 1979:44)

Equally important, perhaps, is the relationship between the structuralism of Lévi-Strauss and that of Piaget (1970:106), as well as that between Lévi-Strauss and the "universal grammar" of the linguist Noam Chomsky. Consider, for example, what Chomsky says of the study of universal grammar:

. . . The study of universal grammar, so understood, is a study of the nature of human intellectual capacities. It tries to formulate the necessary and sufficient conditions that a system must meet to qualify as a potential human language, conditions that are not accidentally true of the existing human languages, but that are rather rooted in the human "language capacity," and thus constitute the innate organization that determines what counts as linguistic experience and what knowledge of language arises on the basis of this experience. Universal grammar, then, constitutes an explanatory theory of a much deeper sort than particular grammar, although the particular grammar of a language can also be regarded as an explanatory theory. (Chomsky 1972:27)

In addition to having been influenced by *depth psychology* and *structural linguistics* Lévi-Strauss has been influenced by *cybernetics.* Thus he not only believes in universal structures of the mind, but also that the most fundamental operation of the mind is to operate in terms of binary oppositions (that is, to continually divide things into two categories, to dichotomize—for example: raw vs. cooked; sacred vs. profane; and, the most fundamental opposition of all, nature vs. culture). This tendency gives the clue, he thinks, that enables us to understand many things which have heretofore eluded understanding. Lévi-Strauss has applied his mode of analysis to kinship, *totemism*, and mythology, and in each area has made valuable contributions and stimulated much further work and controversy. His well-known general work, *Structural Anthropology* (1963) has been influential. Although he probably has more critics than admirers in anthropology, he does not lack for the latter. His *Festschrift*, titled *Echanges et Communications* (Pouillon and Maranda 1970) is the largest volume of its kind ever published. No less a figure than Edmund Leach, a most distinguished member of the British structural-functional school, has become a defender of Lévi-Strauss and has also attempted the same kinds of analyses (Leach 1967b; 1969; 1970). This is not to say that Leach accepts uncritically everything Lévi-Strauss says, or that Lévi-Strauss is necessarily correct. There is a long way to go before a truly convincing case will be made for this type of analysis. The implications for a theory of culture, however, are profound.

Lévi-Strauss uses what is essentially the comparative method of the early evolutionists. He believes that the study of existing "primitives" tells us something about the past, something about our own development:

. . . The anthropologist respects history, but he does not accord it a special value. He conceives it as a study complementary to his own: one of them unfurls the range of human societies in time, the other in space. And the difference is even less great than it might seem, since the historian strives to reconstruct the picture of vanished societies as they were at the points which for them correspond to the present, while the ethnographer does his best to reconstruct the historical stages which temporally preceded their existing form. (Lévi-Strauss 1966:256)

Yet, at the same time, as Leach points out, Lévi-Strauss has a way of looking at history and at the past that differs from most others: ". . . Lévi-Strauss insists that when history takes the form of a recollection of past events it is part of the thinker's present, not of his past" (Leach 1970:16). Likewise, Lévi-Strauss omits the value judgments of the early evolutionists:

The presuppositions of 19th-century anthropologists were protohistorical, Evolutionist or Diffusionist as the case might be. But Lévi-Strauss' time sense is geological. Although, like Tylor and Frazer, he seems to be interested in the customs of contemporary primitive peoples only because he thinks of them as being in some sense primeval, he does not argue, as Frazer might have done, that what is primeval is inferior. In a landscape, rocks of immense antiquity may be found alongside sediments of relatively recent origin, but we do not argue on that account that one is inferior to the other. So also with living things (and by implication human societies). (Leach 1970:17)

Thus, for Lévi-Strauss, there is no essential difference between the minds of primitive men and those of contemporary men. It is to his credit that he so quickly rejected the idea of "stages" of intellectual development. The human mind, for Lévi-Strauss, has always worked in the same way and what was present in the past is with us still in one form or another: "for the thinking human being all recollected experience is contemporaneous; as in myth, all events are part of a single synchronous totality" (Leach 1970:16). But since Lévi-Strauss has yet to demonstrate this proposition, and since it so clearly related to concepts such as the collective conscience, the unconscious, archetypes, archaic remnants, and the like, it is easy to see why the critics react so strongly. Even so, the question of the human mind and its organization remains one of our greatest puzzles:

Just as the human body represents a whole museum of organs, each with a long evolutionary history behind it, so we should expect to find that the mind is organized in a similar way. It can no more be a product without history than is the body in which it exists. By "history" I do not mean the fact that the mind builds itself up by conscious reference to the past through language and other cultural traditions. I am referring to the biological, prehistoric, and unconscious development of the mind in archaic man, whose psyche was still close to that of the animal. (Jung 1968:57)

While we may be unable to accept the assertions of Freud, Jung, or Lévi-Strauss on the nature of the mind, we cannot, as some would have us do, simply throw out the problem. And we may be getting much closer to the time when we will be better able to solve it.

Lévi-Strauss was also influenced by Marx. He says of this:

. . . rarely do I tackle a problem in sociology or ethnology without having first set my mind in motion by reperusal of a page or two from the *18 Brumaire of Louis Bonaparte* or the *Critique of Political Economy*. Whether Marx accurately foretold this or that historical development is not the point. Marx followed Rousseau in saying—and saying once and for all, as far as I can see—that social science is no more based upon events than physics is based upon sense-perceptions. Our object is to construct a model, examine its properties and the way in which it reacts to laboratory tests, and then apply our observations to the interpretation of empirical happenings: these may turn out very differently from what we had expected.

At a different level of reality, Marxism seemed to me to proceed in the same way as geology and psycho-analysis (in the sense in which its founder understood it). All three showed that understanding consists in the reduction of one type of reality to another; that true reality is never the most obvious of realities, and that its nature is already apparent in the care which it takes to evade our detection. In all these cases the problem is the same: the relation, that is to say, between reason and sense-perception; and the goal we are looking for is also the same: a sort of *super-rationalism* in which sense-perceptions will be integrated into reasoning and yet lose none of their properties. (1961:61)

Lévi-Strauss shares the Marxian doctrine that all the *superstructures* of culture stand on an economic base *(infrastructure)*, that "true reality" is never the obvious reality, and thus that informants' statements about their social structure or culture cannot be trusted as true accounts. But in spite of his ties to Marx, Lévi-Strauss is not a materialist. This distinction has led some of those influenced by both Lévi-Strauss and Marx to attempt to create a new theoretical approach, *Structural Marxism*.

STRUCTURAL MARXISM

Structural Marxism attempts to combine elements of structuralism with elements of materialism in such a way as to be able to penetrate below mere surface phenomena into the "real" structure. The nature of infrastructural causality is somewhat ambiguous, for some structural Marxists avoid facing the issue directly and others redefine infrastructure to make it significantly different from what Marx himself presumably had in mind. Some structural Marxists, for example, are willing to accept kinship ideologies which, as ideologies, are mental rather than material. This mentalism is, of course, anathema to cultural materialists (Harris 1979).

This major point of linkage between Marx and Lévi-Strauss appears to be the emphasis they both place on getting beyond the superficial aspects of social relations. For an example that does not attempt to go into detail, Marx argued that capitalist economic categories like wages, profit, and income express only the visible relations between owners of land, labor, and capital and thus mask the real fact that profit for one person is the unpaid labor of another. For Lévi-Strauss, as well as for Marx, structures are not directly observable but exist, rather, beneath the surface structure and constitute the "deeper logic of a social system—the underlying order by which the apparent order must be explained" (Godelier 1977:45).

Harris argues that the above linkage between Marx and Lévi-Strauss is basically trivial because "all research strategies (including cultural materialism) seek in one way or another to get away from surface appearances and to find the inner 'secret' of phenomena" (1979:219). The more important issue for Harris is the fundamental relationship between infrastructure and superstructure. He presents the gist of the problem as follows:

. . . Marx's formulation of the principle of infrastructural determinism refers to the mode of production as consisting of forces of production and relations of production. The concept of forces of production seems fairly unambiguous and corresponds to etic behavioral techno-environmental interactions; relations of production, however, pose a serious definitional problem, since they are concerned with the emic and etic arrangements by which access to resources, control over labor inputs, and distribution of output are regulated. This means that social relations of production for Marx included items ordinarily discussed under such rubrics as ownership, class and caste stratification, employment and even the ideological aspects of these components. (1979:219)

Harris believes that Marx gave clear causal priority to the productive forces, whereas the structural Marxists do not. The latter argue that

Marx left room for ideological as well as material causes and that the relations of production are at least as important as the forces of production. Thus they do not assert the priority of infrastructure and do not believe that superstructure emerges from it. Rather, as one of the chief proponents has stated it:

> Unlike a number of materialists, we do not suppose that the different levels of a social formation emerge one from another. On the contrary, the variation and development of the subsystems depend directly on their internal structures and their intrasystemic contradictions. (Friedman 1975:163)

Harris cannot accept the antimaterialist implications of the nonreduceability of "structures":

> . . . When structuralists—Marxist as well as pure Lévi-Straussians—refer to "structures," they intend not to make any distinction between emic and etic, or mental and behavioral, components. Thus what Friedman is proposing as the dominant determinism impinging upon sociocultural systems consists of elements that in the cultural materialist strategy are not only structural rather than infrastructural, but superstructural, mental, and emic rather than structural, behavioral, and etic. (1979:223)

The arguments for either side in this controversy continue with little hope of resolution. Harris, Berger (1976) and other cultural materialists on the one side and scholars such as Maurice Bloch (1975), Jonathan Friedman (1974, 1975), Maurice Godelier (1977), the converted materialist Marshall Sahlins (1976) and others on the opposite side. The concept of culture is integral in both views and it can be hoped that whatever the specific outcome may be our understanding of culture itself will be improved.

SYMBOLIC ANTHROPOLOGY

In recent years anthropologists in growing numbers have turned to an approach to culture through the analysis of symbols and systems of symbols. As Melford Spiro pointed out at an early conference on symbolic anthropology, it is difficult to characterize this as a new approach, although some of its practitioners seemed to believe that it was:

> In rereading these papers, I was struck, too, with their implicit neglect of the ancestors of our own clan, and with their refusal to forge alliances with members of other clans. From these papers alone a neophyte to anthropology would never know that symbolic anthropology (if we wish to use that term) is the heir to a rich

heritage, that it is descended from a line that includes Durkheim and Leslie White, Lloyd Warner, A. I. Hallowell, Geza Roheim and Edward Sapir—to name but a few of the distinguished predecessors of this new field. It is as if, rather breathlessly, we were all, for the first time, discovering America; as if we were entering a brave new world on whose soil no anthropological foot had, until recently, ever trod. In fact, however, the terrain is filled with many ancestral tracks, some of them well beaten, at that. (1969:209)

Subsequently Raymond Firth traced symbolic analyses back into the eighteenth century (1973). Colby, Fernandez, and Kronenfeld have recently pointed out that "There is hardly a problem in modern symbolic anthropology that is not overt or implicit in the work of Durkheim and Freud" (1981:432). Even so, it remains true even now that symbolic anthropologists do not always consult the work of others, either peers or ancestors. It is one of the shortcomings of this rapidly expanding field that virtually everyone who might be seen as a symbolic anthropologist has his or her largely idiosyncratic approach to it. Nonetheless it is a very significant development in the study of culture and, indeed, might be said to have potentially revolutionary consequences. For purposes of convenience only let us say there are four major traditions of symbolic anthropology.

PSYCHOANALYTIC ANTHROPOLOGY

This tradition of symbolic analysis began with Freud and has always been part of psychoanalysis and of what can fairly be called a psycho-analytic anthropology. Freud himself ventured into anthropology early with *Totem and Taboo* (1918). Other well-known practitioners of this tradition, all employing the theory of symbols stemming from Freud's *The Interpretation of Dreams* (1900) include Geza Roheim, George Devereux, Weston LaBarre, and others. And, of course, there are many anthropologists who employ psychoanalytic concepts at times.

Perhaps one of the best examples of this type of symbolic analysis would be Roheim's *The Eternal Ones of the Dream* (1945), his monumental analysis of Australian Aboriginal totemism and ritual. A less ambitious but more recent similar analysis, for a brief example, is Les Hiatt's discussion of "Secret Pseudo-Procreation Rites Among the Australian Aborigines" (1971) in which he argues that such rites take place because there are two points of male insecurity—two points that is, where it is difficult for males to sustain their otherwise dominant posture: "the evident and peculiar ability of females to produce babies and the fond relationship between women and their male offspring" (1971:79). "So men," Hiatt continues, "uncertain of their natural contribution to human reproduction, assert an ordained and pre-eminent supernatural contribution; and, envious of the carnal bond between mother and son, force them apart in the name of a spiritual imperative" (1971:80). Hiatt then attempts to show that the rites for the first point tend to be primarily phallic in their symbolism and highlight male potency, whereas for the second they tend to be uterine in their symbolism and arrogate female fecundity. The secrecy itself he explains as a result of the male attempt to affirm male priorities in "areas where women are in a naturally strong position" (1971:80).

A more recent example is Gananath Obeyesekere's *Medusa's Hair* (1981) in which he employs anthropological and psychoanalytic theories of symbols to demonstrate that current notions about the differences of personal and cultural symbols are inadequate. He also argues cogently for symbols to be analyzed in context rather than on the more abstract and theoretical level employed by some contemporary symbolic anthropologists. *Medusa's Hair* attempts to bridge the perennial and crucial problem of how individual psychology is related to culture:

> On the analytical level my study of personal symbols hinges on the view of culture that stems from Max Weber and on the theory of unconscious motivation that stems from Freud. For Weber culture is the result of the human tendency to impose meaning on every dimension of existence. Nevertheless, Weber neglected one area of human existence: those critical experiences that lie outside conscious awareness. This is where psychoanalysis comes in, with its theory of unconscious or deep motivation. It depicts the way motives are linked with "symbols" or images, generally of a private nature, either in dreams or in fantasy. Yet in spite of Freud's own interest in culture it is rare to come across psychoanalysts or social scientists, with the notable exception of culture and personality theorists, who deal with the interdigitation of deep motivation and public culture. The bias is strong in the social sciences that culture must deal exclusively with group processes rather than with individual motivation (1981:1).

Inasmuch as *The Interpretation of Dreams* (1900) still remains the only comprehensive theory of symbols, it is somewhat strange that many symbolic anthropologists attempt to ignore it. Psychoanalysts, of course, have always been interested in symbols and their interpretation. It is perfectly fitting that anthropologists should attempt to use the experience of psychoanalysts in the study of cultural symbols. For another recent and fine work attempting to blend psychoanalysis with structuralism and symbolic anthropology see Robert A. Paul's *The Tibetan Symbolic World* (1982).

FRENCH SYMBOLIC ANTHROPOLOGY

The analysis of symbols is an integral feature of Lévi-Strauss's structuralism and thus Lévi-Strauss and many of his followers can also be
considered symbolic anthropologists. For one relatively simple way in
which Lévi-Strauss is seen as a symbolic anthropologist consider how he
approaches one of the classic interests of anthropology, the question of
totemism:

> The term totemism covers relations, posed ideologically, between two series,
> one *natural*, the other *cultural*. The natural series comprises on the one hand
> categories, on the other *particulars*; the cultural series comprises *groups* and
> *persons*. All these terms are arbitrarily chosen in order to distinguish, in each
> series, two modes of existence, collective and individual, and in order not to
> confuse the series with each other. But at this preliminary stage any terms at all
> could be used, provided they were distinct.

NATURE	Category	Particular
CULTURE	Group	Person

> There are four ways of associating the terms, two by two, belonging to the
> different series, i.e., of satisfying with the fewest conditions the initial hypothesis
> that there exists a relation between the two series:

	1	2	3	4
	1	2	3	4
NATURE	Category	Category	Particular	Particular
CULTURE	Group	Person	Person	Group

> To each of these four combinations there correspond observable phenomena
> among one or more peoples. Australian totemism, under "social" and "sexual"
> modalities, postulates a relation between a natural category (animal or vegetable
> species, or class of objects or phenomena) and a cultural group (moiety, section,
> sub-section, cult-group, or the collectivity of members of the same sex). The
> second combination corresponds to the "individual" totemism of the North
> American Indians, among whom an individual seeks by means of physical trials
> to reconcile himself with a natural category. As an example of the third combina-
> tion we may take Mota, in the Banks Islands, where a child is thought to be the
> incarnation of an animal or plant found or eaten by the mother when she first
> became aware that she was pregnant; and to this may be added the example of
> certain tribes of the Algonquin group, who believe that a special relation is estab-
> lished between the newborn child and whatever animal is seen to approach the
> family cabin. The group-particular combination is attested from Polynesia and
> Africa, where certain animals (guardian lizards in New Zealand, sacred croco-
> diles and lion or leopard in Africa) are objects of social protection and veneration;
> it is probable that the ancient Egyptians possessed beliefs of the same type, and to
> such also may be related the *ongon* of Siberia, even though there they concern

not real animals but figures treated by the group as though they were alive. (1963:16–17)

Logically speaking, as Lévi-Strauss goes on, the four combinations are equivalent, since they are all the results of the same operation, the use of "nature" as a metaphor for "cultures." He goes on to argue that previous studies of totemism dealt with only the first two of these and were therefore in error. Whether that opinion is so or not is not our concern here. One can see, in brief, how Lévi-Strauss attempts to make sense out of the wealth of symbolic terms and acts relating to totemism. Lévi-Strauss quotes Radcliffe-Brown to point out "the resemblances and differences of animal species are translated into terms of friendship and conflict, solidarity and opposition. In other words the world of animal life is represented in terms of social relations similar to those of human society" (1963:87).

For Lévi-Strauss, as for most anthropologists, it is culture that sets man apart from other creatures. Culture is made possible through the human capacity for symbolic thought and communication. Human action itself communicates:

. . . When an individual acts as an individual, operating upon the world outside himself—e.g. if he uses a spade to dig a hole in the ground—he is *not* concerned with symbolization, but the moment some other individual comes onto the scene *every* action, however trivial, serves to communicate information about the actor to the observer—the observed details are interpreted as signs, because observer and actor are in relation. From this point of view the animals in any human environment serve as things with which to think *(bonnes à penser)*. (Leach 1970:43)

Lévi-Strauss believes that certain binary concepts are just naturally part of the human condition: left and right, male and female, nature and culture, up and down, and the like. These natural sets come to be infused with cultural significance and thus can symbolize good-bad, permitted-not permitted, sacred-profane, and the like. Also, as humans exist only in relations with each other the relations themselves communicate: father-son, employer-employee, upper class-lower class, and similar pairs all have symbolic as well as practical significances. In fact, everything in nature can come to have symbolic significance although some things, like blood or semen, for example, quite probably are the most commonly employed for symbolic purposes. In any case, Lévi-Strauss thinks that the key to understanding culture is to understand the way the human mind apprehends nature, categorizes, and imparts meaning, and thus allows shared understanding and communication both conscious and unconscious.

While it cannot be said that there exists in France a genuine tradition of symbolic anthropology as such, the work of Pierre Bourdieu (1977) as well as that of Lévi-Strauss can be seen as in that general current. There is, however, a long tradition of *semiotics* which can be traced to Marcel Mauss and Ferdinand de Saussure, among others, which influenced the creation of the Musée de l'Homme and the development of surrealism as well as the beginnings of a symbolic anthropology (Clifford 1981). Indeed, as Milton Singer has pointed out (1978), virtually all of the current interest in cultures as systems of symbols and meanings, in France and everywhere else, has been influenced either by de Saussure (1954) or Charles S. Peirce (1931) or both. Singer has suggested a "semiotic anthropology" based on the philosophy of Peirce to get at problems of culture theory (1978:223) but so far the term has not been widely adopted. All of the symbolic anthropologists to follow can be linked to this shift to the more semiotic view of culture that occurred in the 1960s.

BRITISH SYMBOLIC ANTHROPOLOGY

There is, of course, no "school" of British symbolic anthropology any more than there is a French or American one, and obviously British and American anthropologists have been influenced by the French and vice versa, but British anthropologists in recent years have been in the forefront of symbolic anthropology and the better known ones will be mentioned here together.

Perhaps the best-known of the British symbolic anthropologists is the late Victor Turner, whose book *The Forest of Symbols* (1967) sets forth his approach in clearer language than some of his other and later work. He follows the *Concise Oxford Dictionary* in his definition of "symbol": ". . . a thing regarded by general consent as naturally typifying or representing or recalling something by possession of analogous qualities or by association in fact or thought." He then goes on to say, "the symbols I observed in the field were, empirically, objects, activities, relationships, events, gestures, and spatial units in a ritual situation" (1967:19).

Turner believed that the structure and properties of ritual symbols must be inferred from three classes of data: (1) external form and observable characteristics; (2) interpretations offered by specialists and laymen; (3) significant contexts largely worked out by the anthropologists (Turner 1967:20). Thus the meaning of symbols is entirely understood through observation and questioning. This approach combines comparisons of emic with etic descriptions—observations of overt behavior with statements pertaining to "inner states" and meanings. It also compares the interpretations of anthropologists with those of the persons being studied.

While this procedure might in some sense seem obvious, straight-forward, and logical, except for Turner such a systematic procedure has seldom been followed by symbolic anthropologists. In the psycho-analytic approach, for example, the dream symbols are imposed by the theory and the analyst. For Lévi-Strauss, while the actual content of ritual or myth can vary enormously, the underlying binary dichotomy and the "true meaning" can be known only to the investigator. In neither case does it matter what symbolic significance the individuals themselves understand.

When applied to individual cases this type of analysis spreads out to include both technoenvironmental and biological factors. The best illus-tration of this quality, which must suffice for our purposes here, comes from Turner himself:

Here is an example. At *Nkang'a,* the girl's puberty ritual, a novice is wrapped in a blanket and laid at the foot of a *mudyi* sapling. The *mudyi* tree *Diplorrhyn-cus condylorcarpon* is conspicuous for its white latex, which exudes in milky beads if the thin bark is scratched. For Ndembu, this is its most important characteristic, and therefore I propose to call it "the milk tree" henceforward. Most Ndembu women can attribute several meanings to this tree. In the first place, they say that the milk tree is the "senior" *(mukulumpi)* tree of the ritual. Each kind of ritual has this "senior" or as I will call it, "dominant" symbol. Such symbols fall into a special class which I will discuss more fully later. Here it is enough to state that dominant symbols are regarded not merely as means to the fulfillment of the avowed purposes of a given ritual, but also and more impor-tantly refer to values that are regarded as ends in themselves, that is, to axiomatic values. Secondly, the women say with reference to its observable characteristics that the milk tree stands for human breast milk and also for the breasts that supply it. They relate this meaning to the fact that *Nkang'a* is performed when a girl's breasts begin to ripen, not after her first menstruation, which is the subject of another and less elaborate ritual. The main theme of *Nkang'a* is indeed the tie of nurturing between mother and child, not the bond of birth. This theme of nur-turing is expressed at *Nkang'a* in a number of supplementary symbols indicative of the act of feeding and of foodstuff. In the third place, the women describe the milk tree as "the tree of a mother and her child." Here the reference has shifted from description of a biological act, breast feeding, to a social tie of profound significance both in domestic relations and in the structure of the widest Ndembu community. (1967:20–21)

Turner's brand of symbolic anthropology is much more soundly grounded in careful ethnographic fieldwork—in *empiricism*—than is Lévi-Strauss's structuralism. It also emphasizes context:

I found that I could not analyze ritual symbols without studying them in a time series in relation to other "events," for symbols are essentially involved in social process. I came to see performances of rituals as distinct phases in the social processes whereby groups became adjusted to internal changes and adapted to their external environment. From this standpoint the ritual symbol becomes a factor in social action, a positive force in an activity field. The symbol becomes associated with human interests, purposes, ends, and means, whether these are explicitly formulated or have to be inferred from the observed behavior. The structure and properties of a symbol become those of a dynamic entity, at least within its appropriate context of action. (Turner 1967:20)

This emphasis is in a remarkable contrast with Lévi-Strauss, who in his later works such as *The Raw and the Cooked, From Honey to Ashes, The Origin of Table Manners,* and *The Naked Man* analyzes folk tales and other material drawn from a wide variety of cultures and sources, and thus totally removes them from context. For examples of how the failure to properly consider context and empirically grounded information leads Lévi-Strauss into trouble see Harris's discussion of Lévi-Strauss in *Cultural Materialism* (1979:202–215), Paul Shankman's "Le Roti et le Bouilli: Lévi-Strauss's Theory of Cannibalism" (1969), and Melford Spiro's "*Whatever Happened to the Id*" (1979).

Another of the great British anthropologists who has done exceptionally creative work in the analysis of symbols is Mary Douglas. Douglas fully accepts the idea that nature is put to social uses. The challenge, she asserts, "is to examine the social relations it masks" (1975:6). As she is primarily interested in religion, and as all religions deal with pollution and hygiene, she takes beliefs about these concepts as her starting point:

> Hygiene . . . turns out to be an excellent route [to the understanding of religious ritual], so long as we can follow it with some self-knowledge. As we know it, dirt is essentially disorder. There is no such thing as absolute dirt: it exists in the eye of the beholder. If we shun dirt, it is not because of craven fear, still less dread or holy terror. Nor do our ideas about disease account for the range of our behavior in cleaning or avoiding dirt. Dirt offends against order. Eliminating it is not a negative movement but a positive effort to organize the environment. (1966:2)

In her book *Purity and Danger* Douglas attempts to show that "rituals of purity and impurity create unity in experience" and, "by their means symbolic patterns are worked out and publicly displayed" (1966:2–3). Then, "as we examine pollution beliefs we find that the kind of contacts which are thought dangerous also carry a symbolic load . . . a more interesting level at which pollution ideas relate to social life" (1966:3). Douglas believes that some of the ideas about diet and pollution are actually analogies for a general view of the social order:

. . . For example, there are beliefs that each sex is a danger to the other through contact with sexual fluids. According to other beliefs only one sex is endangered by contact with the other, usually males from females, but sometimes the reverse. Such patterns of sexual danger can be seen to express symmetry or hierarchy. It is implausible to interpret them as expressing something about the actual relations of the sexes. I suggest that many ideas about sexual dangers are better interpreted as symbols of the relation between parts of society, as mirroring designs of hierarchy or symmetry which apply in the larger social system. What goes for sex pollution also goes for bodily pollution. The two sexes can serve as a model for the collaboration and distinctiveness of social units. So also can the processes of ingestion portray political absorption. Sometimes bodily orifices seem to represent points of entry or exit to social unity, or bodily perfection can symbolize an ideal theocracy. (1966:3–4)

With this theoretical scheme Douglas analyzes our own western European idea of dirt and pollution and demonstrates that, contrary to the claims of Robertson Smith or of Frazer, we are not different from "primitives" in this respect. She has also done fascinating analyses of the Lele cult of the pangolin and how animals feature in Lele religious symbolism, as well as cross-cultural analyses of body symbolism, jokes, and other such things (1975).

Still another distinguished British social anthropologist has devoted increasing amounts of time in recent years to symbolic analysis. Edmund Leach has been much influenced by Lévi-Strauss and, in addition to his own symbolic and structural analyses of biblical texts and other phenomena, he has produced a book, *Culture and Communication* (1976), which attempts to deal with the logic by which symbols are connected. The main thrust of this work is to argue that:

. . . culture communicates; the complex interconnectedness of cultural events itself conveys information to those who participate in those events. That granted, my purpose is to suggest a systematic procedure by which the participant observer anthropologist can set about decoding the messages embedded in the complexities which he observes. (1976:2)

Leach argues that communication among humans takes place through "expressive actions which operate as *signals, signs,* and *symbols*" (1976:9). He further assumes that:

. . . *all* the various non-verbal dimensions of culture, such as styles in clothing, village lay-out, architecture, furniture, food, cooking, music, physical gestures, postural attitudes and so on are organized in patterned sets so as to incorporate coded information in a manner analogous to the sounds and words and sentences of a natural language. (1976:10)

And he also assumes that "it is just as meaningful to talk about the grammatical rules which govern the wearing of clothes as it is to talk about the grammatical rules which govern speech utterances" (1976:10). That is, there are *cultural* rules basically similar to the rules of language which anthropologists should be able to comprehend. The problems to be solved have to do with the fact that (1) "a sign is always a member of a set of contrasted signs which function [only] within a specific cultural context," (2) "a sign conveys information only when it is combined with other signs and symbols *from the same context*" [emphasis is mine] (1976:13), and (3) in real life, signals, signs, and symbols get constantly mixed up (1976:32). Leach's definitions are presented in diagram form here but in order to fully understand them and his overall analytic scheme it is necessary to pay very close attention to the book *Culture and Communication* itself. Leach's position on spoken language and on how human psychology is related to structural analysis is not entirely clear or satisfactory but it is certainly stimulating and useful. Leach considers his position to be compatible with that of both Mary Douglas and Victor Turner but not with that of Raymond Firth.

Leach's objection to Firth has to do ostensibly with Firth's treatment of "Hair Symbolism," "Food Symbolism," "Bodily Symbols of Greetings and Parting," and other categories as separate and distinct, itemized by particular examples, and thus failing to recognize that "each of these codes is potentially a transformation of any of the others" (1976:96). The reason is that Leach, like Lévi-Strauss, believes the concept of *structural transformation* is fundamental to structural analysis, a position that Firth would certainly not accept without much more evidence than either Lévi-Strauss or Leach have been able to muster to date. The real issue, which is the most fundamental to contemporary cultural anthropology, is, in Leach's terms, whether one is an "empiricist" or a "rationalist." While this is not identical with Harris's use of idealist vs. materialist there is a basic similarity that is worth noting.

In brief, Leach argues that the subject matter of all social anthropology is cultural and social variation and that the anthropologist's task is both to describe this variation and to explain it. Some anthropologists attempt causal explanations and try to find antecedent events that explain the phenomena at issue. Still others concentrate on interdependencies in the cultural or social system and offer functional explanations. For a third category, according to Leach, "the object of the exercise is to show how any particular cultural institution, as actually observed, is only one set of possible permutations and combinations, some of which can also be directly observed in other cultural settings. These last offer structuralist explanations—using the term 'structuralist' in the sense favored by Lévi-Strauss" (1976:3–4).

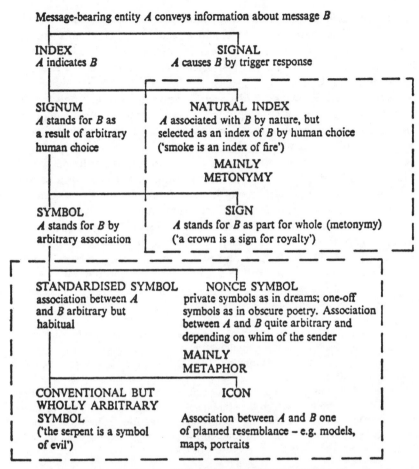

Message-bearing entity *A* conveys information about message *B*

INDEX	SIGNAL
A indicates *B*	*A* causes *B* by trigger response

SIGNUM	NATURAL INDEX
A stands for *B* as a result of arbitrary human choice	*A* associated with *B* by nature, but selected as an index of *B* by human choice ('smoke is an index of fire') MAINLY METONYMY

SYMBOL	SIGN
A stands for *B* by arbitrary association	*A* stands for *B* as part for whole (metonymy) ('a crown is a sign for royalty')

STANDARDISED SYMBOL	NONCE SYMBOL
association between *A* and *B* arbitrary but habitual	private symbols as in dreams; one-off symbols as in obscure poetry. Association between *A* and *B* quite arbitrary and depending on whim of the sender MAINLY METAPHOR

CONVENTIONAL BUT WHOLLY ARBITRARY SYMBOL	ICON
('the serpent is a symbol of evil')	Association between *A* and *B* one of planned resemblance – e.g. models, maps, portraits

COMMUNICATION DYAD—THE COMMUNICATION EVENT. (From Leach 1976:12)

Until fairly recently, most anthropologists would have considered themselves empiricists and (although it is a bit of an oversimplification) they would have felt, as Leach indicates, "that the basic task of the anthropologist in the field is to record directly-observed, face-to-face behaviours of members of a local community interacting with one another in their day-to-day activities" (1976:4). The term structuralist for the Lévi-Straussians refers to the structure of *ideas* rather than the structure of society. Thus they attend more to what is said than to "objective facts" and they attend to myths and to informants' statements about what ought to be rather than to what "really" is. There is no doubt that Firth is an empiricist whereas Leach claims to be both structuralist and empiricist. Leach also claims that these two approaches are complementary rather than opposed, which is true enough for most anthropologists except when it comes to Lévi-Strauss per se and to ideas about structural transformations. Harris, of course, would object to rationalists as well as idealists.

Firth's book, *Symbols: Public and Private* (1973), is the only one to deal with the history of anthropological inquiry into symbols. He points out, among many other things, that virtually all anthropologists had to and did confront symbols in their research, wherefore, as Spiro also pointed out, the current interest in symbolic analysis is hardly new. Firth also makes it eminently clear just how complex the issue of symbolic representation and analysis really is by drawing not only from anthropology but also widely from art, literature, music, everyday life and whatever. He offers his own definitions (1973:74–75) and reviews the anthropological work up to that time. He is also much concerned with the issue of public symbols as opposed to private ones, which is still a somewhat neglected area. Firth's view of what anthropology can contribute to the study of symbols clearly does not include the structuralism of Lévi-Strauss:

. . . Essentially as I see it, the anthropological approach [to symbolic analysis] is comparative, observational, functionalist, relatively neutralist. It links the occurrence and interpretations of symbolism to social structures and social events in specific conditions. Over a wide range of instances, anthropologists have observed what symbols people actually use, what they have said about these things, the situations in which the symbols emerge, and the reactions to them. Consequently, anthropologists are equipped to explain the meanings of symbols in the cultures they have studied, and to use such explanations as a means of furthering understanding of the processes of social life. (1973:25)

Unfortunately, although symbolic analyses have flourished and multiplied in the past twenty years, we are still not as well equipped as we might be.

AMERICAN SYMBOLIC ANTHROPOLOGY

Certainly much of the interest in symbolic analysis in the United States can be traced to the work of David Schneider, whose book *American Kinship: A Cultural Account* (1968) sets forth with unusual lucidity what a cultural (symbolic) analysis is all about. Following Talcott Parsons, Clyde Kluckhohn, and Alfred Kroeber, as well as having been influenced by Lévi-Strauss and Clifford Geertz, Schneider considers culture to be a "system of symbols." By "symbol" he means "something which stands for something else, or some things else, where there is no necessary or intrinsic relationship between the symbol and that which it symbolizes" (1968:1). A culture is divided into "units" which are said to be "anything that is culturally defined and distinguished as an entity" (1968:2). Thus for Schneider:

> . . . The ghost of a dead man and the dead man are two cultural constructs or cultural units. Both exist in the real world as cultural constructs, culturally defined and differentiated entities. But a good deal of empirical testing has shown that at a quite different level of reality the ghost does not exist at all, though there may or may not be a dead man at a given time and place, and under given conditions. Yet at the level of their cultural definition there is no question about their existence, nor is either one any more or less real than the other (1968:2).

And, although language and words constitute a major part of culture they are not isomorphic with it since other objects and things are part of the symbolic system as well. The task for the anthropologist working through *informants* (as contrasted with respondents, subjects, or patients, for example) is to come to understand the system of symbols and symbolic meanings that constitute the culture of any given group or society. Schneider himself picks American kinship as the cultural system he wishes to analyze and gives an account of that phenomenon that is unprecedented and extremely insightful. While doing so he also discusses the problems of variation in American culture, sampling, and the differences between different *levels of understanding*. He also discusses the paradoxes in American culture as well as our cultural attempts to resolve them. This is not to say that he leaves us with no unanswered questions, not the least of which is whether anyone else, having attempted the same analysis, would come up with the same interpretations.

The same is true of the work of Clifford Geertz, who has come to symbolize this growing trend in cultural anthropology and analysis. Although there are similarities in the approaches of Schneider and Geertz, Geertz's position is a far cry from previous notions of culture. He rejects reified notions of culture as a superorganic of some kind, he does not accept culture as patterns of behavior, and he also rejects the idea that culture is somehow located in the mind. For Geertz's semiotic approach to culture, culture is public because meaning is public (1973:12). Culture is a context within which social events can be described (1973:14). Cultural anthropology is an interpretive rather than experimental science:

> The concept of culture I espouse, and whose utility the essays below attempt to demonstrate, is essentially a semiotic one. Believing, with Max Weber, that man is an animal suspended in webs of significance he himself has spun, I take

culture to be those webs, and the analysis of it to be therefore not an experimental science in search of law but an interpretive one in search of meaning. It is explication I am after, construing social expressions on their surface enigmatical. (1973:5)

Explication, for Geertz, comes through "thick description," which is the goal of ethnography. Thick description is what an anthropologist does when he or she carefully analyzes ethnographic detail, breaking it down further and further to get at the meaning of it for the members of the culture — the native's point of view. But, he goes on, "anthropological writings are themselves interpretations, and second and third order ones to boot (by definition, only a 'native' makes first order ones: its *his* culture)" (1973:15). Even so, Geertz sees these anthropological interpretations as "part of a developing system of scientific analysis" (1973:15). It is over the question of scientific analysis that Geertz is challenged by a host of others who, although appreciative of his work, do not like the direction in which they see him moving the profession of anthropology. Geertz acknowledges that interpretation is not predictive, nor is it verifiable. His theory lacks criteria for evaluating interpretations. Thus, how would anyone know whether any given interpretation is good or bad, valid or invalid or even useful? And how would interpretive anthropologists be able to evaluate other interpretations or explanations of the same thing? Similarly, Geertz does not think that generalization and comparison (fundamental to science, including anthropology up until now) are what anthropologists should be worrying about. His is more a clinical approach:

To generalize within cases is usually called, at least in medicine and depth psychology, clinical inference. Rather than beginning with a set of observations and attempting to subsume them under a governing law, such inference begins with a set of (presumptive) signifiers and attempts to place them within an intelligible frame. Measures are matched to theoretical predictions, but symptoms (even when they are measured) are scanned for theoretical peculiarities — that is, they are diagnosed. In the study of culture the signifiers are not symptoms or clusters of symptoms, but symbolic acts or clusters of symbolic acts, and the aim is not therapy but the analysis of social discourse. (1973:26)

Geertz's approach, whatever its elegance, is primarily descriptive and does not lead to much in the way of theoretical formulations. Part of the cause is Geertz's belief that the distinction between description and explanation is blurred and, in any case, "relative" (1973:27). For those who are disturbed by this, it is an anthropology that is too poetic, novelistic, and humanistic. And there is no doubt that Geertz is interested in the convergence of the social sciences and humanities (Geertz 1980). Paul Shankman and others have reviewed and commented on these problems in a recent issue of *Current Anthropology* that should be read by anyone interested in the study of culture.

As Shankman points out, ". . . In cultural anthropology, symbolic approaches including, but not confined to, Geertz's work now represent a major school among the younger generation" (1984:263). The very attenuated and incomplete discussion here cannot even begin to do justice to either symbolic anthropology or the intellectual ferment being created by structuralism, semiotics, and *phenomenology*, which are of course all related in our intellectual tradition. But it should be clear that the concept of culture has been undergoing still another transformation. There is much agreement even among those who disagree with Geertz that a semiotic approach to culture is not only appropriate but also holds the promise of deepening our understanding of that useful but elusive concept.

SUMMARY

The tendency in the 1960s and 1970s has been increasingly toward a view of culture as a complex web of symbolic meanings and understandings and, related in part to the rise of French structuralism, has developed into what is now usually called symbolic anthropology. This is all related to the development of semiotics as a general theory of signs and symbols, primarily through the work of de Saussure and Peirce. But there is little agreement between various proponents of symbolic analysis beyond the acceptance of culture as symbolic. There is no widely agreed-upon theory of symbols and the tendency has been toward idiosyncratic interpretations that are difficult or impossible in many cases to verify. Some anthropologists, Clifford Geertz in particular, have suggested that anthropology should become an "interpretive science" in search of meaning rather than an experimental one in search of laws, which has been the more traditional view. Although proponents of symbolic analysis were grouped here primarily geographically for convenience there are no genuine schools of British, French, or American symbolic anthropology although individual scholars, Lévi-Strauss and Schneider for example, have attracted and influenced many others. This semiotic anthropology, to use Singer's term, is a far cry from the materialist and ecological positions discussed previously. It clearly demands a more person-centered, emic, psychologically sophisticated researcher than ever before.

FURTHER READINGS

There are many works on French structuralism and Lévi-Strauss. Some of the better ones are Leach's *Claude Lévi-Strauss* and Shalvey, *Claude Lévi-Strauss*. There is also the collection, *Claude Lévi-Strauss: The Anthropologist as Hero*, edited by Hayes and Hayes. For a history of symbolic studies in anthropology see Firth, *Symbols: Public and Private*. A broad collection of papers on symbolic analysis is *Symbolic Anthropology: A Reader in the Study of Symbols and Meanings* edited by Dolgin, Kemnitzer, and Schneider. For critical analyses see Peacock, *Consciousness and Change*; Sperber, *Rethinking Symbolism*; Boon, *Other Tribes, Other Scribes*; and Wagner, *The Invention of Culture*. In addition to Freud, *The Interpretation of Dreams*, see also Jung, *Man and His Symbols*.

CHAPTER VI

Psychological Anthropology

The conventional wisdom has it that in the 1920s and 1930s, specifically in the United States, something emerged called culture-and-personality studies; these have been discussed previously. Subsequently, the term psychological anthropology was suggested (Hsu 1961) and has often been used as a synonym. While Hsu's position did suggest a distinction between psychological anthropology and social and cultural anthropology, it did little to distinguish culture-and-personality from psychological anthropology. Thus it is implied that prior to the 1920s there was an anthropological tradition which was not psychological out of which suddenly emerged a new and unprecedented subdiscipline which was. The continued existence of courses entitled Culture-and-Personality and/or Psychological Anthropology reinforces this belief as do the periodic position statements of cultural materialists (Harris 1968) and social anthropologists (Gluckman 1964). That this confusion still exists can be seen in the name of a recent journal devoted to such studies, *The Journal of Psychological Anthropology: A Quarterly Journal of Culture and Personality.** Becker (1971:87) makes this same error. Similarly, Gluckman

*This has been changed to *The Journal of Psychoanalytic Anthropology.*

uses the term psychological anthropology as synonymous with cross-cultural studies of personality (1964:13). Recent histories of anthropology, except for Bock (1980), although they often pay lip service to previous psychological interests, actually do very little if anything to dispel this view (Broce 1973; Darnell 1974; Waal Malefijt 1974; Harris 1968; Kuper 1973; Penniman 1974). This view of the history of anthropology is incorrect and misleading. The terms culture-and-personality and psychological anthropology are not synonymous, the former being merely one relatively recent and local development of the latter, which in fact represents an original and continuing mainstream of anthropology.

Explicit in Marvin Harris's vociferous criticism of the ubiquitous "mentalism" in anthropology is the admission that anthropology has always been "psychological" (1968:394). In a similar vein Melford Spiro has pointed out that culture-and-personality studies, although in his view they represent a distinctive anthropological development, have deep historical roots in anthropological science:

> Since these [culture-and-personality] studies have historical roots both in eighteenth century thought and in nineteenth century scholarship, I do not mean to imply that culture-and-personality represented an unprecedented innovation. Indeed, in addition to its deeper historical roots, it will be remembered that Edward Sapir, Ruth Benedict, and Margaret Mead were all students of Franz Boas, whose psychological interests are well known. But continuity is not identity, and these three pioneers are sufficiently distinct from their intellectual predecessors to warrant our reference to their work as a "new approach." (Spiro 1972:578)

Fred W. Voget, too, has commented briefly (1960) on the psychological interests preceding the emergence of culture-and-personality studies. But what, specifically, was psychological about the anthropological tradition that spawned culture-and-personality studies? How, precisely, did such studies represent a new approach? What, in fact, is the current state of psychological anthropology? How does it relate to symbolic anthropology? To avoid the confusion that has continually surrounded the polemics relating to psychological anthropology it is necessary to begin with a definition of psychology. Psychology, according to the Oxford English Dictionary, is "The science of the nature, functions, and phenomena of the human soul or mind." The contemporary usage need not include the soul and thus deals only with mind. There is nothing intrinsic to this definition that restricts psychology to "the study of the individual." This erroneous claim, apparently associated with what Gilbert Ryle characterized as a fundamental "category mistake" (1949:18) stemming principally from Descartes, was most stubbornly promoted by A. R. Radcliffe-Brown (1957:45) but has been often stated by many others as well. And if, following Ryle and Geertz, we view mind as a disposition, capacity, propensity, or whatever, we do not thereby make it any the less psychological. Likewise note that there is nothing to suggest that "unconscious" phenomena are psychological while "conscious" phenomena are social, a position which, implicitly at least, can also be found in British social anthropology (Gluckman 1964). Finally, it must be made clear that conscious or unconscious thoughts that are somehow "shared" are not thereby a social rather than a psychological phenomenon, a position held by some and often erroneously attributed to Durkheim (1893) because of his concept of the "collective conscience" (Bender 1964).

Psychological anthropology is an anthropology that attempts to deal with mind. It also deals, then, with all those related mentalistic terms and concepts such as "ideas," "beliefs," "thoughts," "motives," "attitudes," "values," "symbols," "reason," "perception," "memory," "cognition," "feelings," "emotions," and so forth. The question here is whether or not anthropology has concerned itself with these dimensions in the study of human beings or whether, somehow, it has avoided a concern with them in favor of a less mentalistic and therefore more mechanistic, materialistic, and/or scientific approach. If it has avoided such concern, has it always done so? Is psychological anthropology, as the conventional wisdom would have it, simply a fad which flourished in the 1930s and 1940s and then began to drop off?

Let us begin again with the "early evolutionists," and within that category with Lewis Henry Morgan. We ordinarily think of Morgan as interested in cultural evolution, specifically the evolution of the family, government, and property. He was also, of course, interested in "progress" and "civilization." It would be equally reasonable, however, to think of him as interested in the evolution of mind or intelligence. Note, first of all, that Part I of *Ancient Society* (1877) is entitled "Growth of *Intelligence** Through Inventions and Discoveries." Morgan makes his intentions clear at the beginning of the first chapter:

> An attempt will be made in the following pages to bring forth additional evidence of the rudeness of the early condition of mankind, of the gradual evolution of their *mental* and moral powers through experience, and of their protracted struggle with opposing obstacles while winning their way to civilization. It will be drawn, in part, from the great sequence of inventions and discoveries which stretches along the entire pathway of human progress; but chiefly from domestic institutions, which express the growth of certain ideas and passions. (1877:3)

Morgan's interest in mind would seem clear enough from this passage alone; but an examination of his previous work makes the conclusion inescapable. It is not always mentioned in anthropological circles that Morgan wrote a book entitled *The American Beaver and His Work* (1868) prior to *Ancient Society*. Nor is it mentioned that the major thesis of *The American Beaver* is that beavers react and adapt to their environment through the application of *mental principles* in essentially the same way people do. They are not, that is, "instinctual" rather than "cultural," as most of the other scholars of Morgan's period would have had it (Moore

---

*Emphasis is mine, as it is throughout this discussion unless otherwise specified.

1974). Thus *Ancient Society* can be seen as a continuation of Morgan's lifelong interest in mind and reason, and the mental behavior of humans correspondingly seen as essentially only quantitatively different from that of other animals. Carl Resek, Morgan's biographer, makes this very clear:

> He never paid much attention to the history of ideas because he was certain that since the dawn of creation men, indeed all animals, were guided by *plain reason*. This postulate of a *rational* history he would attempt to prove over and over again by studies in animal psychology that were climaxed by his great book on the American beaver. Now he sent an article to the Knickerbocker entitled "Mind or Instinct," in which he sought to show that animals adjust to their environment through *thought*, not instinctually as most writers claimed. From Buffon's *Natural History*, farmer's almanacs, and neighbors' tales he culled numerous examples illustrating the capacity of animals to memorize, ponder, and decide. Metaphysicians denied them a "thinking principle," he wrote, because they forgot that man himself had progressed from a mental level akin to that of the beasts. (Resek 1960:18)

It might also be pointed out that Parts II, III, and IV of *Ancient Society* are entitled, "Growth of the *Idea* of Government," "Growth of the *Idea* of the Family," and Growth of the *Idea* of Property," respectively.

> In any just estimate of the magnitude of the achievements of mankind in the three sub-periods of Barbarism, they must be regarded as immense, not only in number and in intrinsic value, but also in the *mental* and moral development by which they were necessarily accompanied . . . .
> With the production of inventions and discoveries, and with the growth of institutions, the *human mind* necessarily grew and expanded; and we are led to recognize a gradual enlargement of the brain itself, particularly of the cerebral portion. The slowness of this *mental growth* was inevitable in the period of savagery, from the extreme difficulty of compassing the simplest invention out of nothing, or with next to nothing to assist *mental* effort . . . . (1877:35–36)

Although Morgan may have been naive in his belief that inventions and discoveries could influence brain size with the directness and rapidity he suggested, he did imply the important feedback system involved over time between brain and behavior or, if you will, between thought and culture. He did not believe you could study cultural evolution (progress towards civilization, in his terms) independently of mind. In this respect he was more sophisticated than some of his later admirers —Leslie White for example, who believes that culture evolves on its own and quite independently of mind (1969). Marvin Harris, of course, takes a position somewhat similar to that of White.

While other great evolutionists may not have been quite so explicit about their interest in mind they were as much interested in it as Morgan was. Edward B. Tylor, generally recognized as one of the first anthropologists and as the individual who introduced the term culture into our language, conceived of all aspects of culture as being essentially products of human reason—indeed, so much so that Morris Opler has characterized Tylor's position as "rationalistic determinism." He has summarized it as follows:

It is essential to understand the significance and primacy that Tylor attached to the acquisition of *rational thought* and *logic* and, in addition, the degree to which he saw in this the gateway to knowledge and to the control of life forces. Historical materialists and technological determinists subordinate mind to matter and see mental life as the consequence or "superstructure" of the mode of production. In Tylor's view, *mental life* has an evolution of its own and one that has enormous implications for all the rest of culture and for the further progress of culture. I emphasize this because Tylor's attention to progress in the material arts is sometimes taken to mean that he was a materialist and because his references to man's increasing control over nature are interpreted as evidence of his espousal of technological determinism. Yet Tylor's general position is obviously one of philosophical idealism. It is true that he said that man's first need "is to get his daily food." But, as we have seen, he also taught—and this is central to his evolutionism—that man's food quest and all his other endeavors remain on a humble, brutish level until certain *intellectual goals* are reached and obstructing *mental confusions* are eliminated. (Opler 1964:135–136)

It has elsewhere been suggested that Tylor took the development of science as his model for culture evolution so that ". . . culture, in its gradual course towards perfection, is characterized by false and inadequate knowledge which is slowly but relentlessly swept aside" (Hatch 1973:25). Tylor's idealism and psychological interest has been acknowledged by others as well (Waal Malefijt 1974; Harris 1968).

James George Frazer, too, was basically interested in mind. His principal task was to demonstrate how religion and science evolved from magic, each of these being essentially a mode of problem-solving thought that was superior to its predecessor. *The Golden Bough* (1890) deals with the evolution of explanations and beliefs as well as of ritual and behavior, and, as Edmund Leach has made clear, there is little doubt about Frazer's primary interest:

Frazer called himself a social anthropologist, but the bias of his interest was in psychology rather than sociology. He took over from Bastian the assumption that the fundamental psychology of human beings will everywhere be reflected by similar customary behaviors, or conversely, that similar customs always have the same symbolic implications, regardless of the context in which they appear.

But Frazer coupled this belief with a curious contempt for his subject matter. If Tylor's "savage" sometimes seems to be a primitive philosopher struggling to solve the problems of existence, Frazer's "savage" is a lunatic at large—a child of nature, whose ignorance evokes our amusement rather than our sympathy . . . . (Leach 1961:377-378)

R. R. Marett, another of the famous early evolutionists, states in his book *The Threshold of Religion* that his special interest is of a psychological nature (1909) and in *Faith, Hope and Charity in Primitive Religion* he begins his discussion of religion, "Following psychology," by asserting that the religious life (indeed, all life) is made up of feeling, thinking, and acting (1932:3). Westermarck, too, had psychological interests, and engaged in a dispute with W. H. Rivers over explanations for blood feuds. Westermarck attempted to explain them in terms of the psychological concept of revenge. Rivers objected on the grounds that examples could be found in which revenge was not the motive. Eventually Rivers was forced to the question of "how can you explain the workings of the human mind without a knowledge of the social setting which must have played so great a part in determining the sentiments and opinions of mankind?" You might say this is the most fundamental question of cross-cultural psychology which was pioneered by Rivers and his colleagues (Price-Williams 1975).

Rivers, of course, was a psychologist, but in this early phase of the development of anthropology there seems to have been no controversy over the relationship of psychology to anthropology. Rivers surely had a legitimate claim to being an early anthropologist as well as a psychologist. In his book *Psychology and Ethnology* (1926), he states: "To me, as to most students of the subject, the final aim of the study of society is the explanation of social behavior in terms of psychology." In these pre-Radcliffe-Brown days there is no record of anyone attempting to drum Rivers out of the Anthropological Society for this "reductionist" statement nor is there any indication in Brenda Seligman's review of *Psychology and Ethnology* that the intimate relationship between the two was even in question (1927). In fact, Rivers was not a psychological reductionist, as he also acknowledged: "It is only by the combination of ethnological and psychological analysis that we shall make any real advance" (1926).

It is fair to say, I believe, that this general statement is far more representative of most of the English anthropologists of this early period than is any belief in reductionism. In fact, it appears that the early evolutionists attempted to adhere to their aims, which were, as stated in the prospectus for the Anthropological Society in 1893, "to study man in all his leading aspects, physical, *mental* and historical; to investigate the laws of his origin and progress; to ascertain his place in nature and his relations to the inferior forms of life, and to attain these objectives by patient investigation, careful induction, and the encouragement of all researches tending to establish a de facto science of man" (Burrow 1963:142). There is simply no question that the English anthropologists of the formative period of anthropology were committed to the study of mental evolution no less than physical and material evolution.

This interest in mental capacities was not unique to English anthropologists. The Germans, too, shared this interest albeit for slightly different reasons. Less influenced than their English counterparts by evolutionary theory, their interest in mind was more in terms of basic and universal aspects of thought. Theodore Waitz devoted much effort to the question of psychic unity and in his early *Introduction to Anthropology* examined, among other things, the question of whether, psychologically, man was all of one species (1863). Adolf Bastian referred to these potential basic aspects of thought as *Elementargedanken* (1895) and felt he encountered them "with monotonous regularity in his far-flung field investigations" (Fogelson 1977:4). The Germans, like the French sociologists in this respect, were likewise more concerned than the English with what can be termed "group psychology." As Raymond Fogelson has pointed out, these interests were foreshadowed in the work of Fichte, Herder, and the brothers Grimm, then sharpened by Morits Lazarus and Heymann Steinthal on *Volkerpsychologie.* In 1860 appeared the *Zeitschrift für Volkerpsychologie und Sprachwissenschaft,* which might, again according to Fogelson (1977), be considered the first journal of psychological anthropology. German interest in *Volkerpsychologie* continued into the early twentieth century, reaching a climax with Wilhelm Wundt, who produced a still untranslated ten-volume work on the subject.

You do not escape the interest in psychology by turning to the later German diffusionists even though that might be expected. Wilhelm Schmidt's *The Cultural Historical Method of Ethnology* (1939), a thorough and critical exposition of the historical method of ethnology based primarily on the work of Fritz Graebner, defines ethnology as follows:

A science which has for its object the study of the development of the *mind* and of the exterior *rational activity* of man in racial life. (1939:8)

If that is not convincing, how about the following:

Ethnology is a science of the *mind*. All that it deals with has proceeded from the *mind*, has gone through the *mind* and bears its impress, and it is precisely through this process that it becomes a culture object . . . . (1939:7)

Later in his work Schmidt goes on to discuss more precisely how it is that psychology is of use to anthropology.

The French sociological tradition has often been held up as a clear example of an explicitly nonpsychological social science, although Inkeles (1959) and others have exposed the implicit psychological assumptions that were employed by Durkheim and his followers, and Nisbet (1974) has argued that Durkheim anticipated issues that would later have been included under the category of psychological anthropology. This claim, like so many such, is clearly oversimplified, and the status of such concepts as the *conscience collective,* as has been indicated previously, has never been made entirely clear.

It is more than fair to say that the actual nature of the *conscience collective* and the *conscience individuelle* to this day has never been made clear, nor has the relationship between the two been made clear. Even if one agrees that there is something like a collective conscience it would seem that the only access to it would be through the individual conscience in any case. This, in fact, is probably the basis for much of the confusion. Consider this recent statement from the Laboratory of Comparative Human Cognition:

The confusion that has suffused this topic from its inception has several sources which are our major concern here. The first involves the term "modes of thought" (or "mentality") as it appears in this discussion. In principle, anthropologists have followed Durkheim in maintaining a distinction between the formal properties of cultural belief systems ("collective representations") and the mental operations of individuals when thinking about (or "with") these belief systems. In practice, however, the distinction is difficult to maintain, as shown in the writings of Lévy-Bruhl (46–47). "Collective representations are social phenomena, like the institutions for which they account; . . . social phenomena have their own laws, . . . which analysis for the individual *qua* individual could never reveal" (46, p. 63). This statement is followed by a multitude of assertions that are virtually impossible to interpret as being about other than individual thought processes: for example, "The preconnections, preperceptions, and pre-conclusions which play so great a part in the mentality of uncivilized peoples do not involve any logical activity; they are simply committed to memory." (46:93) There is little wonder that Boas and others could conclude that Lévy-Bruhl was making statements about the operation of individual thought processes and admonish him with his own principle that there is no justification in concluding illogicality of individual thought from the falseness of cultural belief systems! (Laboratory of Comparative Human Cognition 1978:57)

Lévy-Bruhl, however misunderstood, was clearly pursuing what were psychological issues. Marcel Mauss was interested in bringing psychological studies more into line with sociological ones, extending in this way the work of his famous uncle. Mauss was particularly interested in such things as obligation, motives, and in general the meaning of gift giving to participants themselves. As we have seen, out of his interest in this "inside" view, Mauss came to realize that there may be absolutely fundamental "structures" of some kind in the mind. The link to Lévi-Strauss here is obvious and his interest in the mind is well known. Although it may not be as clear as one would like, a distinct pattern of interest in the psychological aspects of culture starts with Comte and continues through French social science to the present.

We might get a hint about the psychology of "historical particularism" in Marvin Harris's objection to Boas's "mentalism." It is well known that Boas was interested in psychology and in the individual. If there is any doubt about this, consider the following from a paper Boas published in 1910 entitled: "Psychological Problems in Anthropology":

The science of anthropology deals with the biological and *mental manifestations* of human life as they appear in different races and in different societies . . . . We are also trying to determine the *psychological laws* which control the *mind of man* everywhere, and that may differ in various racial and social groups . . . .

The fundamental problem on which all anthropological inquiry must be founded relates to the *mental equipment* of the various races of man. (1910:371)

Boas in fact employed the term "psychological anthropology" at least as early as 1904:

In psychological anthropology the important questions are the discovery of a system of the evolution of culture, the study of the modifications of simple general traits under the influence of different geographical and social conditions, the question of transmission and spontaneous origin, and that of folk psychology *versus* individual psychology. (1904:513)

It has long been maintained that Boas's interest in psychology was transmitted through Sapir-Benedict-Mead into the study of culture-and-personality. The implication seems to be that no other of Boas's students or colleagues either had or pursued such interests, that American anthropology, aside from Boas's peculiarity on this score, was somehow either anti- or nonpsychological. Let us consider this more carefully.

Alexander Chamberlain, who was Boas's first student and produced two books on the comparative study of childhood, can be considered "a neglected pioneer in psychological anthropology" (Fogelson 1977:7). Clark Wissler, along with Boas, one of the best-known anthropologists of the period, received his Ph.D in psychology under Cattell at Columbia in 1901. Although he subsequently worked as an anthropologist he never lost his interest in psychology and he did not hesitate to invoke psychological principles in his study of culture. For example, in a short paper published in 1906 he postulated a psychophysical element operating in the development of primitive art (as opposed to the then current notion that ornamental art was the result of degeneration from representational art). He says:

The hacking and scratching occurring in daily activity must have made an impression upon man. A feeling for symmetry of form, and regularity, which seems quite fundamental in the mind of man, is a sufficient basis for the working up of these scratches into ornamentation. (Wissler 1906:191)

In "The Psychological Aspects of the Culture-Environment Relation" he suggests that:

. . . It seems that American anthropologists have taken a position involving the conscious construction origin for cultures as opposed to a sociologic-evolutionary theory. Upon such assumption it is difficult to see how the mere external world could be an important factor in determining cultures. On the other hand there seems to be a *psychological cultural environment* that is a factor of the first importance. The geographical area seems to be a factor only in so far as it tends to offer bounds or barriers to a cultural environment, but on the other hand, it seems that the inner geographical character of the area has little weight in determining the particular form of culture produced therein, that being dependent upon *peculiar psychological conditions* and apparently such conditions as are over and above the fundamental human level. (Wissler 1912:224–225)

In an address in 1915 to Section H, Anthropology and Psychology, American Association for the Advancement of Science, Wissler took a much more negative view toward psychology. But even here he did not reject psychology and concluded by saying "Psychology can be of the very greatest service to anthropology by discovering the relations between man's innate and cultural equipments" (1916:201). Wissler was actually more opposed to instinct psychology specifically than to psychology in general. One can see in these two papers Wissler struggling to find the meaning of the concept of culture and, like others of his time, he was concerned that anthropology not be "reduced" to psychology. But to say that anthropology cannot be reduced to psychology is not to say that there can be no relationship at all—no psychological anthropology, if you will. Wissler thought there might be an inborn psychophysical basis for the universal features of culture and he refers to a human "drive to culture beyond man's power to arrest."

Robert Lowie, too, expressed his interest in the relationship of psychology to anthropology. He discussed this in a paper entitled

"Psychology and Sociology" (1915) and then at considerable length in his book *Culture and Ethnology* (1917). Lowie, like the others, argued that anthropology could not be reduced to psychology, but he also agreed that the anthropologist needed psychology in the study of culture:

> Yet, when all is said and done, the spirit of skepticism that has invaded sociological and ethnological circles may be carried too far. I venture to believe that some facts may not only become more intelligible when viewed from the angle of individual psychology, but it may be advisable not to defer this mode of looking at them until an indefinitely remote future. Even where individual psychology has not yet advanced far enough to give a solution of the problem, the new data may well prove a goad for further development of that branch of the science. And again an ethnologist conversant with psychology may give a more accurate description of his observations than his less sophisticated colleague (1915:219).

Alexander Goldenweiser was struggling with the culture-environment question at about the same time as Wissler. In his article "Culture and Environment" he comes to much the same conclusion as Wissler:

> . . . Again, we may allow for the possibility that certain features in the environment, which we know not, may favor or check the development of those traits of the human mind which stand for the reception and faithful reproduction of ideas. But *psychic inertia is a general trait of human, nay animal, psychology*, and, as such, is quite independent of any specific environment. What is to be assimilated is determined by culture; the mechanism of reception, assimilation, reproduction of ideas *is determined by human psychology;* environment has nothing whatever to do with it. (1916:632)

Later, in his book *History, Psychology, and Culture*, he has this to say:

> *The Most General Relation between Psychology and Culture.* —To a superficial view the relation between the individual mind and culture seems paradoxical: on the one hand, culture springs from the individual mind; on the other, the mind itself is determined by culture.
>
> When this proposition is expanded, the paradox disappears. If we had the knowledge and patience to analyze a culture retrospectively, every element would be found to have its beginning in the creative act of an individual mind. There is, of course, no other source for culture to come from, for what culture is made of is but the raw stuff of experience, whether material or spiritual, transformed into culture by the creativeness of man. An analysis of culture, if fully carried out, leads back to the individual mind.

The content of any particular mind, on the other hand, comes from culture. No individual can ever originate his culture—it comes to him from without, in the process of education.

In its constituent elements culture is psychological and, in the last analysis, comes from the individual. But, as an integral entity culture is cumulative, historical, extra-individual. It comes to the individual as part of his objective experience, just as do his experiences with nature, and, like these, it is absorbed by him, thus becoming part of his psychic content. (1933:59)

Speaking for the "American school of historical ethnology" in 1925, Goldenweiser states bluntly: "The American school of historical ethnology must be characterized as critical, historical, and psychological." He then goes on to say:

While there is, of course, such a thing as uncritical psychologizing, no interpretation or reconstruction of history can be critical unless it is also psychological. If it is not psychological, it must also be uncritical. Therein lines the cardinal sin of the mechanical diffusionists. (1925:38)

A. L. Kroeber, who gave us the concept of culture as a superorganic, would seem to be thereby committed to a nonpsychological anthropology. But no one who has examined much of Kroeber's work could possibly believe this. Kroeber wrote a famous and controversial article in 1909 entitled "Classificatory Systems of Relationship" in which he argued that kinship terminologies, contrary to what Morgan had said, were not linked to social structure. They were, he argued, linguistic and psychological rather than sociological. Most of Kroeber's work was subsequently proven wrong but as late as 1952 he still clung to a psychological element. He said then that what he should have said was "that as part of language, kin term systems reflect unconscious logic and conceptual patterning as well as social institutions" (1952:172).

In Kroeber's Introduction to Elsie Clews Parsons' *American Indian Life* (1922), he asserted that anthropologists knew more about the minds of Indians than did others and he obviously believed they could communicate this in prose.

In a paper in 1928, some time after his superorganic paper (1917), he also employs the "impulse of destructiveness" and discusses the role of emotion with reference to culture. The revised edition of his massive text *Anthropology* (1948) has a rather encyclopedic chapter entitled "Cultural Psychology," in which Kroeber's acceptance of the legitimacy of psychological anthropology is perfectly clear. Kroeber, like all of his peers, only cautions that anthropology cannot be reduced to psychology.

In this chapter Kroeber takes up the issue of the "psychic unity of mankind," as the starting point for the reciprocal interrelation between anthropology and psychology. He acknowledges that cultural happenings are also personal and psychological happenings and that considering the psychological would deepen our understanding of culture:

> The recognition of personality and personality relations is of real significance in enhancing the understanding of culture by giving it body and reality — a stereoscopic sense of depth. (1948:242)

Perhaps the following statement best represents his position:

> It is true, as Linton points out, that at present it is equally impossible to explain culture in terms of individual psychology and to understand it without some reference of psychology. After all, culture exists only through persons, in or by their behavior. Yet when we study culture, we concern ourselves primarily with those aspects of their behavior which are more than individual. Our generalizations, and therefore our specific scientific findings, are obviously on a more-than-individual level. But the individual and personalized substratum is still there. So far as we remain aware of the substratum, our depictions and analyses of culture retain a certain color and body and impression of life. So far as we are unaware of the underlying psychology, or indifferent to its suffusion, our cultural findings may be exact, but they tend to be arid, mechanical, and lacking in interest. (1948:242)
>
> Any and every cultural phenomenon therefore has also a psychological aspect or coloring: it is necessarily imbued with something psychological. It cannot however be satisfactorily reduced to purely psychic terms, which are in their nature individual. There is always a large and definitely significant irreducible communal residue that is specifically cultural. (1948:255)

His basic contention seems to have been: although any cultural phenomenon has a psychological substratum, anthropology should not be reduced to psychology. The psychological must be related to the cultural and be interpreted ultimately within the cultural context or framework in which it occurs. Kroeber's view does not differ much from that of many contemporary psychological anthropologists.

There is little point in discussing either Radin or Sapir in this context, as their commitment to psychological anthropology, like Goldenweiser's, is obvious. Nor is there much point in continuing with most of the subsequent generation of well-known American anthropologists—those such as Benedict, Mead, Hallowell, Linton, Kluckhohn, Jacobs, DuBois, Goldfrank, Herskovits, Reichard, Spier, Speck, and others touched by Boas and who, if they did not have specific psychological interests of their own, certainly did not object to such interest on the part of their students and others.

It appears that what we see in this attenuated examination of the history of psychological anthropology is that prior to the first generation of Boas's students there was little or no concern over the question of anthropology versus psychology. This is quite likely due to the fact that there was little or no interest in the culture concept itself until this time. Those who formed the Anthropological Society and formally created the discipline were interested in a comprehensive science of man and simply assumed that the study of mind was an integral and vital part of such a science. Later, as the concept of culture began to be consciously elaborated, and as anthropology had to find an academic niche for itself, the culture concept came to the forefront. But there is little or no evidence during this period that psychology was considered unnecessary or irrelevant to anthropology. Indeed, as we have seen, quite the contrary. There was near universal agreement that anthropology had to proceed with the help of psychology. There is nowhere a rejection of psychology, only the constant and understandable reiteration that anthropology could not merely be reduced to psychology. Where there are criticisms of psychology these are invariably focused on specific psychological traditions, particularly instinct and associational psychologies. Thus, while Ernest Becker may be correct in bemoaning the "fetishism" of the behavioral sciences, there was certainly no total rejection of psychology by the new and growing field of anthropology (1971).

This link is not difficult to understand. If, as Becker has also observed, the science of man grew out of the moral crisis resulting from industrialization, one of the most basic questions can be seen to be the relationship of the individual to his or her society. This was, in fact, one of the basic questions that informed anthropology from the beginning, right on up at least to the Sapir-Benedict-Mead era. The question we must now consider is what happened to this issue? And what happened to the related issue of psychological anthropology? Is it true, as Burridge remarked some time ago (1965:17), that for culture-and-personality studies, "the writing is on the wall?" And if it is true, what are the alternatives?

Those who have argued that there is no place for psychology in anthropology are well known. We have already mentioned Kroeber, whose idea of culture as superorganic would seem to preclude a psychological interest—but whose other work shows him to have been in some respects an active psychological anthropologist.

Almost as well known as Kroeber is Leslie White, self-proclaimed culturologist and one of the most fervid polemicists for nonpsychological anthropology. In his own words:

All of this means that culture has, in a very real sense, an extrasomatic character. Although made possible only by the organisms of human beings, once in existence and under way it has a life of its own. Its behavior is determined by its own laws, not by the laws of human organisms. The culture process is to be explained in terms of the science of culture, of culturology, not in terms of psychology. (1969:140)

Although both Kroeber and White were influential and although the latter especially had for some time a small but loyal band of followers, their extreme superorganicism was not widely accepted. The obvious reification involved, along with the uncompromising cultural determinism, has been difficult for others to accept. And, in the case of White, his position is paradoxical because of his beliefs about symbolization:

Man is unique: he is the only living species that has a culture. By *culture* we mean an extrasomatic, temporal continuum of things and events dependent upon symbolizing . . . . In the course of the evolution of primates *man* appeared when the ability to symbol had been developed and become capable of expression. We thus define man in terms of the ability to symbol and the consequent ability to produce culture. (1969:3)

A. R. Radcliffe-Brown is another of those who argued for the total separation of psychology and anthropology. In his posthumously published lecture notes he asserts:

How do I meet the criticism that social science and psychology both observe the same entities, acts of behavior of individuals? If the subject matter, the data, constituted the only difference between two sciences, then there would be no difference between the sciences of the psychologist and of the sociologist. You can, however, take an act of behavior and observe it in two totally different systems. The social scientist and the psychologist are not concerned with the same system and its set of relations. The social scientist is concerned with relations he can discover between acts of diverse individuals; the psychologist with relations between acts of behavior of one and the same individual.

Psychology deals with the system we call *mind*. Mind (and I think this is the only justifiable definition) is the name of a system of mental relations, a system of which the units, individual acts of inner and outer behavior, are connected with one another by relations of interdependence. (1957:45–46)

Followers of Radcliffe-Brown, most notably Max Gluckman, carried this notion of systems even further and argued that the various systems should be regarded as "closed." That is, the student of social systems need not be concerned with any other system and, indeed, should even be "naive" about them (1964). This argument raises many questions, however, most of which are not answered, and it is difficult at times to understand what really was the proponents' objection to psychological anthropology.

First, there is the question of whether systems can be so easily separated even analytically. Second, even if they can, *should* they be? That is, as many have argued, if your goal is to understand human customs (a goal that Gluckman for example would accept), can you best understand them purely sociologically, or by a combination of both social and psychological approaches? The answer would seem obvious. Even if you accept the analytical distinctions between social and psychological systems, is it reasonable to proceed believing that what goes on in individual minds is totally irrelevant to the social acts they engage in? Were Radcliffe-Brown's motives, whatever they might have been, irrelevant to the sociology of anthropology? Are motives and functions isomorphic? Finally, neither Radcliffe-Brown nor his followers are at all consistent in their use of the term psychology or even in what they claim about the relationship of psychology to anthropology. Radcliffe-Brown, for example (1957:51), acknowledges that there are areas in which psychology and sociology might come together (in the future) to form an intermediate science (of *social psychology!*). Gluckman's use of psychological terms and concepts is virtually impossible to follow at times. What, for example, is one to make of the following:

> Different disciplines may study the same events, and even some of the same regularities in those events: but they look for different kinds of interdependencies between the regularities, i.e., for different kinds of relations. Thus a social anthropologist, like a psychologist, may study events of mental and emotional life—the actions and thoughts and feelings of individuals, and (if he has the techniques to collect the necessary information) even "unconscious" thoughts and feelings. The psychologist seeks to find the relations between these events as they occur in the life of single individuals, what Radcliffe-Brown called "individual mental or physical system." The social anthropologist seeks to find relations between these events as they link together mental systems within a physical environment, i.e., he studies them within social systems. (1964:160)

Are we seriously to believe that if a social anthropologist studies the feelings and thoughts of individuals, and even unconscious ones, they are thereby no longer psychological but become merely part of the social system? And how are we to reconcile Radcliffe-Brown's assertion that "It would be perfectly possible to build up a social science without paying the least attention to the internal relations of human beings" with the letter to Robert Lowie quoted previously?

Not all of the British structural functionalists shared Radcliffe-Brown's extreme position in this question. Meyer Fortes, for example, with a Ph.D. in psychology, readily acknowledges that he turned to psychoanalysis for guidance during his first fieldwork (1978:8). He also points out that his structuralist approach was perfectly consistent with his early training as·a psychologist:

> The "structuralist" approach I later adopted in association with Radcliffe-Brown and Evans-Pritchard at Oxford grew directly out of repeated, objectively presented field observations. As it happened, this was also consistent with my earlier training as a psychologist, with its emphasis on behavior and conduct, notably of course verbal behavior and moral conduct, as significant indices of the social and personal relationships that are the basic substance of social reality (1978:9)

Raymond Firth, too, was sympathetic to the importance of individuals and psychology and, in fact, it could probably be argued that he developed his concept of social organization (as different from social structure) at least in part for this reason.

S. F. Nadel, also with training in psychology, was far more sophisticated in his treatment of the anthropology-psychology relationship than were most of his peers. Although we cannot go into this treatment in detail here, consider a few of Nadel's statements on this topic from *The Foundations of Social Anthropology:*

> Needless to say, anthropological literature is full of observations of a psychological nature. Actions are liberally described as expressing motives, emotions, thoughts, interests, states of consciousness or, for that matter, the impact of the unconscious. We read that members of a group are conscious of their unity or proud of their status; that there are bonds of sentiment between parents and children or between kinsmen; that people are afraid of witchcraft; or that a group encourages or represses violent emotions. (1951:56)

> If social psychology represents a separate field of enquiry, then it must either be concerned with a range of phenomena not accounted for by the other branches of psychology, or approach phenomena common to all branches under a special aspect. In the sense of the first alternative social psychology is commonly contrasted with individual psychology. This distinction would be meaningful only if individual psychology could be said to examine mental events peculiar to isolated individuals—thoughts or emotions which live, in unique form, in the minds of selected persons but disappear or change into something else in man in the aggregate. This seems to be absurd. Apart perhaps from personality studies or psychopathological case-histories, "individual" psychology is concerned, not

with *one* individual, or a few selected ones, but with *the* individual; it aims at the discovery of regularities valid, with whatever variations, for man at large. Everything, then, that individual psychology records is true also of the human beings who live in and make up society; and the individual whose perceptions, memory or thought processes are examined in the laboratory sustains, by these same mental faculties, his social behavior. (1951:290–291)

John Kennedy demonstrated quite convincingly in an exchange with Gluckman that, contrary to Gluckman's claims, E. E. Evans-Pritchard's classic study, *Witchcraft, Oracles, and Magic among the Azande* (1937), was much more of a psychological than a sociological document (1967). Indeed, if you peruse the book at all, I do not see how this could fail to be perfectly plain to anyone but the most absolutely closed-minded. For example:

The Zande, as it seems, retains his *infantile aggressive instincts* through life, but unlike so many savages, he does not *project* [Langness's emphasis] these on to a more or less well-defined High God or on to the spirits of his ancestors, but rather on his fellows, especially on such as are spiteful, dirty, unmannerly, or physically deformed. (1937:xvii)

Social anthropology flourished for quite a long time following Radcliffe-Brown's strictures but has now come to what is essentially a dead end. British anthropologists have turned more and more to one or another form of symbolic analysis, stubbornly implying if not insisting that symbols, like social structures, can be analyzed apart from the individuals for whom they have meaning. Indeed, Ioan Lewis has recently argued (for reasons only indirectly related to psychological anthropology) that social anthropology was in reality only a myth! (1974)

The most vociferous of the recent critics of psychological anthropology is Marvin Harris, who devotes much of his book *The Rise of Anthropological Theory* (1968) to the thesis that the development of a scientific anthropology has been actively hindered because of its mentalistic bias. He goes on to discuss the "pervasiveness of emic and psychological categories" (1968:395). He deplores the fact that ethnographers from Tacitus down to the present have employed a psychological idiom and he gives examples from Firth, Fortes, White, and others. It should be pointed out here that Harris's own ethnographic work, particularly *Town and Country in Brazil* (1971), suffers from exactly the same thing. Harris's objection, however, seems to be directly toward those who unthinkingly confuse emic and etic statements and who attempt purely

psychological explanations for cultural phenomena rather than toward
psychological anthropology. He says of this, first:

. . . it must be made clear at the outset that whoever operates with a strong implicit or explicit bias in favor of emics is committed to an epistemological tradition shared by the culture and personality school. (1968:395)

And then he goes on to acknowledge that "psychologizing is a deeply
rooted habit among cultural anthropologists" (1968:397). Then, he says,
"this merely confirms Mead's point that there is no sharp line in practice between personality and culture and traditional ethnography"
(1968:398). One gets from this the impression that Harris would like to
see "psychologizing" eliminated from anthropology entirely. But in his
later discussion of psychological anthropology, particularly the work of
Whiting and his followers, he sees much to be gained by combining their
approach with his own cultural materialism. Apparently, if technoenvironmental factors are automatically awarded first causal priority,
psychologizing in some sense may be acceptable.

It appears, then, that a number of points can be emphasized:

(1) In the early formative years of anthropology there was no concern
with separating psychology from anthropology; they were merely accepted as necessary and interrelated aspects of a single grand integrated
science of man.

(2) When concern turned to the epistemological status of the culture
concept (and anthropology was establishing itself as a separate academic
discipline) it was generally acknowledged that anthropology could not
be "reduced" to psychology, but that the two disciplines had an intimate,
necessary, and crucial relationship.

(3) There did arise in the 1930s, specifically in the United States, a
distinguishable subdiscipline called culture-and-personality studies. This
can be distinguished precisely as the name implies—its proponents were
interested specifically in *personality*. And their almost exclusive preoccu-
pation with *culture* as a *determinant* was undoubtedly related to the
attempt to make culture the *key concept* of anthropology (and thus
distinguish it from other social and behavioral sciences). As we have
seen, there are other psychological dimensions in the study of culture and
have been from the beginning.

(4) Even those who have been the most explicitly antipsychological in
their approach to anthropology have tended toward ambivalence while
at the same time regularly employing implicit psychological assumptions
and concepts.

(5) Those who have argued that anthropology should be nonpsychological have always been a minority and can all be said to have failed to

establish themselves as leaders of permanent traditions. In my view this is inevitable since they are attempting to do something which is contrary to what anthropological reality, both theoretically and methodologically, is all about.

(6) The present strong trend in anthropology toward various forms of symbolic analysis (and away from cultural materialism and cultural ecology), the more phenomenological "interpretations" of culture, and the growing re-emergence of cognition as a specific anthropological interest would seem to absolutely demand a psychological dimension. There is not a more illustrative example of this demand than Spiro's discussion in "Whatever Happened to the Id?" in which he takes Douglas, Lévi-Strauss, and Leach to task for insisting that:

. . . the body, or its drives, or the affects and motives to which they give rise —but most especially those related to sex and aggression—are seldom the concern of cultural symbol systems. If the latter appear to be concerned with sex or aggression, it is the job of the anthropologist to uncover the reality behind the appearance. (1979:5)

Leach and Douglas continue to insist that body and other symbols which explicitly refer to sex or aggression are really statements about social structure ("the reality behind the appearance"):

I would instance, for example, Leach's contention [Leach 1967a]* that the denial of physiological paternity in Australia and parts of Melanesia, or the denial of a human genitor to Jesus in parts of Christendom, are statements not about biological sex but about rules of descent. Again, I would instance the contention of Mary Douglas that the (widely held) belief that males are endangered by the vagina and vaginal fluids is not a belief about "the actual relations of the sexes" but is, rather, a symbol of the hierarchical stature of the social system [Douglas 1966:4]; or that rituals concerning excreta, breast milk, saliva, and other bodily emissions are concerned not with the body but with the powers and dangers credited to the social structure, for which the body is a symbol [Douglas 1966:115]; or that rituals of genital bleeding, such as sub-incision rites, are concerned not with sex, or blood, or the penis but with society; what is being carved in human flesh [the penis] is an image of society; and when they are performed by tribes with moieties these genital mutilations "are concerned to create a symbol of the symmetry of the two halves of society" [Douglas 1966:116]. (Spiro 1979:5-6)

The approaches of Leach and Douglas, are, of course, in the tradition of British social anthropology with its (on the part of some) deliberate

---

*Bracketed source notes in this quotation and the next are redated from Spiro's to fit the References in this book.

denial of the necessity for any psychologizing. The foundations for this
denial are very shaky:

Now what is even more remarkable about the Leach-Douglas theory itself is
that it is widely accepted as received anthropological wisdom. It is all the more
remarkable because this counterintuitive theory is presented by its proponents as
self-evident truth requiring no support other than assertion. Consider the following examples, taken at random from Douglas. Item: the notion that beliefs
concerning sexual pollution may actually be concerned with sexual pollution is
simply "implausible" [1966:3]. Item: "we cannot possibly" take rituals concerning
excreta, milk, and the like to be in fact concerned with these bodily fluids and
emissions (1966:115]. Item: "I insist" that the seeming "obsession" of the Yurok
with notions of pollution must be related to the "fluid formlessness" of their social
structure [1966:127]. That is all. No argument or evidence is offered in support of
these contentions. (Spiro: 1979:6)

Spiro has dealt with these issues elsewhere as well (1968a; 1968b). My
point here is not to prove Spiro's own psychological interpretations of
these fascinating human phenomena as opposed to the interpretations of
others. It is merely to point out how much more fruitful it would be to
attempt to combine the approaches into one.

(7) To continue to confuse culture-and-personality studies, which
have faded, with psychological anthropology, which continues as an
inevitable component of the study of culture if not as the mainstream,
leads to much confusion on the part of everyone and threatens to impede
the development of a more viable and useful concept of culture. As
Spindler has commented:

One reason why this kind of anthropology [psychological anthropology]
continues, despite attack and discouragement, is that psychologizing is central to
cultural anthropology, even to anthropologists who are not explicitly psychologically oriented. (1978:20)

Philip Bock begins his text on psychological anthropology with the
simple assertion that "all anthropology is psychological" (1980:1) and
then proceeds throughout attempting to show how and why it is. In this
he and Spindler echo Nadel's earlier chastising of anthropologists for
"officially disregarding psychology" while at the same time "smuggling it
in the back door" (1951:289).

It should be obvious that Lévi-Strauss's structuralism and symbolic
anthropology, along with that of Leach and Douglas, as well as the
ethnoscientists' approach, in spite of whatever protestations are made to
the contrary, are all heavily psychological—or mentalistic, rationalistic,
or idealistic if you prefer. Indeed, how could a semiotic anthropology

—the study of symbols and meaning—be otherwise? Anthropologists can no longer take the easy way out by either denying a science of culture, by denying the crucial significance of psychological concepts and variables, or by arbitrarily restricting its subject matter to only observable behavior. It should be clear by now that there is no easy way to understand human nature and culture. It is, in fact, a tragedy that academic psychology has attempted to build theories of human behavior overwhelmingly on white rats and college sophomores while anthropologists most often implicitly smuggled commonsense psychologies into their analyses rather than the real thing.

This is not to suggest that a closer relationship between anthropology and psychology would solve all the problems of culture theory, nor is it to suggest that other disciplines should be ignored. What is obviously needed is an even more conjunctive approach.

SUMMARY

The confusion of the two terms, culture-and-personality and psychological anthropology, gave the impression to many that as culture-and-personality faded so too did psychological anthropology. This impression assumes that there was previously and could be again a nonpsychological anthropology, which in the view expressed here is a virtual impossibility. Anthropologists of whatever persuasion inevitably make psychological assumptions and use psychological terms and concepts. Since they make them, it would be far better to admit it and attempt to do so in a more sophisticated manner. This becomes all the more crucial as anthropologists and others are turning more and more to a semiotic view of culture. Contrary to the more conventional view expressed in recent years, psychological anthropology thrives and, in fact, constitutes a mainstream of cultural anthropology. It is unfortunate that more anthropologists apparently do not wish to admit to this fact.

FURTHER READINGS

Aside from Bock's *Continuities in Psychological Anthropology: A Historical Introduction*, and Spindler's *The Making of Psychological Anthropology*, there is very little that bears specifically on this issue. But take virtually any anthropological classic, whether by a social or a cultural anthropologist, and examine it closely after reading Inkeles, "Personality and Social Structure." See also Spiro, *Theoretical Papers*, for various arguments on the relationship of psychology to anthropology.

CHAPTER VII

Behavioral Science and Behavioral Evolution

The study of culture has not, of course, gone on in a vacuum. The culture concept has been influenced by events and discoveries outside the field of cultural anthropology itself. The relationship between archeology, physical anthropology, linguistics and cultural anthropology, which has always existed, has been strengthened by recent developments in all these fields. Developments in paleoanthropology, ethology, cybernetics, and evolutionary biology have been important in bringing about a new view of man and culture. A broad, new, conjunctive approach to the study of humans and culture—*behavioral science*—emerged in the late 1940s and early 1950s, one in which the relationship between human biology and culture can be better understood. We see clearly now that biological and cultural evolution are not separate processes as had been implicitly assumed in the past. It is also obvious now that to truly understand the process of evolution and our species' position in the overall scheme of things we need to overcome our tendency to fragment and compartmentalize, but instead to attack the questions using whatever theories, concepts and methods are required to do the job. It is an exciting time for students of human nature and culture, what with the wealth of new information and the many new ideas about how they all fit together.

We have discussed the history of the culture concept up to this point almost as if it were unrelated to developments outside cultural anthropology. In fact, until about 1950 this is very much the way the concept developed. This historical process is related to Ernest Becker's thesis in *The Lost Science of Man,* and worth noting.

Becker argued that the science of man, and by this he means essentially the general idea that it was possible to study man scientifically at all, began as a "grand vision." The purpose of this grand vision—this science of man—was to enable people to overcome the moral crisis brought about by the breakdown of medievalism and the absence of anything to take its place. In order to have a sound basis for a new social order, it appeared necessary to understand what had happened to the old, and what kinds of laws or rules governed human progress in general. Thus the concepts we still employ—culture, society, social system, and their likes—began to emerge.

But, Becker asserts, this grand vision got lost along the way. The science of man became bogged down by the tendency of its practitioners to fragment, to invent new concepts and then found new disciplines around them. Thus sociology took for its subject matter, as we see so clearly in Durkheim and Radcliffe-Brown, the concepts of society and social system. Political science attempted to carve out its own distinctive subject matter. Psychology took the psyche as its proper subject matter.

Workers in all of these newer sciences were at the same time careful not to intrude on the subject matter of economics, which was somewhat older and better established. Anthropology took the concept of culture. An attempt was made, then, however unconsciously or unknowingly, to create a science of culture that would have its own distinctive subject matter and that would not be reducible to other like disciplines such as biology, psychology, or whatever. This attempt had the effect, and is still with us, of creating independent departments of specialists ("fetishists," in Becker's terms), which came to exist largely for their own self-interest—hence the grand, all-encompassing science of man, which was to solve the moral crisis resulting from industrialization, became lost. While it is obvious that universities must be organized in some fashion for administrative purposes and logistics, there is an unfortunate tendency for organizations to solidify and maintain themselves in ways that are not necessarily conducive to the most efficient pursuit of knowledge. Indeed, it is not at all far fetched to note that traditional university departments are like dinosaurs that have not quite yet disappeared but are getting dangerously close to it. (As an anthropologist, for example, I work in a Neuropsychiatric Institute where I am a professor of psychiatry and biobehavioral science, coordinate a group of sociobehavioral scientists, and participate in a program for psychocultural studies!

In the same building there is a neurophysiology group and even a neuro-biochemistry group!)

The history of the study of culture reflects an overwhelming attempt to demonstrate *cultural* influences as opposed to others. Anthropologists have consistently argued against race as a factor in producing different cultural traditions or as a factor affecting intelligence or evolution. They have, likewise, tended to oppose purely biological explanations for human or cultural differences, and they have opposed instinct theories as well. Kroeber's attempt to establish culture as a "superorganic" phenomenon, one totally unrelated to psychology or biology, is the best and simplest example of these oppositions. The result of this overwhelming attempt was that we studied culture, until recently, independently of biology, genetics, physiology, and so on. The relationship of cultural anthropology to psychology has not been quite so distant, as we have seen, but even here there has been great resistance. Biologists and geneticists, as well as psychologists and others, were guilty of the same thing —they studied their subject matter as if it were unrelated to culture. Even archeologists and physical anthropologists for a time tended to drift away from the cultural anthropologist. We now recognize that this trend is no longer possible, that fragmenting the science of man was responsible for a terribly distorted view of humans and culture, psychology, genetics, biology, and evolution, in addition to helping the science of man to become "lost." This realization has led, in recent years, to a new more interdisciplinary approach.

BEHAVIORAL SCIENCE

Although there is some confusion about the history of the term behavioral science, and even more about its proper definition, it appears that it came into prominence at the University of Chicago in the late 1940s:

> About 1949 a group of faculty members at the University of Chicago, some of whom have now moved to the University of Michigan, began to consider whether a sufficient body of facts exists to justify developing empirically testable general theories of behavior. This group used the term behavioral science to cover the diverse areas of their interests, primarily because its neutral character made it acceptable to both social and biological scientists (Alexander, Bavelas, et al. 1956:2)

The term was also apparently in use at Yale at the same time as George Peter Murdock retitled his third edition of his *Outline of Cultural*

Materials (1950; 1st edition 1938), calling it *Behavioral Science Outlines* (Senn 1966:113). It was also in use in a less formal way by 1943 and probably even earlier (Senn 1966:110).

In any case, there were at least two different major definitions of the term, one of which was more comprehensive than the other and included "an array of biological, psychological and social sciences in collaborative inquiry concerning the behavior of man." The other view restricted behavioral sciences primarily to sociology, anthropology and social psychology (Group for the Advancement of Psychiatry 1962:40). The first textbook (in social psychology) employing the term was published in 1953, *Research Methods in the Behavioral Sciences* (Festinger and Katz 1953). In the same year the Ford Foundation set up the Center for Advanced Study in Behavioral Sciences and in the following year both Harvard and the University of North Carolina published surveys using the term. In 1956 the journal *Behavioral Science* appeared (Senn 1966).

Behavioral science was very controversial and many scientists rejected the term. Nonetheless, behavioral science gained a foothold and was established and generously funded by government agencies. The movement created jobs for behavioral scientists in colleges and medical schools throughout the United States, although in many cases the new professionals did not get along well and had trouble in becoming integrated into medical and other departments. In this sense it could be said that the "behavioral science movement," as it came to be called, was less than a resounding success. And from a purely practical or political sense this is probably the case. In a purely intellectual sense, however, it has stimulated and helped to bring about a much broader conception of human nature and culture.

In anthropological circles this approach has sometimes been called "behavioral anthropology," "evolutionary anthropology," "biological anthropology," "Darwinian anthropology," and even "human biology." I refer to it in this book as "behavioral evolution," this being the term used by A. Irving Hallowell, one of the early proponents of such a view, in a pioneering paper:

In this paper I have attempted to give the broad outlines of a *conjunctive* approach to human evolution. The organic, psychological, social, and cultural dimensions of the evolutionary process are taken into account as they are related to underlying conditions that are necessary and sufficient for a human level of existence. I have also devoted some attention to earlier opinions to bring into sharper focus the problems that need reconsideration in the light of contemporary knowledge. "Behavioral evolution" is, perhaps, the term which best defines the framework of a conjunctive approach. (Hallowell 1963:440)

The conjunctive approach to human behavior, evolution, culture, society, and personality tends to put all of these subjects in a new light. In addition to the vast amount of interdisciplinary stimulation provided by the behavioral sciences movement, causing scholars of many different persuasions to seriously rethink their position, this approach was also aided by five important recent developments: (1) the "rediscovery" of Darwin and evolution, (2) new discoveries in the field of *paleoanthropology*, (3) the increasing importance of *ethological* studies, particularly those dealing with nonhuman primates and carnivores, (4) the accumulation of more and more cross-cultural data on a larger number of human groups, and (5) the discovery of cybernetics.

EVOLUTION AND BEHAVIOR

As we have seen, when the early evolutionary theories were mostly discredited by the newer generations of anthropologists, the concept of evolution itself was neglected. Psychologists likewise, when the recapitulation hypothesis was discredited, turned away from the study of evolution. This general attitude toward evolution was unfortunately encouraged by the discovery and rapid development of genetics— Darwin had written before the science of genetics was established. Within a short time after his death, critics began to challenge much of what Darwin had said, especially his views of the inheritance of acquired characteristics (which were very similar to Lamarck's), and even his theory of natural selection. By the early 1900s the geneticists had attained a dominant position that they held until fairly recently (Freeman 1970).

To understand the significance of this turn it is necessary to understand that the early theories of biological evolution, both Darwin's and Lamarck's, importantly emphasized *behavior* as a significant variable in the process of evolution. This emphasis is most obvious in the Lamarckian view, where the behavior of the organism is what is believed to bring about the subsequent changes in the species (the giraffe has a long neck because its ancestors had to stretch to reach the trees on which they fed, for instance); but behavior is equally important in the theory of natural selection. Darwin had argued that inasmuch as all species had more young than could survive there was a factor of *overproduction*. There was also, he observed, *variation*—that is, individuals of the same species are not identical in every way. Overproduction meant that there was *competition* for things, including the opportunity to reproduce. Because there was variation, some creatures could do better than others in this competition, wherefore their characteristics survived and those of others did not. Clearly, in this scheme, the behavior of creatures is of great importance.

The geneticists, in their early and most enthusiastic period, virtually did away with behavior as a relevant consideration and attempted to explain evolution simply as a result of a kind of genetic programming that operated independently of the behavior of the animal. George Gaylord Simpson has put it very nicely:

> Samuel Butler said that a hen is an egg's way of producing another egg. Thus in the Darwinian epoch he foreshadowed a reorientation of evolutionary studies that did later occur. Without expressing it in that way, the evolutionary scientists of Butler's and earlier times held the common-sense view that an egg is a hen's way of producing another hen. They were trying to explain the evolution of the hen, not of the egg. It was the geneticists, after 1900, who came around to Butler's view that the essence of the matter is in the egg, not in the hen. (Simpson 1958:7)

The result of turning away from behavior was to turn away from Darwinism as well. The turn also contributed to the separation of genetics and biology from the study of culture. Now there is a new synthetic theory that incorporates the more useful features of Darwin, of genetics, and of various other views and that, most importantly, once again recognizes behavior as a factor of great significance (Campbell 1974; Freeman 1970; Hallowell 1963; Roe and Simpson 1958). Darwin has thus been rediscovered and the evolutionary theory "has emerged saliently as the unifying paradigm of all the biological sciences, from biochemistry to ecology" (Freeman 1970:51).

PALEOANTHROPOLOGY

Perhaps even more dramatic with respect to a new view of humans and culture are the recent discoveries from paleontology and archeology. These have raised questions about the fundamental definitions of human beings and culture, definitions that had been for the most part unchallenged for a long period. What, after all, in evolutionary perspective, *is* a "human being"? If we find, in the course of archeological excavations, the bones of creatures which are more or less like those of modern people but not exactly like them, how do we determine whether or not they are "men" as opposed to nonmen? Until fairly recently this issue was not regarded as critical. Remember that well into the nineteenth century no human fossils had been found at all. The first fossil formally recognized as such was a *Neanderthal* found in 1856. Even the true significance of this fossil lay in limbo for another thirty years—until two similar skeletons were uncovered in association with the remains of extinct animals and a number of crude stone tools (Daniel 1962; Howell 1965; Oakley 1964). Neanderthals, however, are classified along with modern man as *Homo sapiens*. The classification is based upon morphological features, one of the most important of which is the size of the skull and brain case. Thus Neanderthals, being recent and large-brained, did not importantly affect our definition of man.

Things became considerably more difficult after the 1890s, when a young Dutch doctor and student of early man, Eugene DuBois, discovered what turned out to be a more primitive fossil human—Java man. This fossil was subsequently termed *Homo erectus*, since it was quite different from anything previously known, but still basically human in form. This discovery caused so much controversy in anthropological circles and was subject to so much disbelief that DuBois locked up his finds and refused to let others see them. After other *Homo erectus* finds were made, in Java, China, Algeria, and East Africa, DuBois was eventually given credit for his find and *Homo erectus* was seen to be a separate, far-ranging, and successful species (Howell 1965).

Although Java man created a sensation when first discovered, and although it was more "primitive" or "ape-like" than Neanderthal, it still did not seriously shake our beliefs about what the fundamental criteria for being human were—Java man was bipedal, had humanlike dentition, and had other physical features similar to those of modern people. More importantly, however, Java man proved to have approximately 1000 cubic centimeters of brain, 900–1000 cubic centimeters being an implicitly held "critical point" for man as opposed to ape (modern man ranges from 1000 to 2000 with a mean of 1300). That is, if one had a fossil find otherwise humanlike, it was considered human only if it also had not less than 900–1000 cc of brain case. One further reason the finding of Java man did relatively little to shake our established beliefs about human evolution is that the fossils could not be adequately dated, since the geology of Java was so little known at the time of DuBois's discovery. Although Java man was established as older than Neanderthal, just how much older was not clear until many years later.

Archeological sites, however, do not always contain fossil materials. In the absence of such evidence, how does one establish that the site was occupied by humans as opposed to some other creature? The common solution was to use the presence of tools—if there were tools, they must have been made by humans, because it was universally believed that only humans made and used tools. Evidence of fire, too, could be used in the same way. Brain size was linked with these latter two criteria. To make fire and to make and use tools, it was long believed, required having a brain of the proper "human" size. For a long time nothing much happened to challenge this view.

But this way of thinking received a severe jolt with the discovery of an entirely unprecedented group of fossils, the *Australopithecines*. The first of these, the famous Taung baby, was discovered in 1924 by the anatomist Raymond Dart in South Africa. At first, as in the case of Java man, the scientific community reacted with surprised disbelief. Part of the skepticism stemmed from the fact that Dart's find was a child only five or six years of age. To establish it as an entirely new and radically different fossil it was necessary to find more evidence, preferably adults. Then, in the 1930's, the paleontologist Robert Broom found enough materials to reconstruct several adult skulls along with various other body bones. Broom's fossils were slightly different from Dart's original, but close enough to establish the authenticity of the Australopithecines. Since these early discoveries there have been many more such finds so that there are now thousands of Australopithecine specimens from East Africa as well as South Africa. Although there are many professional disputes over whether certain finds are older than others, whether certain types are different species or merely variants of a single species, and the like, both the general features of the Australopithecines and the crude dates of their appearance are quite clear—and the implications for theories of humans and culture are most profound (Campbell 1974; Pfeiffer 1984).

Most authorities seem to agree that the earliest genus of the family Hominidae was *Ramapithecus*. This fossil has many very ape-like features but it also has characteristics of man. If this controversy is ever settled and *Ramapithecus* continues to be classified as Hominidae it would mean that the Hominidae became a distinct line approximately fifteen million years ago.

The genus *Australopithecus* is most likely a descendant of *Ramapithecus*. The specimens that represent this genus constitute two separate but apparently contemporary lineages, *Australopithecus boisei* and *Australopithecus africanus*. The former, with fossils dating from about 3 million to 1.2 million years, apparently became extinct. *Australopithecus africanus*, with fossil evidence ranging from about 5.5 million to 1.5 million years, is believed to be ancestral to man.

In the Australopithecines we have creatures who are erect and bipedal, with a humanlike pelvis and leg formation. The dentition and skull are remarkably manlike although the creature is so old it was first thought that it had to be an ape. *Australopithecus africanus* was a relatively small-brained creature. With a skull smaller than that of a chimpanzee it had a cranial capacity which varied from 435 to 815 cc, a brain about as large as a gorilla's. Unlike the fossils of *Ramapithecus*, which are found in forest environments, Australopithecines are associated with grassland and savanna. What made the Australopithecines such an unprecedented, startling, and challenging discovery was the evidence that they must have hunted and apparently made stone tools (M. Leakey 1970; 1971). This evidence obviously challenged the prevailing view that the large brain of *Homo erectus* or *Homo sapiens* was a necessary requirement for making and using tools. Since tools were routinely taken as evidence of culture, their tools meant that the Australopithecines must have possessed the rudiments, at least, of culture. Thus we are now forced to believe that tool making and tool using actually preceded the large brain and, in fact, appear to be factors involved in the evolution of the brain. As a consequence, then, in a specifically biological frame of reference, humans become in important measure a *product of culture*—of their own thought and behavior, that is—as well as the creator of it. The large brain *and* culture, contrary to what we always believed, must have evolved *together* over a long period of time, with the behavior associated with tool using feeding back on the organism itself and helping to bring about a change in dentition, in the shape of the face and skull, in the pelvis, and hence in the size of the brain (Campbell 1974; Howell 1965; Hallowell 1963; Pfeiffer 1969; Roe and Simpson 1958; Spuhler 1959).

The earliest fossils thus far recovered that can be placed in our own genus, *Homo*, can be dated approximately one million years ago. The earliest of these are from Africa and Java and are designated *Homo erectus* to distinguish them from modern man. From about 600,000 years ago we have fossils appearing from the Old World—scattered from Germany to Hungary to China and Algeria. It is known that *Homo erectus* knew how to control fire approximately 500,000 years ago and became an increasingly successful hunter. The earliest people who can be said to be truly like us most probably did not appear until about 60,000 years ago.

Although experts continue to argue about the details and precise classifications of the various kinds, fossil evidence grows larger each year and there is little argument over the general course of events. We cannot know exactly when fire first appeared, or true language, or who conceived of the first funeral ceremony, or whatever, but there is little doubt about the evolutionary process that produced us. Clearly, some relatively small-brained, erect, bipedal "protohuman" was responsible for making and using tools hundreds of thousand if not millions of years before we had previously thought possible.

ETHOLOGY

It is strange that although people knew for a long time that animals other than humans used tools and made things—for what, after all, is involved in the spider's construction of a web, a bird's making a nest, a primate's using a stick to probe for insects or a rock to break things, a hermits crab's using a discarded shell, and the like—they continued to define themselves as *the* tool makers and to assume that this capacity set humans apart clearly and completely from other creatures. It is true, however, that we knew suprisingly little about the behavior of animals in their natural state.

Paleontology is not the only development to bring about changes in the way we think about ourselves and culture. In recent years the science of ethology has made tremendous contributions to our thought along these lines. Indeed, the Nobel prize for medicine in 1973 was shared by three ethologists—Konrad Lorenz, Nikolaas Tinbergen, and Karl von Frisch. We now have, for the first time, solid data that bears upon the behavior of many species of animals *in their natural environment,* and it seems incredible, in looking back, that until about fifty years ago we had virtually no such information. Furthermore, even the information that might have been available was not ordinarily used by students of the human species. Although there are over 200 species of monkeys and apes, we had no adequate observations of any of them in their natural environment until 1931 when, under the tutelage of Robert M. Yerkes, H. W. Nissen did a field study on the chimpanzee (Carpenter 1964:3).

Even so, it was not until the 1950s that such studies became accepted and important parts of anthropology, biology, psychology, and zoology. Man, defined by himself as the tool-making, unique, and distinctive culture-bearing creature, had apparently no need for such information! Indeed, some even today do not believe that such information has any relevance whatsoever to understanding the behavior of humans; others, at the opposite extreme, naively believe one can generalize directly from animals to people. In between are those more cautious scholars who recognize that while one cannot generalize directly from animal to human behavior, one can learn a great deal about behavior in general. This information about behavior in general is, in turn, most helpful in trying to understand human behavior in particular. We study chimpanzees, gorillas, monkeys, wolves, lions, or whatever, not because *our* behavior is like theirs but, rather, because the behavior of our ancient prehuman forebears must have been more similar to that of certain present-day animals than to our own present-day behavior. Likewise, we do not study contemporary hunting and gathering peoples because they behave as our ancestors did, but because they must behave more nearly as our ancestors did than as we do. These assumptions are fundamental to any study of humans and culture in phylogenetic perspective—but they must not be abused; as anthropologist Alexander Alland said:

A renewed interest in the application of Darwinian biology to human behavior has developed in the last several years. This interest has opened an exciting field for theory and research specifically because it operates without the assumption that, since men are animals, they must behave like other animals. Instead, those interested in this approach search for both continuities and discontinuities in those processes which gave rise to man and which continue to influence his development.

Books like *African Genesis, The Territorial Imperative, On Aggression,* and *The Naked Ape* (there are several more) obscure the real scientific progress that has been made in this area. These books oversimplify both Darwinism and the human condition. Their focus on hypothetical biological determinants of human social existence does not offer a plausible theory of human origins. Furthermore, these authors have been singularly unable to offer insights into the reasons for behavioral differences between groups, or to explain the complexities of human social patterns.

It is important to salvage those aspects of biological theory which can contribute to an understanding of man. The works named represent an intellectual dead end at a time when the complexities of human behavior can and must be probed in depth. The political and ecological situation in the world has reached a level of crisis approaching disaster. Outworn analyses such as those which equate war with innate aggression can only offer comfort to those who wish to maintain the *status quo.* (Alland 1972:2-3)

Recent studies of animal behavior have told us many things we did not previously know and have also caused us to consider much more systematically and deeply some of the things we thought we already knew. The exciting work done on the chimpanzee by Jane van Lawick-Goodall, for example, has made us aware of a number of new facts. Chimpanzees make and use simple tools. They have been observed picking up twigs, stripping the leaves from them, and then using what remains to dip into termite nests to get the termites for food. They also have been observed making sponges of soft leaves in order to drink water they could not otherwise have reached. They routinely make nests to sleep in at night. What is more, we know now for the first time that chimpanzees, contrary to what has always been believed about them, occasionally hunt and kill other animals for food. We have detailed information on the sexual life of chimpanzees which has exploded many of the myths that formerly surrounded the subject. The chimpanzees, far from fighting over sexually receptive females or allowing them to mate with only the dominant male, calmly take turns (Lawick-Goodall 1971:96).

George B. Schaller's work with the mountain gorilla is another case in point. Probably no animal in history has been subject to so many myths, distortions, and outright fabrications as this peaceful, placid beast. And, again, the information sheds new light on former beliefs:

Some scientists have maintained that monkey and ape groups remain together over long periods of time because the males have continuous and ready access to receptive females. But from my observations it seems the gorilla groups remain stable, on the whole, even though there may be no receptive females for months at a time, indicating that sex is of little or no importance here. Gorillas always gave me the impression that they stay together because they like and know one another. The magnanimity with which Big Daddy shared his females with other males, even though some were only temporary visitors, helped to promote peace in the group. (Schaller 1964:122)

Similarly, with respect to the widely advertised belief that territoriality is an "instinctive" phenomenon:

The fact that several gorilla groups occupy the same section of the forest, and that, when groups meet, their interactions tend to be peaceful was of considerable interest to me. Once it was generally thought that each monkey and ape group lived in a territory, the boundaries of which were defended vigorously against intrusions by other members of the same species. But the gorilla certainly shares its range and its abundant food resources with others of its kind, disdaining all claims to a plot of land of its own. (Schaller 1964:201)

This is not to say that territoriality is not important in many animals; it is, but what is emerging clearly from ethological studies is that all of those phenomena we have tended to take for granted—sexual exclusiveness, territoriality, instinctive aggressiveness, and the like—are immeasurably more complex than we had heretofore imagined. Previous views of animal behavior have been oversimplified, as have been previous views of man and culture. We have, until recently, attributed remarkable abilities to *Homo sapiens* with no regard for the complexities of animal social organization, tool using, or "proto-culture" that preceded them. It was as if a human had suddenly emerged, from an ancestor that possessed none of these characteristics at all, as a radically different, dominant, large-brained, culture-bearing creature. While chimpanzees and gorillas do not tell us directly of our own behavior, they suggest much about the kinds and ranges of behavior that must probably have been involved in the evolution of our behavior.

Recent years have seen much research on the language abilities of apes, mostly chimpanzees and gorillas, and claims have been made for their capability for symbolic thought and communication (Fouts and Mellgren 1976; Gardner and Gardner 1969; Laidler 1978; Patterson 1978; Premack 1976; Rumbaugh 1977). The early somewhat exaggerated claims have more recently been called into question (Bindra, Patterson, and Terrace 1981; McGonigle 1980; Savage-Rumbaugh, Rumbaugh and Boysen 1980; Sebeok and Umiker-Sebeok 1980; Terrace 1979a, 1979b); but even so, it is obvious that nonhuman primates have a much greater symbolic capacity than anyone previously would have expected. They do not have language in the sense that humans do but they can learn to manipulate signs and symbols up to a point. They apparently do not learn to use a sound code made up of essentially meaningless elements that can be infinitely combined. Although the gap between *Homo sapiens* and the great apes seems to be less the more we learn, and although both monkeys and apes might be said to have hints of culture, it remains true that a full-fledged cultural mode of life is distinctively human.

But studies of the behavior of monkeys and apes, however much they are closer to humans than other animals are, must not be taken as the only ones of relevance. As Schaller has made clear, from an ecological point of view there are cogent reasons to study other kinds of animals, particularly group-dwelling carnivores:

When trying to deduce the social system used by *Australopithecus* and other early hominids, anthropologists have usually looked for clues among nonhuman primates. This is logical on phylogenetic grounds but not on ecological ones. Social systems are so strongly influenced by the ecological conditions under which an animal lives that even the same species may behave differently from area to area as Rowell (1967) has shown for several primates and Kruuk (1970) for hyenas. Monkeys and apes are essentially vegetarians living in groups which confine themselves to small ranges. Man and his precursors, on the other hand, have been widely roaming scavengers and hunters for perhaps two million years, a way of life that has diverged so drastically from the nonhuman primates that similarities in the social systems of the two may well be accidental. More can probably be learned about the genesis of man's social system by studying phylogenetically unrelated but ecologically similar forms than by perusing nonhuman primates. The social carnivores provide an obvious choice. (Schaller 1972:378)

Studies of such animals as lions, hyenas, jackals, wild dogs, and wolves have suggested, among other things, that it is the social behavior of these animals that enables them to exploit the particular environments they inhabit (Kruuk 1972:275). This is strong evidence for those who hold that cooperation and the evolution of sociability are of far greater importance in evolution than a creature's innate aggressiveness or some kind of situation of "all against all." These studies have demonstrated nothing conclusive as yet, but, again, they show the enormous complexity of the issues and they force us to consider our assumptions more carefully.

Nor are the relevant studies confined only to nonhuman primates and carnivorous predators. The behaviors of all creatures—insects, amphibians, reptiles, and birds—are all of great interest now to students of man.

Again, not because they necessarily tell us about human behavior per se, but because they tell us so much about *behavior* itself, particularly those forms of behavior we label communication, adaptation, sociability, territoriality, and even what we term "intelligence." Information from both paleontology and ethology is coming in so fast at the present time that one has difficulty keeping abreast of it. It combines to put us on the threshold of a new, comprehensive, and significant science of human beings.

CROSS-CULTURAL STUDIES

Ethnography is generally defined as the scientific description of human life. Ethnography can easily be thought of as the ethology of humans. As in the case of ethological studies in general, it may seem incredible not to realize how little we actually knew about our non-Western human peers until well into the twentieth century. Remember that the only sources of information available to the early evolutionists —and to all scholars before them—were the usually biased accounts of travelers, missionaries, prospectors, traders, and adventurers. Systematic scientific studies of non-Western peoples began in earnest only in the twentieth century—in fact, only about fifty years ago. That all theories of behavior, society, culture, and evolution were based upon the behavior of western Europeans or on biased accounts of other people is a fact of great significance in the history of science and should not be ignored. The related factor of assuming that existing "primitive" people could be taken as representative of our prehistoric ancestors is perhaps of no less importance.

In recent years we have accumulated a wealth of detailed ethnographic information of a substantial number of different cultures all around the globe. We know from this information, plus the archeological record, that currently existing hunters and gatherers are marginal types not representative of those hunting and gathering populations who existed in previous times and who exploited the vast herds of miscellaneous ungulates that populated their environments in such staggeringly large numbers. The Eskimo, Australian Aborigines, African Bushmen, and other hunter-gatherers that we have studied most intensively all occupy relatively remote and sparse environments. Their requirements for making a living are far different, for example, from the requirements of those who lived in close proximity to the estimated thirty million bison that inhabited the North American continent at the time of first European contact (McHugh 1972). Archeological evidence indicates that many of our ancestors must likewise have been blessed with an abundance. Nonetheless, the information acquired from studies of existing hunter-gatherers has often been a critical factor in allowing archeologists to interpret the meaning of their finds. To have some idea, say, of the way contemporary people make use of stone tools or housing sites, how and why they move over the land, what kinds of refuse they leave behind, and other such things, is obviously of value when an investigator is confronted by limited evidence of such activity in the past. This kind of combination of ethnography with archeology is a part of the exciting "new archeology" that is still developing.

Ethnographic studies have gone much further, however, to give us insight into the workings of culture and cultural evolution and the essential human condition. It was, for example, as we have seen, the cross-cultural record that converted Freud's brilliant but parochial and essentially culture-bound psychoanalytic theory into a newer, more powerful, more comprehensive and more useful theory which, however inadequate some might consider it, still remains the only psychological therory of personality "adequate thus far to cope with the enormous complexities of the human psyche" (Spiro 1972:574).

Although anthropologists have been accused in the past, perhaps rightly so, of concentrating too exclusively on the differences between human cultures and thus neglecting the similarities, it is also the case that the information to establish true human universals has come from the cross-cultural record. We now recognize, for example, that if there be such a thing as an Oedipus complex, it results not from memory traces in the species, not from biology, but rather from universally similar factors of infancy, childhood, the family, and the requirements of child-rearing. We know that human beings, for reasons which are now beginning to become clear, have chosen only a few from an infinite number of possible kinship systems (Murdock 1949b). We know, likewise, that however much cultures may differ in their specifics, each human culture has a normative dimension and constitutes, in that sense, a moral order. And we know that such things as aggression, territoriality, war, and the like are not absolute human universals but are dependent upon circumstances of technology, environment, personality, culture, and history. We also know that most of those various behavior patterns that we have attempted to define as "normal" or "abnormal" are, in fact, relative to the cultural context in which they occur and that, with the exception of only the most extreme pathologies, no definite scale exists whereby we can measure behavior in such terms. Recent ethnographic and cross-cultural work on homosexuality (Herdt 1981, 1982), excessive drinking (Marshall 1979), child abuse (Korbin 1981), cannibalism (Brown and Tuzin 1983), and other such "problems" give new dimension to our understanding and add to the already substantial ethnographic literature bearing on the human experience.

The full range of human behavior "in its natural state" is at once awesome and beautiful. We are not very close to understanding this vast panorama of behavior, but we now in the twentieth century are much more aware that it exists and we have a much better understanding of its dimensions that ever before. If critics condemn anthropologists for having neglected their own culture and their own social problems for the esoteric and bizarre, let these critics tell us where else we would have acquired *any* valid information on the richness and beauty of human life as it has expressed itself around the world. Or perhaps we would somehow be better off not knowing of the infinite wonder of human life?

CYBERNETICS

One development of recent years that has helped to bring about the new view of culture and evolution is the discovery of cybernetics — essentially the study of the control functions of communication. In at least three ways, the development of cybernetics has influenced the science of man: by challenging the absolute laws of Newtonian physics and thus demonstrating that the social sciences need not be less scientific than physics, by opening our eyes to the complexities of feedback and thus allowing us to see the process of evolution in a more useful perspective, and by providing us with computers that enable us to handle masses of data not otherwise manageable.

According to Newtonian physics, which had dominated science for at least two hundred years, the universe operated according to precise, rigid laws in which the future depended strictly upon the past; everything was deemed perfectly predictable and there were, in principle, no uncertainties. It was this model that students of human beings—anthropologists, sociologists, psychologists, political scientists, and others—attempted to emulate in their attempts to become scientific. This model influenced Boas and Durkheim, Radcliffe-Brown and Malinowski, and virtually all others. For years, members of the so-called "hard sciences" argued that the various social sciences could never become sciences at all—that human behavior was fundamentally unpredictable and hence that the study of it could not be the same as the study of the laws of the universe. The new view of physics, arising out of the Heisenberg *"principle of uncertainty"* (S. F. Mason 1962:557) and utilizing as it does statistics and probability theory instead of absolutes and immutables, renders this criticism untenable and thus opens up new possibilities for a true science of human beings which is just that—a science:

> Newtonian physics, which had ruled from the end of the seventeenth century to the end of the nineteenth with scarcely an opposing voice, described a universe in which everything happened precisely according to law, a compact, tightly organized universe in which the whole future depends strictly upon the whole past. Such a picture can never be either fully justified or fully rejected experimentally and belongs in large measure to a conception of the world which is supplementary to experiment but in some ways more universal than anything that can be experimentally verified. We can never test by our imperfect experiments whether one set of physical laws or another can be verified down to the last decimal. The Newtonian view, however, was compelled to state and formulate physics as if it were, in fact, subject to such laws. This is now no longer the dominant attitude of physics . . . . (Wiener 1954:7)

Cybernetic explanations, according to anthropologist Gregory Bateson (1972), have peculiarities which make them much more useful to social and behavioral scientists than the explanations of classical physics. First of all, they deal with "form" rather than with the "substance" that the laws for energy and matter were concerned with. That is, cybernetic explanations deal in the relations between things rather than in what actually composes or makes up the things. They are similar in this way to Lévi-Strauss's structuralism, which is not surprising inasmuch as Lévi-Strauss was influenced to some extent by cybernetic theory. Cybernetic explanations are also concerned with the order of things rather than in what is being ordered. But they are thus interested in order not purely for its own sake but rather for the information that is associated with or emerges from the order—what message is conveyed, that is. Such explanations are further concerned with "context" in a way that physics is not. There is, of course, a hierarchy of contexts within which communications must be understood. The same message can obviously mean different things in different contexts. This becomes absolutely crucial for studies of emics, where we are led to "understand" in terms of larger and larger contexts. As Bateson says, "without context there is no communication" (1972:408). Cybernetic explanations are negative rather than positive:

> Causal explanation is usually positive. We say that billiard ball B moved in such and such a direction because billiard ball A hit it at such and such an angle. In contrast to this, cybernetic explanation is always negative. We consider what alternative possibilities could conceivably have occurred and then ask why many of the alternatives were not followed, so that the particular event was one of those few which could, in fact, occur. The classical example of this type of

explanation is the theory of evolution under natural selection. According to this theory, those organisms which were not both physiologically and environmentally viable could not possible have lived to reproduce. Therefore, evolution always followed the pathways of viability. As Lewis Carroll has pointed out, the theory explains quite satisfactorily why there are no bread-and-butter-flies today. (Bateson 1967:29)

Thus cybernetics deals with "restraints." The assumption is that without restraints of some kind, change would be regulated only by chance.

. . . For example, the selection of a piece for a given position in a jigsaw puzzle is "restrained" by many factors. Its shape must conform to that of its several neighbors and possibly that of the boundary of the puzzle; its color must conform to the color pattern of its region; the orientation of its edges must obey the topological regularities set by the cutting machine in which the puzzle was made; and so on. From the point of view of the man who is trying to solve the puzzle, these are all clues, i.e., sources of information which will guide him in his selection. From the points of view of the cybernetic observer, they are *restraints*. (Bateson 1967:29)

Likewise, there are restraints that result from "feedback." That is, the information one receives from having attempted something not only enables one to try it again somewhat differently, but also reduces the chances of trying still other things. The concept of feedback has helped us to understand that human evolution was not a completely predetermined process independent of the actions of organisms, but rather that it depended upon the actions of organisms for its continuation. Adaptive change, such as that required by evolution, has many dimensions. It involves responding, learning, ecological succession, biological change, and so on, depending upon how we wish to view it. But in all cases, if it is to be truly adaptive change, it must involve trial and error, and there must be a way of comparing one attempt with another. Because some errors must always be made, and because errors are "always biologically and/or psychically expensive" (Bateson 1972:274), certain things continually drop out of the system and thereby change the context. A new situation exists and the process continues.

This view of evolutionary change is far more sophisticated than that held by Darwin or by the early cultural evolutionists. It combines with the other recent developments we have mentioned to put us on the brink of a comprehensive, meaningful, and, we must hope, useful science of human beings. This newly emerging view combines features of all of the views that have gone before. It is, above all, evolutionary. It recognizes

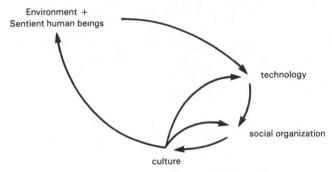

CYBERNETICS IN THE EVOLUTION OF CULTURE

the importance of history and diffusion and also insists upon the crucial significance of an ecological point of view. It recognizes the significance of technoenvironmental factors, but does not believe that these are the sole determinants of cultural phenomena or cultural change. Finally, it recognizes what Bateson has recently termed the "ecology of mind" (1972)—that is, the question of how ideas interact both with themselves and with the environment to produce a viable system. Thus the new view goes well beyond arguments involving history versus science, idiographic versus nomothetic, functionalism versus historical reconstruction, sociology versus psychology, group versus individual, idealism versus materialism, and the like. It retains as a most useful convenience, however, the concept of culture—albeit in a revised form. In its simplest form it might look something like the diagram.

People inevitably exist in some environment. Out of their interaction with their environment emerges a technology. Technology, we can say, is not the absolutely unique possession of human beings, since animals, too, in some sense have technologies. The spider's web, the nests of birds, the use of simple tools by many creatures, and other such things are examples of technology. But in humans technology is developed to an extraordinary degree. Out of man's interaction with the environment and the emerging technology are implications for the way people can order themselves with relation to others—social organization. All of these things in turn—the interaction with the environment, technology, and social organization, come to carry both private and public symbolic meanings which influence and feed back into all of the other dimensions. However much technoenvironmental factors are determinants of behavior, the relationship between human beings and their environment and technology is mediated by their ideas and beliefs about themselves, their fellows, and, indeed, the universe itself. The Mennonites, a religious group in the United States, resist automobiles, television, and modern technology in general not because they are unaware that such things exist, but rather because of their religious beliefs. Likewise, as the venerable historian Arnold J. Toynbee has recently pointed out (1973), there is surely some relationship between people's attitudes toward the world and how they have treated it. Witness a Judeo-Christian attitude:

And God blessed them, and God said to them, Be fruitful, and multiply, and fill the earth, and subdue it; and have dominion over the fish of the sea and over the fowl of the air and over every living thing that moves upon the earth. (Genesis 1:28)

Compare this with the following attitude expressed by the Shahaptian medicine man Smohalla:

My young men shall never work. Men who work cannot dream, and wisdom comes to us in dreams . . . . You ask me to plough the ground. Shall I take a knife and tear my mother's bosom? You ask me to dig for stone. Shall I dig under her skin for her bones? You ask me to cut the grass and make hay and sell it and be rich like white men. But dare I cut off my mother's hair? (Quoted in Haines 1955:169)

Or consider one of the many comments of the remarkable Nez Perce leader, Chief Joseph:

The white men were many and we could not hold our own with them. We were like deer. They were like grizzly bears. We had a small country. Their country was large. We were contented to let things remain as the Great Spirit made them. They were not, and would change the rivers if they did not suit them. (Quoted in Brown 1970:304)

The price we are paying for our arrogance toward nature and other creatures is becoming increasingly apparent as the current environmental and ecological issues before us now cannot be further evaded or pushed aside. Campbell has stated part of the problem very well:

It is a very important characteristic of material culture that in relation to its creator it is not only an extra-bodily organ but also part of the environment, and it is a part of the environment that affects man closely. When man's culture "evolves," therefore his environment changes, and a new adaptation of the organic body will be selected. We therefore find man living in a fast-changing culture. No sooner does the culture adapt than the environment has changed, and further adaptation is selected. In face of this ever increasing rate of environmental change, man's physical evolution runs far behind (Dobzhansky 1963), which suggests that man is ill-adapted genetically to his environment. In at least one sense that is true: without the barrier that his material culture forms between man and his environment, he would be unable to survive. But it is also open to question whether man is fully adapted in any sense, for the rate of change in his environment may appear to be outstripping even his cultural adaptations. (1974:330)

CHARACTERISTICS OF MAN AS AN ANIMAL

Humankind's kinship with the rest of nature has become more and more apparent as the behavioral sciences have shown. We recognize the continuity of biological and cultural evolution and the complex feedback between the two. Anthropological works like Weston LaBarre's *The Human Animal* (1954) and Ashley Montagu's *The Direction of Human Development* (1955) attempted to present more integrated pictures of the process of human development and the central role of culture in that process. The picture becomes clearer each year. Nowadays we have no trouble recognizing that humankind is animal; then as animals we are *mammals*, primates, and hominids. Each of these classifications implies certain things for the way humans relate to their environment and to other creatures.

Being mammals, people share with all other mammals certain features or "adaptive complexes" (Campbell 1974) that are generally regarded as particularly important in understanding evolution and culture. Mammals have the ability, for example, for constant and lively activity. This capacity contrasts mammals with both reptiles and amphibians, which become relatively inactive at night and during periods of cold weather. Their difference would presumably give the mammals an advantage over reptiles and amphibians, and it would also have allowed mammals to move northward into colder latitudes and thus exploit more of the earth's surface. This kind of capacity for constant activity is made possible through the phenomenon of *homoiothermy*—the ability to maintain a constant and appropriate body temperature. This ability may date back as much as 150 million years (Campbell 1974; LaBarre 1954).

To maintain a constant body temperature it is necessary to have a reliable supply of food for energy. Mammals solved this problem in part by evolving a new kind of dentition. Whereas reptiles have what is called *homodont* dentition, mammals have *heterodont* dentition. A snake's teeth are nearly all of the same shape (fangs excepted) and have the same function—namely to trap. Mammalian teeth, on the other hand, are more specialized, some being for tearing, others for chewing, cutting, or grinding. With such teeth many more kinds of food could be exploited than had been with homodont teeth, and the efficency of the digestive process was increased as well.

Still another factor of great importance for the mammals was reproductive economy. Reptiles maintain themselves by producing large numbers of eggs, only a few of which hatch offspring that live to maturity. Placental mammals, by retaining the egg and nourishing the infant or infants inside the mother, cut down on losses and thus improve reproductive economy. There is a postnatal factor here as well as a prenatal one. It is of the utmost importance for the development of culture. Mammals are fed by the mother for long periods of time after they are born. Remaining in close association with the parent, instead of being abandoned as the offspring of most reptiles are to shift for themselves, they are relatively safe. More important by far is that this long period of dependency allows for a much greater transfer of learned behavior:

> The intimate relationship between generations resulting from suckling and caring for the young makes possible the transmission of learned behavior by imitation. Behavior patterns learned by trial and error have been recognized among lower vertebrates and invertebrates, but the simplicity and origin of such behavior puts it into a different class from that of mammals. It is the transmission of complex learned behavior by imitation that makes it unnecessary to learn solely from direct experience—a dangerous process . . . . Instead, the experience of generations can be assimilated in a short time with reduced danger to the young. Thus the mammals have the great advantage [shared to some extent by birds] of being able, as it were, to "inherit" [by imitative learning from parent] "acquired" [i.e., learned] behavior characters. The inheritance of acquired characters makes possible a high rate of evolution of those characters, and thus the behavior patterns of mammals have evolved fast and increased in complexity in such a way as to put them in that respect at a different level from all other living organisms. (Campbell 1974:52)

The "different level" here is culture. It is in this factor of increasing postnatal dependence upon adults that we find the real basis for what becomes in hominids an overwhelmingly cultural mode of existence.

The greater ability to imitate, and to learn in general, is largely due to the increase in brain size that we find in mammals. Even relatively ordinary mammals like the sheep, for instance, have large brains in proportion to their body weight when compared with reptiles. This ratio of brain weight to body weight increases in the primates; within the primates it increases very dramatically in hominids, especially in *Homo sapiens*. Not only does the brain increase in size, but in addition most of the increase is in the cortex, the part of the brain that seems to be involved specifically in both memory and problem-solving activities. It is this high brain-to-body ratio, along with the period of infant dependency, that allows for the extragenetic transmission of information, the most fundamental requirement for culture (Montagu 1955; LaBarre 1954; Campbell 1974).

Being not merely mammals but primates and the most highly developed of primates, humans share with other primates further things of great significance for an understanding of the human species. Foremost of these is the ancient but more highly developed and exceedingly useful five-fingered hand. The evolution of the hand was accompanied by a host of other changes. Evolution is an exceedingly complicated process, even the slightest change in one organ being accompanied by corresponding changes in many others. This is not very well understood as yet although we have many ideas as to how changes most probably occurred. Consider what John Pfeiffer has to say on the hand:

> The retreat of the snout was also accompanied by the loss of prosimian tactile whiskers or "feelers." The hands acquired a considerably richer supply of nerve cells and fibers concerned with the sense of touch. Hands and sense organs evolved together, each development accelerating the other in an involved feedback relationship. Fingers became more and more mobile, capable not only of moving faster but also of assuming a far greater variety of positions. Devices designed originally for grasping and holding on were used increasingly to get food and, even more important, to pick up objects, bring them closer, and turn them around to examine from all angles. The ability to manipulate in this way was new in the history of terrestrial life, reached a high point in the monkey family. (Pfeiffer 1969:30)

In comparison with other mammals, primates have in general much greater maneuverability of the limbs, with a well-developed collarbone enabling them to move the arm in all directions. There is also a much improved sense of balance and improved motor control. Primates typically bear one offspring at a birth, a development which, it is believed, must be associated with dwelling in the trees; it would be difficult or impossible for a mother to get around in the trees with large numbers of infants. Also, with fewer infants, much better care can be given them. The primate mother, then, with only two teats placed high on the chest and having the ability to use forelimbs and hands, can hold her infant, observe it carefully, and fondle it in a way no nonprimate mother can. This situation may have much to do with the development of emotional attachments between them which could, perhaps, then be generalizable to other animals later in life. In the primates we see continued cortical expansion, an increasingly long period of infant dependency, the development of stereoscopic vision, a complicated social organization, and other factors that are found in a somewhat modified form in hominids (LaBarre 1954; Campbell 1974).

The argument is that hominids evolved out of creatures similar though not identical to contemporary primates, and this evolution was associated with changes in behavior and environment leading eventually to *Homo sapiens*. The omnivorous nature of primates, particularly their chewing and digestive processes, it is argued, made it possible for them to evolve from forest-living to plains-living creatures. The necessity for this adaptation may have been a change in climate, but there may have been other factors as well. The flexibility of primate food habits allowed an adaptation in food-finding behavior such that the early hominids could bring about a fundamental change in their environment by spreading out into other climates and temperatures. Among other things, there appears to have been a change toward cooperative hunting, a development of central importance for further human evolution. And it is believed there must have been developing also at the same time an increasingly complicated technology, mode of communication, and social organization. The facts of all these developments are by no means complete; indeed, much of the evidence is scanty. But that a process of this kind occurred, involving creatures of this kind, over an exceedingly long period of time, is no longer open to serious dispute. It is the details of occurrence that are not clear, not the process or the fact.

Being not merely a primate but moreover a hominid, a human has certain characteristics as a hominid that must not be overlooked. First, humans are the most generalized of animals. They have no highly specialized organs, no heavy fur, no hooves, no wings, no multiple stomachs like the ungulates, no weapon teeth, no natural body armor. In sum, evolving humans did not make the dangerous specializations, like the dinosaur or saber-tooth tiger, that led to extinction. The best example of this is the human hand, of which LaBarre has said:

> The primate hand, which man has removed from all probable future specialization, may yet afford the most elegant example in all evolutionary history of Cope's law of "the survival of the unspecialized." (1954:31)

Even more:

> . . . The human hand is the adaptation to end all adaptations: *the emancipated hand has emancipated man from any other organic evolution whatsoever.* With man, genetic evolution and organic experiments have come to an end. Without involving the animal body and its slow, blind genetic mechanisms, man's hands make the tools and the machines which render his own further physical evolution unnecessary; they replace the slow, cumbrous, expensive, uncertain, and painful mechanism of organic evolution with the swift, conscious, biologically free, and painless making of machines.

Nothing like this has ever happened before in evolution. Machines not only can do man's flying, diving, and superhuman seeing and hearing for him, but also *they do his evolving for him.* (Indeed, in a cybernetic "feed-back" machine like a thermostat—in which the results of its action are automatically scanned by the machine to correct and modify its future action according to man's preconceived, built-in intentions—man is already creating a quasi-organism, with one sense and part-brain, after his own image. Nor does it invite disrespect to realize that with his brain man can build mathematical thinking machines better than his own for their particular purpose.) The critical fact is that the making of machines is done with no narrow and irreversible commitment whatever of man's body. With hands, the old-style evolution by body adaptation is obsolete. All previous animals had been subject to the *autoplastic* evolution of their self-substance, committing their bodies to experimental adaptations in a blind genetic gamble for survival. The stakes in this game were high: life or death. Man's evolution, on the other hand, is through *alloplastic* experiments with objects outside his own body and is concerned only with the products of his hands, brains, and eyes—and not with his body itself. True, a flaw in the design of an experimental jet plane may kill a pilot, but that does not make the human race extinct or even wipe out aeronautical engineers as a species. (LaBarre 1954:89-90)

Humans have a distinctive form of sexual behavior characterized by an absence of oestrus. Most animals mate only at certain times of the year. Indeed, often the males and females of a species are not together at all except during the brief mating season. Some animals have one breeding period a year, others have more than one. Humans can and do breed at any time during the year. Accordingly, humans experience no such period of sexual excitement and disruption of social behavior as is found in many other primates—no period of "sexual mania." This sexual behavior appears to be associated with a longer period of child-rearing without loss of reproductive ability, with the possibility of a more permanent male-female relationship, and with sexual drives more readily subject to cortical rather than purely hormonal control. All of these characteristics, in turn, are presumably related in ways that are not well understood to the presence of the permanent breast in humans, to a manner of copulation in which the partners can face and embrace each other, and to the capability for female orgasm, which is not generally believed to occur in nonhuman creatures. There are hints here, it is believed, as to the factors involved in bringing about the complex emotional life of human beings.

Still other factors are also related to sex. In many species the female is much smaller than the male. This difference in size allows, in creatures like the baboon, a greater number of females to survive in a limited amount of territory and hence to better maintain the size of the group. In humans, as we know, the difference in size between males and females is not very great. The reasons for this smaller difference in humans are not completely clear, but they may have to do with the need for the female pelvis to be large enough to accommodate the large-brained human fetus, and with the fact that human males do not need a larger size to cope with predators or with each other. All of these distinctive human characteristics are related, in turn, to the phenomenon of fetalization —that is, to the fact that man retains in the adult form characteristics that are found in the fetal form of lower animals. Physically, humans have become increasingly infantilized—this infantile physique can be seen in the smallness of the human face and the large brain case, and also in such features as the long neck, small teeth, thin nails, thin skull bones, and the like. What appears to be involved here is that in order for brain and intelligence to grow, humans need more time for learning—it simply takes more time to become human than to become some other kind of mammal. It is the brain and learning which gain an advantage by this slowed-down process.

The human hominid begins extrauterine life equipped with a basic human structure and few reflexes, but with no complex given patterns of behavior that can emerge despite *socialization*. As a human, an individual must learn goals and also the techniques for attaining them. Contrast this need for learning with the rather complex behavior patterns of honeybees or other social insects (Allee 1958) that do not seem to involve learning. Or contrast it, if you will, with the behavior of salmon, driven somehow to the precise spot where they were hatched, even after having traveled thousands of miles in the ocean and even though their parents died before they were hatched. Humans, although they have the same basic drives that other animals have, do not have these more elaborate patterns that emerge without learning (Spiro 1954).

Finally, humans alone, as we have previously noted, have developed the capacity for symbolic behavior to its most complex form. The human brain—developed to such a remarkable culmination from the large and complex brain of the mammals—allows humans to invent and transmit symbols and thus creates a vast chasm between humans and other animals. And it is symbols, of course, that make culture possible. Although we know that some nonhuman creatures have a simple technology, that they can communicate, that they might be said to have the rudiments of a cultural way of life and even perhaps the rudiments of the ability to symbolize, they cannot truly be said to live in a symbolic cultural world as we humans do.

Reviewing the catalogue of human characteristics (diet and dentition, primate reproduction and nurturance, brain development, generalized capacities rather than specializations, infantile physique, learned rather than reflex behavior patterns, capacity to use symbols), we see thàt culture is not a mere happenstance sort of thing—it is a necessary, inevitable and indispensable human requirement. The necessity for culture is a result of the unique psychobiological characteristics of the human animal. Humans have drives as all animals do, but being primates, and being hominids, above all, they have no biologically given ways of satisfying these drives—they must invent, modify, and transmit extragenetically the symbolic means which enable them to survive and, indeed, to reflect upon and appreciate their survival. There is no better statement of this necessity for culture than that by the anthropologist Clifford Geertz:

. . . there is no such thing as a human nature independent of culture. Men without culture would not be the clever savages of Golding's *Lord of the Flies* thrown back upon the cruel wisdom of their animal instincts; nor would they be the nature's noblemen of Enlightenment primitivism or even, as classical anthropological theory would imply, intrinsically talented apes who had somehow failed to find themselves. They would be unworkable monstrosities with very few useful instincts, fewer recognizable sentiments, and no intellect: mental basket cases. As our central nervous system—and most particularly its crowning curse and glory, the neocortex—grew up in great part in interaction with culture, it is incapable of directing our behavior or organizing our experience without the guidance provided by systems of significant symbols. What happened to us in the Ice Age is that we were obliged to abandon the regularity and precision of detailed genetic control over our conduct for the flexibility and adaptability of a more generalized, though of course no less real, genetic control over it. To supply the additional information necessary to be able to act, we were forced, in turn, to rely more and more heavily on cultural sources—the accumulated fund of significant symbols. Such symbols are thus not mere expressions, instrumentalities, or correlates of our biological, psychological, and social existence; they are prerequisites of it. Without men, no culture, certainly; but equally, and more significantly, without culture, no men.

We are, in sum, incomplete and unfinished animals who complete and finish ourselves through culture—and not through culture in general but through highly particular forms of it; Dobuan and Javanese, Hopi and Italian, upper-class and lower-class, academic and commercial. Man's great capacity for learning, his plasticity, has often been remarked, but what is even more critical is his extreme dependence upon a certain sort of learning: the attainment of concepts, the apprehension and application of specific systems of symbolic meaning. Beavers build dams, birds build nests, bees locate food, baboons organize social groups, and mice mate on the basis of forms of learning that rest predominantly on the instructions encoded in their genes and evoked by appropriate patterns of external stimuli: physical keys inserted into organic locks. But men build dams or shelters, locate food, organize their social groups, or find sexual partners under the guidance of instructions encoded in flow charts and blueprints, hunting lore, moral systems, and aesthetic judgements: conceptual structures molding formless talents.

We live, as one writer has neatly put it, in an "information gap." Between what our body tells us and what we have to know in order to function, there is a vacuum we must fill ourselves, and we fill it with information (or misinformation) provided by our culture. The boundary between what is innately controlled and what is culturally controlled in human behavior is an ill-defined and wavering one. Some things are, for all intents and purposes, entirely controlled intrinsically: we need no more cultural guidance to learn how to breathe than a fish needs to learn how to swim. Others are almost certainly largely cultural: we do not attempt to explain on a genetic basis why some men put their trust in centralized planning and others in the free market, though it might be an amusing exercise. Almost all complex human behavior is, of course, the vector outcome of the two. Our capacity to speak is surely innate; our capacity to speak English is surely cultural. Smiling at pleasing stimuli and frowning at unpleasant ones are surely in some degree genetically determined (even apes screw up their faces at noxious odors); but sardonic smiling and burlesque frowning are equally surely predominantly cultural, as is perhaps demonstrated by the Balinese definition of a madman as someone who, like an American, smiles when there is nothing to laugh at. Between the basic ground plans for our life that our genes lay down (the capacity to speak or to smile) and the precise behavior we in fact execute (speaking English in a certain tone of voice, smiling enigmatically in a delicate social situation)* lies a complex set of significant symbols under whose direction we transform the first into the second, the ground plans into the activity. (Geertz 1965:112–114)

However much anthropologists may fall into or out of camps, schools, fads or fancies, and however much they may continue to disagree with each other over how to approach the study of culture, they would all pretty much agree with the general view expressed in this chapter and with Geertz's eloquent statement. And everyone would have to agree that this view of human nature and culture is very different from what we began with in the 1800s. Much has been accomplished and the profession of anthropology has grown rapidly and, for the most part, done well. Even so, when it comes to the study of culture, there has been a tendency, in practice, to take the easier of two contrasting views. Culture can be viewed as a kind of superorganic phenomenon and, in that sense, it is something external to the human animal. Generations of anthropologists have returned from the field to describe the culture of "their people," writing descriptions which deal most typically with recurrent patterns of behavior that characterize the behavior of the so-and-so. The more complex problem of culture, posed by Sapir, of how culture comes to be in and influence individual human beings in particular contexts, a concept of culture as a more internal phenomenon, has tended to be neglected. As anthropologists have made vociferous claims for

*Parentheses inserted; source publication has dashes.

cultural determinism (not as extreme in their neglect of biology as some current writers such as Freeman would have it), or at least for intense cultural influences on human behavior, both individual and collective, it behooves us now to demonstrate just how these various cultural processes actually work. How well this can be done will quite probably determine where anthropology will be in the future.

SUMMARY

The concept of culture—foreshadowed by Turgot and others, introduced into English by Matthew Arnold and Edward Tylor, pluralized by Boas, clarified by Kroeber and Sapir, spurned by Radcliffe-Brown, but popularized by Benedict, utilized more importantly by Malinowski, White, Harris, Schneider, and scores of others—remains the key concept of anthropology. But the problem of how individual human beings actually internalize or otherwise acquire and use this distinctive capacity remains little understood (Schwartz 1981). Current definitions and approaches tend to concentrate on culture as symbolization and communication although a few scholars cling to strictly behavioral definitions. It is obvious that as human beings we are utterly dependent upon the complicated symbolic systems—cultural tradition and meanings—that we somehow come to know and transmit extragenetically from one generation to the next.

While there remain those who insist that technoenvironmental factors are basic, causal, and relatively unaffected by human thought or belief, there are increasing numbers of those who are more and more willing to concede that unless human cognitive abilities are taken more fully and consciously into account we shall never truly understand the mysteries of human nature and culture. As Roheim put it: "Thus the problems of the origin of culture and of the origin of mankind, of the specific features of the human species are really only one problem" (1971:19). The conjunctive approach we have briefly sketched includes in one form or another all of the major approaches that went into making anthropology what it is today. We recognize evolution; indeed, evolution has become the most central unifying feature of modern social and biological sciences. We recognize that there was and is diffusion. History is regarded as crucial, both oral and written. Psychological factors are an integral feature of this new view. Social organization is recognized as basic. The new ecological perspective includes not only environmental and technological variables but also insists on recognizing the input of the creature itself. While our understanding of culture either as public or private, individual or collective, is still in its infancy, we have surely come a long way since the emergence of anthropology as an academic discipline. Whatever the future holds for academic departments the concept of culture must remain a central focus for all students of the remarkably complex human species.

We can no longer be content with describing culture as merely the context in which an individual exists; we must now also concentrate on how it "gets inside" and affects the individual and we must try to understand what it means to say "the true locus of culture is in the individual."

FURTHER READINGS

A. I. Hallowell's paper, "Personality, Culture and Society in Behavioral Evolution," also *Instinctive Behavior*, edited by Schiller, Allee's *The Social Life of Animals*, and Roe and Simpson, *Behavior and Evolution*, must be consulted. *Evolution after Darwin*, edited by Sol Tax, is also of great interest. Simpson's *The Meaning of Evolution* remains an excellent work on evolution in general. For human evolution see Campbell's book of that title and also Pfeiffer's *The Emergence of Man*. *Evolution and Human Behavior* by Alland is also of note.

For ethology, the volume edited by Eibl-Eibesfeldt, *Ethology*, is outstanding. But see also *Instinctive Behavior*, edited by Schiller, Allee's *The Social Life of Animals*, and Tinbergen's *Social Behaviour in Animals*. Studies of a single species of particular interest include Mech's *The Wolf*, McHugh's *The Time of the Buffalo*, Schaller's *The Year of the Gorilla*, and Jane van Lawick-Goodall's *In the Shadow of Man*. Jolly's *The Evolution of Primate Behavior* is quite exceptional for primates in general.

For work on early man consult Howell, *Early Man*; Howells, *Mankind in the Making*; and Campbell, *Human Evolution*.

For cybernetics and its importance see Wiener, *The Human Use of Human Beings: Cybernetics and Society*, and also Bateson's *Steps to an Ecology of Mind*. *Steps to an Ecology of Mind* is also of immense value on the question of man's relationship to his environment. See also *The Impact of Civilization on the Biology of Man* (Boyden 1970).

The significance of cross-cultural studies as such has not really been treated in a single volume. But again, see Hallowell's paper mentioned above, and Geertz's collection of essays, *The Interpretation of Cultures*. Also see Melford Spiro's papers "Human Nature in Its Psychological Dimension" (1954) and "Culture and Human Nature" (1978).

For the best treatment of current culture theory see the appropriately titled volume *Culture Theory: Essays on Mind, Self, and Emotion*, edited by Shweder and LeVine (1984).

Glossary

a priori Prior to experience, presumptively, reasoning from axioms. That kind of reasoning which deduces consequences from axioms presumed to be true without verification by experience.

age-area hypothesis The notion that a culture trait diffuses outward in the various directions from its origin point at an equal rate. Thus the distance of a trait from its origin point can be taken as an indication of its age.

alienation A condition said to be particularly associated with large industrialized societies. There are several meanings, the most important being a sense of powerlessness, meaninglessness, normlessness, isolation, or self-estrangement.

animism The notion that the phenomena of life are produced by an immaterial *anima*, or soul, which is distinct from matter. Tylor's minimum definition of a religion.

anomie From Durkheim. The condition of being only loosely integrated into society so that individuals lack interpersonal ties.

anthropology The science of human beings in the widest sense. Often divided into social or cultural anthropology, physical anthropology, archeology, and linguistics.

anthropomorphic Having human form or personality; said of nonhuman beings or nonliving things.

antiquarian Someone who studies antiquities.

archeology That branch of anthropology that studies artifacts and other material remains of older cultures.

artifact Something made by human beings.

Australopithecus A fossil manlike creature who lived in Africa during the Pleistocene era.

basic personality structure A matrix in which character traits develop. Not to be confused with *national character* or *modal personality*. See Kardiner 1945:24.

behavior   Observable interaction between an organism and its environment. Or, as for the physicist, change of state over time.

behavioral science   The attempt to blend the best of social science with psychology and biology in an attempt to create a unified theory of behavior.

behaviorist   One who believes the only legitimate object of psychological, anthropological, or sociological investigation is observable behavior (as opposed, for example, to mind, ideas, or thoughts).

civilization   A human condition or state of being presumably elevated in some way above other states or conditions of being. Opposed to the condition of being primitive or barbarous. A qualitatively high level of cultural or technological complexity.

clan   A unilineal descent group, either patrilineal or matrilineal, within which the specific genealogical connections with the founding ancestor are unknown so that many of the members are unable to say precisely how they are related to one another. The founding ancestor can be either real, or imaginary, such as an animal or plant.

collective conscience   From Durkheim. "The totality of beliefs and sentiments common to average citizens of the same society, which forms a determinate system which has its own life . . . ."

community   An independent collectivity of individuals living permanently in a geographically limited area and characterized by a given culture.

community studies   Studies for which a bounded community such as a village or localized group of some kind is taken as the unit.

comparative method   A procedure by which different classes of phenomena (deemed on various criteria to be comparable) are examined to determine their similarities and differences and the cuases of these similarities and differences.

configuration (of culture)   The basic integrative "theme" of a culture. That overriding orientation that gives to a culture its distinctive "stamp" or character. See Benedict 1934.

convergent evolution   The process by which similar cultural traits in different cultures are believed to have originated independently and evolved through dissimilar phases.

coup de poing   A simply flaked triangular stone tool, one of the first formal implements; probably used for a variety of purposes.

couvade   The imitation of some of the concomitants of childbirth by the father, at around the time of birth. This may include retiring into bed, seclusion, and the observance of food taboos, all of which are believed to help the child.

craniometry   The science of measuring skulls.

cross-cultural survey   The use of the Human Relations Area Files or other ethnographic information to see what is known about a given topic in a number of diverse cultures.

cultural anthropology The branch of anthropology that has for its subject matter the study of culture (as contrasted with the study of physical, biological, or other characteristics).

cultural ecology From Julian Steward. This term attempts to recognize that "the mutual relations between organisms and their environment," the most usual definition of ecology, must especially emphasize, in the case of humans, their basic, adaptive characteristic—culture.

cultural lag The retardation of the rate of change in one element of a culture as contrasted with other elements. It is often said, for example, that religious beliefs change more slowly than technology.

cultural materialism An approach, in anthropology, whereby technoenvironmental and technoeconomic variables are assumed to be primary and independent variables causing cultural variability. Social organization and ideology are considered to be dependent variables.

cultural relativism The belief that there is no single scale of values for all cultures, hence that particular customs, beliefs, practices, and other items must be judged relative to the cultural context in which they appear.

culture There is no standard, commonly accepted definition. The most important criteria are that culture is shared behavior and ideas which are cumulative, systemic, symbolic, and transmitted from generation to generation extragenetically.

culture-and-personality That area of research that attempts to bring together the study of culture and the study of personality, the effects of one upon the other. Culture being an anthropological concept and personality a psychological one, this is an interdisciplinary approach to human variability. See *psychological anthropology*.

culture area A region in which a majority of cultural traits and practices are shaped by the different groups that live within its boundaries. In the Great Plains culture area, for example, inhabitants shared buffalo hunting, the horse, the tepee, and other items.

culture center The place where a particular trait or complex is found in its defined and most ideal form.

culture circle The area, geographically, within which a culture complex is found.

culture climax The point in space at which a type of culture (Plains culture, Northwest Coast culture, or the like) has its maximum intensity.

culture complex The fundamental and organically related culture traits that are found within a culture circle. Often spoken of as the cattle complex of East Africa, the pig complex of Melanesia, and the like.

culture trait The simplest, most basic unit into which a culture can be broken down and analyzed.

culturology The study of cultural phenomena "in their own right." This term is used by Leslie White, its foremost proponent, to distinguish the study of culture from sociology.

cybernetics The study of control and communication in living and mechanical systems.

deductive Said of the process of reasoning from generals to particulars, or inferring particulars from known or assumed generalizations. Contrasted with *inductive*.

dependent variable In controlled experimentation, the dependent variable is the one whose behavior is assumed to be predictable from the behavior of another called the *independent variable*.

depth psychology That branch of psychology which explains behavior in terms of the unconscious.

descent A relationship mediated by a parent between a person and an ancestor; *ancestor* is defined as a genealogical predecessor, of the grandparental or earlier generation.

diffusion The process by which an item of culture spreads from one area to another. Essentially, borrowing by one culture from another.

division of labor The division of a task into parts, each of which is performed by a separate person. This should not be equated directly with specialization.

ecosystem The total system of components that meaningfully interact and affect one another and characterize a given population.

emic Descriptive of the meaning of something as it is perceived and understood by participants in a culture rather than by the observers or outsiders.

empiricism The practice or principle of basing conclusions solely upon experience. In science it implies conclusions drawn from observation and experiment only.

enculturation The process by which a human being acquires culture.

ethnocentric Assuming or believing that one's own group's standards, mode of living, values, beliefs, and the like are superior to those of others.

ethnographic present The time at which an ethnographic description is thought to be frozen. For example, an account of an American Indian culture said to be "at the time of European contact."

ethnohistory A method for studying the history of a culture through the use of written and oral traditions.

ethnology In its most comprehensive usage, the science of peoples and cultures. Ethnology is contrasted with ethnography in that the latter is purely descriptive whereas the former is analytic and seeks to find generalizations.

ethnoscience Basically, the system of beliefs and knowledge about the world and things held by groups of "nonscientifically" oriented people. The term is also used for a particular *method* for ascertaining what a people's beliefs are and how they are organized.

ethology The comparative study of animal behavior.

etic Descriptive of the meaning of something in a culture as it is perceived and understood by an observer (outsider) rather than by the participants themselves.

evolutionary stages Arbitrarily defined steps or levels through which, it is proposed, people must have passed in the process of evolution: most usually savagery, barbarism, and civilization, the latter being considered a "higher" stage.

evolutionists   Name given to a group of early anthropologists who believed in a theory of evolutionary stages through which they thought peoples and cultures must pass on their way to becoming "civilized."

Festschrift   A volume of essays written and edited in honor of a distinguished scholar, usually upon his or her sixtieth birthday or upon retirement.

fetishism   The worship of inanimate objects. Irrational reverence or respect for something as sacred or powerful.

folk models   The cognitive schemes that groups of people have for conceptualizing and classifying things in nature (as opposed, for example, to scientific models).

folk-urban continuum   From Robert Redfield. The idea that it is possible to plot communities on a scale which represents the transition from folk society to urban. Folk societies are said to be small, face-to-face, isolated, etc., and urban societies are the reverse.

functionalism   A theoretical position in anthropology that attempts to explain social or psychological phenomena in terms of the contribution they make to sociological or psychological well-being.

geographical determinism   A theoretical position that holds that cultural or social phenomena can be explained by geographical conditions.

grammar   The established or understood rules of speech or writing.

heterodont   Having teeth of different kinds.

historical particularism   Name given to the outlook of a group of early American anthropologists who believed that in order to understand cultural phenomena it was necessary to understand the particular histories of the cultures in which they were found. Franz Boas and his students are said to have held this position.

Hominidae   The family of primates that includes man and fossil species related to him.

homodont   Having teeth which are all of the same kind.

Homo erectus   A fossil species of the genus *Homo* who lived from approximately 250,000 to 1 million years ago.

homoiothermy   The phenomenon of maintaining the body at a constant temperature by means of an internal regulator of some kind.

idealism   A philosophical position which holds that the objects of external perception are ideas of the perceiving mind. Contrasted with *materialism.*

idiographic   Said of a study that attempts to establish a particular or specific factual proposition as opposed to a general one. See *nomothetic.*

idolatry   The worship of idols or images—usually artifacts.

incest taboo   The prohibition of incest—that is, of sexual relations and/or marriage—within the family or a group of kin.

independent invention   The presence of similar or identical things in different cultures in consequence of specific invention in numerous places rather than by diffusion from one invention site to all other sites of occurence.

independent variables. The causal variables that are manipulated in experiments and whose values determine the values of the *dependent variables.*

inductive Said of the process of inferring a law or generalization from a number of particular cases. Contrasted with *deductive.*

informants The individual persons from whom anthropologists acquire information, most usually through conversation and interviewing but also by watching and imitating.

infrastructure The modes of production and reproduction employed by any given group.

kinship The public recognition and expression of genealogical relationships both affinal and consanguineal. Socially recognized relationships can be based on supposed ties as well as actual genealogical ones. The study of *kinship systems* has been fundamental in anthropology from the beginning. It has been suggested by many that *kinship terminologies* are correlated with various features of social organization.

Kulturkreise The presumed origin points for the major culture complexes that are believed to have then diffused outward in a more or less circular fashion. Associated with Wilhelm Schmidt and the German diffusionists.

levels of understanding A given phenomenon can be approached in many different ways such as biological, sociological, psychological, cultural, etc. These are said to be different levels of explanation and render different interpretations which can be linked together although in pure form they are different.

linguistics The comparative study of languages.

maintenance systems The subsistence economy and social structure that combines to enable the family to maintain itself over time. See B. Whiting 1963:5.

mammal An animal of the zoological class Mammalia, characterized by the possession of glands in which milk is secreted for the nourishment of offspring.

material culture The tangible elements of a culture, consisting of artifacts; physically existing objects.

materialism The philosophical position that nothing exists except matter, its movement, and its modification. Also, the position that consciousness is due to the operation of material agencies. Contrasted with *idealism.*

matriarchy A society in which authority is primarily held by females: hypothetical, it appears, as no such society is actually known.

matrilineal descent Descent traced through the female line.

migration Movement from one place to another, either permanently, or recurrently as with the seasons.

modal personality The most representative personality in a given culture.

modernization The process by which previously isolated groups gain modern technology and the know-how to become industrialized and become part of the world community.

monogenesis Development of all life from a single cell, or of all human beings from a single pair.

monotheism Belief in a single god.

morpheme A discrete unit of sound with a definite meaning and function. The smallest structural unit of a language that has meaning.

national character The most representative character type to be found in a nation. Essentially the same as *modal personality.*

Neanderthal A type of fossil human, demonstrably different from modern humans, first found in 1856 in the Neander Valley (now a nature reserve about 10 km east of Düsseldorf).

new ethnography A data-gathering technique developed in recent years for eliciting emic data and consciously separating it from etic data.

nomothetic Said of a study that attempts to derive general propositions that will hold for a number of cases rather than one case. Contrasted with *idiographic.*

nuclear family A married couple along with their children.

Oedipus complex From psychoanalytic theory. The situation (largely unconscious) in which a son is in love (strong sexual desires being involved, according to psychoanalysts) with his mother and is jealous of his father (with resulting feeling of guilt and emotional conflict). When considering daughters rather than sons, this is termed the Electra complex.

onomatopoeia Language phenomenon in which word sounds presumably derive from the sounds of animals and nature. For example *boom* (English), *boum* (French), *rimbombo* (Italian).

paleoanthropology The study of human fossil remains.

parallel evolution A situation in which the same cultural feature evolves in the same manner in more than one culture.

patriarchy A society in which authority is held primarily by males.

patrilocal Said of a residence rule whereby a married couple live in the husband's community.

pattern of culture The combination of distinctive themes or characteristics which give direction and purpose to a culture.

phoneme A basic sound in a language, one that is recognizable regardless of variations in position and can be assigned a symbol. The English language, for example, is said to have 45 phonemes.

phonology The study of speech sounds and their possible combinations in languages.

physical anthropology The systematic study of the physical and biological characteristics of human beings. Human biology.

Pleistocene A geological period, roughly the most recent 2,000,000+ years, which has seen substantial climatic change involving periodic glaciations and in which the development of man and culture took place.

polygenesis Development of mankind from several independent pairs of ancestors.

polytheism   The belief in a number of gods as opposed to just one.

potlatch   A ceremonial destruction or giving away of property to enhance one's status, practiced among the Indians of the Pacific Northwest.

primary institutions   Those customs or ways of behavior that have to do with child-rearing and basic subsistence. See Kardiner 1945:23.

primate   A zoological order that includes lemurs, tarsiers, monkeys, apes, and man.

primitive band   The most fundamental social group beyond the individual family. The type of social organization found where hunting and gathering form the basis for subsistence.

principle of uncertainty   In the study of the behavior of particles, there is always some uncertainty in specifying positions and velocities. From this discovery by Heisenberg, physicists have come to hold the position that nature behaves in such a way that it is fundamentally impossible to make an absolutely precise prediction of what will happen, wherefore we can deal only with probabilities.

projective systems   Those systems of thought that are developed from nuclear traumatic experiences in the life histories of individuals—such things as religion, folklore, and the like. See Kardiner 1945:39.

psychic unity of mankind   The belief that the minds of human beings are basically similar no matter where they are found and that, given the proper conditions, people have the capacity to develop similarly.

psychological anthropology   The name applied to an attempt to understand cultural phenomena by invoking psychological theories and variables. Sometimes confused with *culture-and-personality*, which is merely one type of psychological anthropology.

racial determinism   The belief, totally discredited in anthropology, that cultural differences can be explained by racial characteristics.

reductionism   The practice or principle of explaining something by "reducing" it to another level. Thus, explaining a cultural variable by reducing it to a psychological level of explanation, or explaining behavior by reducing it to the level of physiology or instinct.

reify   To convert something, mentally, into a thing (Latin *res*) when it is not a thing but rather a concept.

relativism (cultural)   See *cultural relativism*.

role   The actual behavior that is said to be required by a particular status holder. See *status*.

salvage ethnography   The attempt to find out as much as possible about a disappearing culture by interviewing the surviving members before they either disappear or forget what the culture was like.

secondary institutions   Those institutional behaviors, like religion and folklore, that are the result of primary institutions and the psychological phenomenon known as projection. See Kardiner 1945:23.

semiotics   The study of signs and their meaning.

shamanism   Religious and curing practices based upon the idea that a spirit or power can be invoked to possess a person (a shaman) and thus endow him or her with supernatural powers of various kinds.

social anthropology   The study of social structure or organization (mostly in preliterate societies) rather than culture. Identified primarily with A. R. Radcliffe-Brown and his followers.

social class   A level within a society, distinguished primarily by economic condition but also by occupation, education, and the like. Examples: lower class, middle class, working class.

socialization   The processes involved in the transmission of culture from one generation to the next.

society   A network of social relations. This can be conceived of as either human beings in general considered as a group or any one of a number of relatively independent human groups.

sociological functionalism   The attempt to explain human customs and behavior by observing the contribution the particular phenomenon makes to the maintenance of the social system.

status   Comparative rank in a community. Ascribed status is that which individuals acquire naturally such as "old man." Acquired status must be established through special effort such as "medical student," "professor," etc.

structural linguistics   That type of linguistic analysis which attempts to study the unconscious structure of language rather than conscious linguistic phenomena. It takes the relations between the terms as the important datum rather than the terms themselves; it assumes that the underlying structure is systemic; and it aims to discover general laws of language.

structural Marxism   An attempt to blend structuralism with Marxism primarily on the grounds that they both attempt to deal with "hidden structures."

structural transformation   In Lévi-Strauss's structural interpretations, the idea that the true meaning of something depends upon transformations from one mode into another and back again.

structuralism   In anthropology, the attempt to analyze the underlying principles of organization rather than the content, as in studying the social structure of a group rather than its culture, or the underlying structures of the mind rather than the actual content of the mind as expressed in dreams or myths. Structuralists seek to understand the relationships between things rather than the things themselves.

subsistence   The means of supporting life. Livelihood. The techniques for insuring a supply of food.

superorganicism   The position in anthropology that holds culture to be superorganic, a thing in and of itself, acting independently of individual human beings. Usually identified with A. L. Kroeber and Leslie White.

superstructure   The thoughts and beliefs of any given group having to do with such things as ritual, music, art, sports, or games.

survival   A culture trait present in a previous period and still present in a contemporary culture where it does not appear to belong.

symbol Something that stands for something else and whose meaning is neither obvious nor intrinsic. The characters in the alphabet are examples of symbols.

symbolic anthropology An approach that attempts to analyze cultures as systems of meaningful symbols that enable human beings to organize their lives and survive.

technoenvironmental determinism The belief that technology and environment are primary and causal in human affairs. Similar to the notion that infrastructure determines structure and superstructure.

themes of culture The basic integrating patterns of behavior that give a culture its character and direction.

theonomy government by God; divine rule. Being subject to the authority of God.

totemism The belief that some form of special relationship exists between a particular plant or animal species or some other natural phenomenon and some particular human group such as a clan, lineage, or moiety.

trait See *culture trait.*

tribe A distinct social or political group that is autonomous and claims a particular territory as its own.

ungulate A hoofed animal.

unilineal evolution A form of evolution in which the attainment of each stage depends upon having passed through the previous stage.

References

Agar, Michael   1973   *Ripping and Running: A Formal Ethnography of Urban Heroin Addicts.* New York: Seminar Press.

Alexander, Franz, Alex Bavelas, et al.   1956   Editorial—"Behavioral Science, A New Journal." Signed by Franz Alexander, Alex Bavelas, David Easton, Ralph W. Gerard, Donald G. Marquis, Jacob Marschak, James G. Miller, Anatol Rapoport, Ralph W. Tyler, Raymond W. Waggoner. *Behavioral Science* 1(1):January, 1956.

Alland, Alexander, Jr.   1967   *Evolution and Human Behavior.* New York: Anchor Books.

Alland, Alexander, Jr.   1972   *The Human Imperative.* New York: Columbia University Press.

Allee, W. C.   1958   *The Social Life of Animals.* Boston: Beacon.

American Ethnologist   1976   Special Issue: *Folk Biology.* Washington, D.C.: American Anthropological Association.

American Ethnologist 1981   Special Issue: *Symbolism and Cognition.* Washington, D.C.: American Anthropological Association.

Arnold, Matthew   1869   *Culture and Anarchy.*

Avebury, Lord   *See* Lubbock, John.

Bachofen, J. J.   1861   *Das Mutterrecht.*

Barnett, H. G.   1953   *Innovation: The Basis of Cultural Change.* New York: McGraw-Hill.

Barnett, H. G.   1957   *Indian Shakers: A Messianic Cult of the Pacific Northwest.* Carbondale, Illinois: Southern Illinois University Press.

Bastian, A.   1895   *Ethnische Elementargedanken in der Lehre von Menschen.* Berlin: Weidmannsche Buchhandlung.

Bateson, Gregory   1936   *Naven.* Cambridge: Cambridge University Press.

Bateson, Gregory   1942a   "Morals and National Character." In *Civilian Morals.* Society for the Psychological Study of Social Issues, Second Yearbook, pp. 71–91.

Bateson, Gregory 1942b "Some Systematic Approaches to the Study of Culture and Personality." *Character and Personality* 11:76–82.

Bateson, Gregory 1944 "Cultural Determinants of Personality." In *Personality and the Behavior Disorders*, vol. 2, Joseph Bell Hunt, ed. pp. 714–735. New York: Ronald.

Bateson, Gregory 1967 "Cybernetic Explanation." *American Behavioral Scientist* 10(8):29–32.

Bateson, Gregory 1972 *Steps to an Ecology of Mind*. San Francisco: Chandler. (The Ballantine paperback edition, also 1972, differs.)

Bateson, Gregory, and Margaret Mead 1942 *Balinese Character: A Photographic Analysis*. Special Publication of the New York Academy of Sciences, New York.

Bateson, Mary Catherine 1984 *With a Daughter's Eye: A Memoir of Margaret Mead and Gregory Bateson*. New York: Morrow.

Becker, Ernest 1971 *The Lost Science of Man*. New York: Braziller.

Bender, Donald Ray 1964 *Early French Ethnography in Africa and the Development of Ethnology in France*. Ph.D. dissertation, Northwestern University.

Benedict, Ruth 1934 *Patterns of Culture*. New York: Houghton Mifflin.

Bennett, John W. 1967 "Discussion and Criticism, On the Cultural Ecology of Indian Cattle." *Current Anthropology* 8(3):251–252.

Berger, Allen 1976 "Structural and Eclectic Revisions of Marxist Strategy: A Cultural Materialist Critique." *Current Anthropology* 17:290–304.

Berland, Joseph C. 1982 *No Five Fingers Are Alike*. Cambridge, Massachusetts: Harvard University Press.

Berlin, Brent, and Paul Kay 1969 *Basic Color Terms: Their Universality and Evolution*. Berkeley: University of California Press.

Berreman, Gerald D. 1966 "Anemic and Emetic Analyses in Social Anthropology." *American Anthropologist* 68(2)(Part 1):346–354.

Berry, William B. N. 1968 *Growth of a Prehistoric Time Scale*. San Francisco: Freeman.

Bidney, David 1967 *Theoretical Anthropology*, second, augmented edition. New York: Schocken.

Biersak, A. 1982 "The Logic of Misplaced Concreteness." *American Anthropologist* 84(4)811–829.

Bindra, D., F. G. Patterson, H. S. Terrace, et al. 1981 "Technical Comments: Ape Language." *Science* 211(4477):86–88.

Bloch, Maurice, ed. 1975 *Marxist Analysis and Social Anthropology*. London: Malaby Press.

Boas, Franz 1887 "The Occurrence of Similar Inventions in Areas Widely Apart." *Science* 9:485–486.

Boas, Franz 1896 "The Limitations of the Comparative Method of Anthropology." Reprinted in Boas, *Race, Language and Culture*, 1940, pp. 271–304. New York: Macmillan.

Boas, Franz 1904 "The History of Anthropology." *Science* 20:513–524.

Boas, Franz 1910 "Psychological Problems in Anthropology." *American Journal of Psychology* 21:371–384.

Bock, Philip K. 1980 *Continuities in Psychological Anthropology: A Historical Introduction.* San Francisco: Freeman.

Boon, James A. 1982 *Other Tribes, Other Scribes.* Cambridge: Cambridge University Press.

Bourdieu, Pierre 1977 *Outline of a Theory of Practice.* London: Cambridge University Press.

Bourguignon, Erika 1979 *Psychological Anthropology: An Introduction to Human Nature and Cultural Differences.* New York: Holt.

Bowers, Alfred W. 1950 *Mandan Social and Ceremonial Organization.* Chicago: University of Chicago Press.

Boyden, S. V., ed. 1970 *The Impact of Civilization on the Biology of Man.* Canberra: Australian National University Press.

Brace, C. L., G. R. Gamble, and J. T. Bond, eds. 1971 *Race and Intelligence.* Anthropological Studies, No. 8, American Anthropological Association.

Brace, C. Loring, and Frank B. Livingstone 1971 "On Creeping Jensenism." In *Race and Intelligence*, C. L. Brace et al., eds.

Broce, Gerald 1973 *History of Anthropology.* Minneapolis, Minnesota: Burgess.

Brown, Dee 1970 *Bury My Heart At Wounded Knee.* New York: Bantam.

Brown, Paula, and Donald Tuzin 1983 *The Ethnography of Cannibalism.* Washington, D.C.: Special Publication of the Society for Psychological Anthropology.

Buel, J. W. 1889 *The Story of Man.*

Burridge, K. O. L. 1965 " 'Culture and Personality' and History: A Review." *Journal of World History* 9:1–29.

Burrow, J. W. 1963 "Evolution and Anthropology in the 1860's: The Anthropological Society of London, 1863–71." *Victorian Studies* 7(2):137–154.

Büttikofer, J. 1893 "Notes." *American Anthropologist* 6:337–339.

Campbell, Bernard 1966 *Human Evolution.* Chicago: Aldine.

Campbell, Bernard 1969 "Just Another 'Man-Ape'?" In *Evolutionary Anthropology*, Hermann K. Bleibtreu, ed., pp. 162–166. Boston: Allyn & Bacon.

Campbell, Bernard 1974 *Human Evolution*, revised edition, Chicago: Aldine.

Campbell, Donald T. 1973 Introduction to *Cultural Relativism* by Melville J. Herskovits, pp. v–xxiii. New York: Vintage.

Carmack, Robert M. 1972 "Ethnohistory: A Review of Its Development, Definitions, Methods and Aims." In *Annual Review of Anthropology*, B. J. Siegel, ed., pp. 227–246. Palo Alto, California: Annual Reviews, Inc.

Carpenter, C. R. 1964 *Naturalistic Behavior of Nonhuman Primates.* University Park: Pennsylvania State University Press.

Chase, Stuart 1948 *The Proper Study of Mankind.* New York: Harper.

Chomsky, Noam 1972 *Language and Mind.* New York: Harcourt.

Clifford, James 1981 "On Ethnographic Surrealism." *Comparative Studies of Society and History* 25:539–564.

Codere, Helen 1950 *Fighting with Property.* Monographs of the American

Ethnological Society, Vol. 18. Locust Valley, New York: J. J. Augustin.

Colby, Benjamin N., James W. Fernandez, and David B. Kronenfeld 1981 "Toward a Convergence of Cognitive and Symbolic Anthropology." *American Ethnologist* 8(3):422–450.

Cole, M., and B. Means 1981 *Comparative Studies of How People Think.* Cambridge, Massachusetts: Harvard University Press.

Cole, M., and S. Scribner 1974 *Culture and Thought: A Psychological Introduction.* New York: Wiley.

Cole, M., J. Gay, J. A. Glick, and D. W. Sharp 1971 *The Cultural Context of Learning and Thinking.* New York: Basic.

Conklin, Harold C. 1955 "Hanunóo Color Categories." *Southwestern Journal of Anthropology* 11(4):339–344.

Crookshank, F. G. 1909 *The Mongol in Our Midst: A Study of Man and His Three Faces.* New York: Dutton.

Cunningham, Clark E., James W. Fernandez, Jane and W. D. Dougherty, and Norman E. Whitten, Jr. 1981 "Symbolism and Cognition." Special Issue, *American Ethnologist* 8(3).

D'Andrade, Roy 1983 "A Folk Model of the Mind." Paper presented to Conference on Folk Models, Institute for Advanced Study, Princeton, New Jersey, May, 1983.

Daniel, Glyn 1964 *The Idea of Prehistory.* London: Watts.

Darnell, Regna 1974 *Readings in the History of Anthropology.* New York: Harper.

Darwin, Charles 1859 *The Origin of Species.* New York: Mentor.

Darwin, Charles 1875 *The Descent of Man and Selection in Relation to Sex.* London: John Murray.

Degérando, Joseph-Marie 1969 *The Observation of Savage Peoples.* Berkeley: University of California Press.

Devereux, George 1956 "Normal and Abnormal: The Key Problem of Psychiatric Anthropology." In *Some Uses of Anthropology: Theoretical and Applied.* Washington, D.C.: The Anthropological Society of Washington.

de Waal Malefijt. *See* Waal Malefijt, Annemarie de.

Diamond, Stanley 1981 "Paul Radin." In *Totems and Teachers,* Sydel Silverman, ed., pp. 67–97. New York: Columbia University Press.

Dobzhansky, T. 1963 "Cultural Direction of Human Evolution: A Summation." *Human Biology* 35:311–316.

Dolgin, Janet L., David S. Kemnitzer, and David M. Schneider, eds. 1977 *Symbolic Anthropology: A Reader in the Study of Symbols and Meanings.* New York: Columbia University Press.

Douglas, Mary 1966 *Purity and Danger.* London: Routledge.

Douglas, Mary 1975 *Implicit Meanings.* London: Routledge.

Down, J. Langdon 1866 "Observations on an Ethnic Classification of Idiots." *Clinical Lectures Reports,* London Hospital, 3:259–262.

Driver, H. E., and Alfred L. Kroeber 1932 "Quantitative Expressions of Cultural Relationships." In *University of California Publications in American Archaeology and Ethnology* 31(4):211–256.

DuBois, Cora   1944   *The People of Alor: A Social-Psychological Study of an East Indian Island.* New York: Harper.

Durkheim, Emile   1893   *The Division of Labor in Society.* New York: Free Press, 1964.

Durkheim, Emile   1912   *Les Regles de la Méthode Sociologique.* Paris: Alcan.

Edgerton, Robert   1976   *Deviance: A Cross-Cultural Perspective.* Menlo Park, California: Cummings.

Eggan, Fred   1950   *Social Organization of the Western Pueblos.* Chicago: University of Chicago Press.

Eibl-Eibesfeldt, Irenäus   1970   *Ethology: The Biology of Behavior.* New York, Holt.

Evans-Pritchard, E. E.   1937   *Witchcraft, Oracles, and Magic among the Azande.* Oxford: Clarendon Press.

Evans-Pritchard, E. E.   1940   *The Nuer.* London: Oxford University Press.

Fenichel, Otto   1945   *The Psychoanalytic Theory of Neurosis.* New York: Norton.

Ferguson, A.   1789 (original 1767)   *An Essay on the History of Civil Society.* Basel, Switzerland: J. J. Tourneisen.

Ferree, Barr   1890   "Climatic Influences in Primitive Architecture." *American Anthropologist* 3:147-158.

Festinger, Leon, and Daniel Katz, eds.   1953   *Research Methods in the Behavioral Sciences.* New York: Holt.

Firth, Raymond   1936   *We, the Tikopia.* London: Allen & Unwin.

Firth, Raymond   1954   "Social Organization and Social Change." *Journal of the Royal Anthropological Institute* 84:1-20.

Firth, Raymond   1957   "Introduction: Malinowski as Scientist and as Man." In *Man and Culture,* Raymond Firth, ed., pp. 1-14. New York: Harper.

Firth, Raymond   1963   *Elements of Social Organization.* Boston: Beacon.

Firth, Raymond   1973   *Symbols: Public and Private.* Ithaca, New York: Cornell University Press.

Fogelson, Raymond   1977   "Notes on the History, Status, and Prospects of Psychological Anthropology." Paper presented at the 76th Annual Meeting of the American Anthropological Association, Houston, Texas, December 1, 1977.

Fortes, Meyer   1945   *The Dynamics of Clanship among the Tallensi.* London: Oxford University Press.

Fortes, Meyer   1949   "Preface." In *Social Structure Studies Presented to A. R. Radcliffe-Brown,* pp. v-xiv. Oxford: Clarendon Press.

Fortes, Meyer   1969   *Kinship and the Social Order: The Legacy of Lewis Henry Morgan.* Chicago: Aldine.

Fortes, Meyer   1978   "An Anthropologist's Apprenticeship." In *Annual Review of Anthropology,* 7:1-30.

Fortune, Reo F.   1932   *Sorcerers of Dobu.* London: Routledge.

Fouts, R. S., and R. L. Mellgren   1976   "Language, Signs, and Cognition in the Chimpanzee." *Sign Language Studies* 13:319-346.

Frake, Charles O.   1961   "The Diagnosis of Disease among the Subanum of

Mindanao." *American Anthropologist* 63(11):13–132.

Frazer, James G. 1890 *The Golden Bough.*

Freed, S. A., and R. S. Freed 1972 "Cattle in a North Indian Village." *Ethnology* 9(4):399–408.

Freed, S. A., and R. S. Freed 1981 "Sacred Cows and Water Buffalo in India: The Uses of Ethnography." *Current Anthropology* 22:483–502.

Freeman, Derek 1970 "Human Nature and Culture." In R. O. Slatyer et al., *Man and the New Biology*, pp. 50–75. Canberra: Australian National University Press.

Freeman, Derek 1983 *Margaret Mead and Samoa: The Making and Unmaking of an Anthropological Myth.* Cambridge, Massachusetts: Harvard University Press.

French, David 1956 "An Exploration of Wasco Ethnoscience." *Yearbook of the American Philosophical Society*, pp. 224–226.

Freud, Sigmund 1900 *The Interpretation of Dreams.*

Freud, Sigmund 1918 *Totem and Taboo*, A. A. Brill, trans.

Freud, Sigmund 1920 *A General Introduction to Psychoanalysis* Garden City, New York: Garden City Publishing Co., 1928.

Freud, Sigmund 1928 *The Future of an Illusion*, W. D. Robson Scott, trans. London: Institute of Psychoanalysis.

Freud, Sigmund 1935 *The Ego and the Id.* Authorized translation by Joan Riviere. London: Hogarth.

Freud, Sigmund 1939 *Moses and Monotheism.* New York: Vintage.

Friedman, Jonathan 1974 "Marxism, Structuralism and Vulgar Materialism." *Man* 9:449–469.

Friedman, Jonathan 1975 "Tribes, States and Transformations." In *Marxist Analyses and Social Anthropology* 11:161–202, Maurice Bloch, ed. London, Malaby Press.

Frobenius, Leo 1898 *Die Weltanschauung der Naturvolker.*

Gardner, B. T., and R. A. Gardner 1969 "Teaching Sign Language to a Chimpanzee." *Science* 165:664–672.

Gardner, B. T., and R. A. Gardner 1971 "Two-Way Communication with an Infant Chimpanzee." In *Behavior of Non-Human Primates*, Alan M. Schreier, Harry F. Harlow, and Fred Stollnitz, eds. New York: Academic Press.

Geertz, Clifford 1965 "The Impact of the Concept of Culture on the Concept of Man." In *New Views of the Nature of Man*, John R. Platt, ed., pp. 93–118. Chicago: University of Chicago Press.

Geertz, Clifford 1966 "Religion as a Cultural System." In *Anthropological Approaches to the Study of Religion*, Association of Social Anthropologists Monograph No. 3, Michael Banton, ed, pp. 1–46.

Geertz, Clifford 1973 *The Interpretation of Cultures.* New York: Basic.

Geertz, Clifford 1980 "Blurred Genres: The Refiguration of Social Thought." *American Scholar* Spring:165–179.

Ginsberg, Herbert, and Sylvia Opper. 1969 *Piaget's Theory of Intellectual Development.* Englewood Cliffs, New Jersey: Prentice-Hall.

Givens, Douglas R.   1977   *An Analysis of Navajo Temporality.* Washington, D.C.: University Press of America.

Gladwin, Thomas   1970   *East is a Big Bird.* Cambridge, Massachusetts: Harvard University Press.

Gluckman, Max   1963   *Order and Rebellion in Tribal Africa.* New York: Free Press.

Gluckman, Max, ed.   1964   *Closed Systems and Open Minds: The Limits of Naivety in Social Anthropology.* Chicago: Aldine.

Godelier, Maurice   1977   *Perspectives in Marxist Anthropology.* London: Cambridge University Press.

Goldenweiser, Alexander   1916   "Culture and Environment."

Goldenweiser, Alexander   1925   "Diffusionism and Historical Ethnology." *American Journal of Sociology* 31:19–38.

Goldenweiser, Alexander   1933   *History, Psychology, and Culture.* Gloucester, Massachusetts: Peter Smith.

Goldman, Irving   1959   "Evolution and Anthropology." *Victorian Studies* September: 55–75.

Goldschmidt, Walter, ed.   1959   *The Anthropology of Franz Boas.* San Francisco: Chandler.

Goodenough, Ward H.   1956   "Componential Analysis and the Study of Meaning." *Language* 32(2):22–37.

Gorer, G., and J. Rickman   1949   *The People of Great Russia: A Psychological Study.* London: Cresset.

Gosse, P. H.   1857   *Omphalos.*

Gould, Stephen J.   1977   *Ontogeny and Phylogeny.* Cambridge, Massachusetts: Harvard University Press.

Gould, Stephen J.   1978   "Women's Brains." *Natural History* 87(8):44–50.

Gould, Stephen J.   1981   *The Mismeasure of Man.* New York: Norton.

Graebner, F.   1911   *Die Methode der Ethnologie.* Heidelberg.

Green, Jesse, ed.   1979   *Zuñi: Selected Writings of Frank Hamilton Cushing.* Lincoln: University of Nebraska Press.

Gronewold, Sylvia   1972   "Did Frank Hamilton Cushing Go Native?" In *Crossing Cultural Boundaries,* Solon T. Kimball and James B. Watson, eds., pp. 33–50. New York: Chandler.

Group for the Advancement of Psychiatry   1962   Report No. 54. *The Preclinical Teaching of Psychiatry.* New York: Group for the Advancement of Psychiatry.

Gruber, Jacob W.   1965   "Brixham Cave and the Antiquity of Man." In Spiro, 1965, pp. 373–402.

Haddon, Alfred C.   1930   "Introduction." In E. B. Tylor, *Anthropology.* London: Watts & Co.

Haddon, Alfred C.   1934   *History of Anthropology.* London: Watts & Co.

Haines, Francis   1955   *The Nez Perce Tribesmen of the Columbia Plateau.* Norman: University of Oklahoma Press.

Hall, G. Stanley   1904   *Adolescence.*

Hallowell, A. Irving   1955   *Culture and Experience.* Philadelphia: University of

Pennsylvania Press.

Hallowell, A. Irving 1963 "Personality, Culture and Society in Behavioral Evolution." In *Psychology: A Study of a Science*, vol. 6, Sigmund Koch, ed., pp. 429–509. New York: McGraw-Hill.

Hallowell, A. Irving 1976 *Contributions to Anthropology: Selected Papers of A. Irving Hallowell*. Chicago: University of Chicago Press.

Hanke, Lewis 1959 *Aristotle and the American Indians*. Bloomington: Indiana University Press.

Harner, Michael 1977 "The Ecological Basis for Aztec Sacrifices." *American Ethnologist* 4(1):117–135.

Harrington, Charles, and John W. M. Whiting 1972 "Socialization Process and Personality." In Hsu, ed., 1972, pp. 469–507.

Harris, Marvin 1964 *The Nature of Cultural Things*. New York: Random House.

Harris, Marvin 1966 "The Cultural Ecology of India's Sacred Cattle." *Current Anthropology* 7(8):51–56.

Harris, Marvin 1968 *The Rise of Anthropological Theory*. New York: Thomas Y. Crowell.

Harris, Marvin 1971 *Town and Country in Brazil*. New York: Norton.

Harris, Marvin 1977 *Cannibals and Kings: The Origins of Culture*. New York: Random House.

Harris, Marvin 1979 *Cultural Materialism: The Struggle for a Science of Culture*: New York: Random House.

Hatch, Elvin 1973 *Theories of Man and Culture*. New York: Columbia University Press.

Hayes, E. Nelson, and Tanya Hayes, eds. 1970 *Claude Lévi-Strauss: The Anthropologist as Hero*. Cambridge, Massachusetts: MIT Press.

Hays, H. R. 1958 *From Ape to Angel: An Informal History of Social Anthropology*. New York: Knopf.

Herdt, Gilbert H. 1981 *Guardians of the Flutes*. New York: McGraw-Hill.

Herdt, Gilbert H. 1982 *Rituals of Manhood*. Berkeley and Los Angeles: University of California Press.

Herdt, Gilbert H., ed. 1984 *Ritualized Homosexuality in Melanesia*. Berkeley: University of California Press.

Herskovits, Melville J. 1924 "A Preliminary Consideration of the Culture Areas of Africa." *American Anthropologist* 26:50–63.

Herskovits, Melville J. 1938 *Dahomey, an Ancient West African Kingdom*. 2 vols. Locust Valley, New York: J. J. Augustin.

Herskovits, Melville J. 1941 *The Myth of the Negro Past*. New York: Harper.

Herskovits, Melville J. 1949 *Man and His Works*. New York: Knopf.

Herskovits, Melville J. 1953 *Franz Boas: The Science of Man in the Making*. New York: Scribner.

Herskovits, Melville J. 1973 *Cultural Relativism* (edited by Frances Herskovits). New York: Vintage.

Heston, Alan 1971 "An Approach to the Sacred Cow of India." *Current Anthropology* 12(2):191–209.

Hiatt, Les 1971 "Secret Pseudo-Procreation Rites among the Australian Aborigines." In *Anthropology in Oceania: Essays Presented to Ian Hogbin,* L. R. Hiatt and C. Jayawardena, eds. San Francisco: Chandler.

Hiatt, L. R., ed. 1978 *Australian Aboriginal Concepts.* Canberra, Australia: Australian Institute of Aboriginal Studies.

Hinsley, Curtis M., Jr. 1981 *Savages and Scientists: the Smithsonian Institution and the Development of American Anthropology 1846-1910.* Washington, D.C.: Smithsonian Institution Press.

Hodgen, Margaret 1964 *Early Anthropology in the Sixteenth and Seventeenth Centuries.* Philadelphia: University of Pennsylvania Press.

Hogbin, Ian 1934 *Law and Order in Polynesia,* 1972. New York: Cooper Square Publishers.

Holland, Dorothy 1983 "Labeling the Opposite Sex: Metaphors and Themes in American Folk Models of Gender." Paper presented to Conference on Folk Models, Institute for Advanced Study, Princeton, New Jersey, May, 1983.

Holmes, G. 1914 "Areas of American Culture Characterization Tentatively Outlined as an Aid in the Study of Antiquities." *American Anthropologist* 16:413-416.

Honigmann, John J. 1961 "North America." In Hsu, ed., 1961, pp. 93-134.

Honigmann, John J. 1967 *Personality in Culture,* New York: Harper.

Honigmann, John J. 1972 "North America," in Hsu, ed., 1972, pp. 121-166. Cambridge, Massachusetts: Schenkman. (Revised from 1961 edition.)

Honigmann, John J. 1976 *The Development of Anthropological Ideas.* Homewood, Illinois: Dorsey.

Howard, Jane 1984 *Margaret Mead: A Life.* New York: Simon and Schuster.

Howell, F. Clark, and the Editors of Life 1965 *Early Man.* New York: Time, Inc.

Howells, William 1967 *Mankind in the Making.* New York: Doubleday.

Hsu, Francis L. K. 1948 (Rev. 1971) *Under the Ancestor's Shadow: Chinese Culture and Personality.* New York: Columbia University Press.

Hsu, Francis L. K., ed. 1961 *Psychological Anthropology.* Homewood, Illinois: Dorsey.

Hsu, Francis L. K. 1971 *Kinship and Culture.* Chicago: Aldine.

Hsu, Francis L. K., ed. 1972 *Psychological Anthropology,* rev. ed. Cambridge, Massachusetts: Schenkman.

Hutchins, E. 1980 *Culture and Inference: A Trobriand Case Study.* Cambridge, Massachusetts: Harvard University Press.

Huxley, Julian 1960 "The Emergence of Darwinism." In *The Evolution of Life,* Sol Tax, ed. pp. 1-21. Chicago: University of Chicago Press.

Hymes, Dell 1972 "The Use of Anthropology: Critical, Political, Personal." In *Reinventing Anthropology.* Dell Hymes, ed. pp. 3-79. New York: Pantheon.

Inkeles, Alex 1959 "Personality and Social Structure." In *Sociology Today,* Robert K. Merton, Leonard Broom, and Leonard J. Cottrell, Jr., eds., pp. 249-276. New York: Basic.

Inkeles, Alex, and Daniel Levinson 1954 "National Character: The Study of

Modal Personality and Sociocultural Systems." In *Handbook of Social Psychology*, second edition, Gardner Lindzey and Elliott Aronson, eds., pp. 977-1020. Cambridge, Massachusetts: Addison-Wesley.

Jarvie, I. C.   1964   *The Revolution in Anthropology*. London: Routledge.

Jarvie, I. C.   1972   *The Story of Social Anthropology*. New York: McGraw-Hill.

Jensen, A. R.   1969   "How Much Can We Boost I.Q. and Scholastic Achievement?" *Harvard Educational Review* 39:1-123.

Jolly, Alison   1972   *The Evolution of Primate Behavior*. New York: Macmillan.

Jung, Carl Gustav   1916   *Psychology of the Unconscious*. London: Kegan Paul.

Jung, Carl Gustav   1923   *Psychology Types*. H. Godwin Baynes, trans. London: Routledge.

Jung, Carl Gustav   1959   *The Archetypes and the Collective Unconscious*. Vol. 9, Part 1, *The Collected Works of C. G. Jung*. London: Routledge.

Jung, Carl Gustav   1968   *Man and His Symbols*. New York: Dell.

Kamin, Leon J.   1974   *The Science and Politics of I.Q.* Potomac, Maryland: Lawrence Erlbaum Associates.

Kaplan, Bert, ed.   1961   *Studying Personality Cross-Culturally*. Evanston, Illinois: Row, Peterson.

Kardiner, Abram   1939   *The Individual and His Society*. New York: Columbia University Press.

Kardiner, Abram   1945   *The Psychological Frontiers of Society*. New York: Columbia University Press.

Kardiner, Abram, and Edward Preble   1961   *They Studied Man*. New York: Mentor.

Kasaipwalova, J.   1973   " 'Modernizing' Melanesian Society—Why and for Whom?" In *Priorities in Melanesian Development*, Sixth Waigani Seminar, Research School of Pacific Studies, Australian National University and University of Papua New Guinea, R. J. May, ed.

Kennedy, John G.   1967   "Psychological and Social Explanations of Witchcraft." *Man* 2(2):216-225.

Kennedy, John G.   1973   "Cultural Psychiatry." In *Handbook of Social and Cultural Anthropology*, John J. Honigmann, ed., pp. 1119-1198. Chicago: Rand McNally.

Kluckhohn, C.   1944   "The Influence of Psychology on Anthropology in America During the Past 100 Years." In *100 Years of American Psychiatry 1844-1944*, J. K. Hall, G. Zilboorg, and H. A. Bunker, eds. Syracuse, New York: Syracuse University Press.

Kluckhohn, C., and O. H. Mowrer   1944   "Culture and Personality. A Conceptual Scheme." *American Anthropologist* 46:1-29.

Kluckhohn, C., H. Murray, and D. Schneider   1955   *Personality in Nature, Society and Culture*. New York: Knopf.

Knight, Rolf   1965   "A Re-examination of Hunting, Trapping and Territoriality among the Northeastern Algonkian Indians." In *The Role of Animals in Human Ecological Adjustments*, American Association for the Advancement of Science, Washington, D.C., A. Leeds and A. Vayda, eds. pp. 27-42.

Korbin, Jill E., ed. 1981 *Child Abuse and Neglect: Cross-Cultural Perspectives.* Berkeley: University of California Press.

Kroeber, Alfred L. 1909 "Classificatory Systems of Relationship." *Journal of the Royal Anthropological Institute* 39:77–84.

Kroeber, Alfred L. 1917 "The Superorganic." *American Anthropologist* 19:163–213.

Kroeber, Alfred L. 1923 *Anthropology.* New York: Harcourt.

Kroeber, Alfred L. 1928 "Sub Human Culture Beginnings." *Quarterly Review of Biology* 8:3 (September):325–342.

Kroeber, Alfred L. 1931 "The Culture-Area and Age-Area Concepts of Clark Wissler." In *Methods in Social Science.* Stuart A. Rice, ed., pp. 248–265. Chicago: University of Chicago Press.

Kroeber, Alfred L. 1948 *Anthropology,* revised edition. New York: Harcourt.

Kroeber, Alfred L. 1952 *The Nature of Culture.* Chicago: University of Chicago Press.

Kroeber, Alfred L., and C. Kluckhohn 1963 *Culture: A Critical Review of Concepts and Definitions.* New York: Vintage.

Kroeber, Theodora 1970 *Alfred Kroeber: A Personal Configuration.* Berkeley: University of California Press.

Kruuk, Hans 1970 "Interactions between Populations of Spotted Hyaenas (*Crocuta crocuta erxleben*) and Their Prey Species. In *Animal Populations in Relations to Their Food Resources,* A. Watson ed., pp. 359–74. Oxford: Blackwell.

Kruuk, Hans 1972 *The Spotted Hyena: A Study of Predation and Social Behavior.* Chicago: University of Chicago Press.

Kuper, Adam 1973 *Anthropologists and Anthropology: The British School 1922–1972.* London: Allen Lang.

Kuper, Adam, ed. 1977 *The Social Anthropology of Radcliffe-Brown.* London: Routledge.

LaBarre, Weston 1954 *The Human Animal.* Chicago: University of Chicago Press.

Laboratory of Comparative Human Cognition 1978. *The Quarterly Newsletter of the Laboratory of Comparative Human Cognition.* University of California, San Diego.

Laidler, K. 1978 "Language in the Orangutan." In *Action, Gesture and Symbol: The Emergence of Language,* A. Lock, ed., pp. 132–155. New York: Academic Press.

Langham, Ian 1981 *The Building of Social Anthropology.* Dordrecht, Holland: D. Reidel.

Langness, L. L. 1965 *The Life History in Anthropological Science.* New York: Holt.

Langness, L. L. 1975 "Margaret Mead and the Study of Socialization." *Ethos* 3(2):97–112.

Langness, L. L., and Gelya Frank 1981 *Lives: An Anthropological Approach to Biography.* Novato, California: Chandler & Sharp.

Lawick-Goodall, Jane van 1971 *In the Shadow of Man.* New York: Dell.

Leach, Edmund 1961 "Golden Bough or Gilded Twig?" *Daedalus* 90(2) (Spring), 1961:371–378, 367.
Leach, Edmund 1965 *Political Systems of Highland Burma*. Boston: Beacon.
Leach, Edmund 1966 "On the Founding Fathers." *Current Anthropology* 7:560–567.
Leach, Edmund 1967a "Virgin Birth." *Proceedings of the Royal Anthropological Institute for 1966*, pp. 39–49.
Leach, Edmund, ed. 1967b *The Structural Study of Myth and Totemism*. London: Tavistock.
Leach, Edmund 1969 *Genesis as Myth and Other Essays*. London: Grossman.
Leach, Edmund 1970 *Claude Lévi-Strauss*. London: Fontana/Collins.
Leach, Edmund 1976 *Culture and Communication*. Cambridge: Cambridge University Press.
Leacock, Eleanor 1954 *The Montagnais Hunting Territory and the Fur Trade*. Memoir 78, American Anthropological Association.
Leaf, Murray J. 1979 *Man, Mind, and Science: A History of Anthropology*. New York: Columbia University Press.
Leakey, M. D. 1970 "Early Artifacts from the Koobi Fora Ansa." *Nature* 226:228–230.
Leakey, M. D. 1971 *Olduvai Gorge, Vol. 3. Excavations in Beds I and II, 1960–1963*. Cambridge: Cambridge University Press.
Lee, Richard B., and DeVore, Irven 1968 *Man the Hunter*. Chicago: Aldine.
Lenneberg, Eric H., and John M. Roberts 1956 "The Language of Experience: A Study in Methodology." Memoir 13 of the *International Journal of American Linguistics*. Bloomington: Indiana University Publications in Anthropology and Linguistics.
LeVine, Robert A. 1973 *Culture, Behavior and Personality*. Chicago: Aldine.
LeVine, Robert A., and Barbara G. LeVine 1966 *Nyansongo: A Gusii Community in Kenya*. New York: Wiley.
Lévi-Strauss, Claude 1949 *Les Structures Élémentaires de la Parenté*. Paris: Presses Universitaires de France. English translation: 1969 *The Elementary Structures of Kinship*. Boston: Beacon.
Lévi-Strauss, Claude 1961 *A World on the Wane* (English translation of *Tristes Tropiques*). New York: Criterion.
Lévi-Strauss, Claude 1962 *Totemism*. Paris: Presses Universitaires de France.
Lévi-Strauss, Claude 1963 *Structural Anthropology*. New York: Basic.
Lévi-Strauss, Claude 1966 *The Savage Mind*. Chicago: University of Chicago Press (first published in French, 1962).
Lévi-Strauss, Claude 1969 *The Raw and the Cooked*. New York: Harper (first published in French, 1964).
Lévi-Strauss, Claude 1973 *From Honey to Ashes*. New York: Harper (first published in French, 1966).
Lévi-Strauss, Claude 1978 *The Origin of Table Manners*. New York: Harper.
Lévi-Strauss, Claude 1981 *The Naked Man*. New York: Harper.
Lewis, Ioan 1974 "The Myth of Social Anthropology." Paper delivered at UCLA Department of Anthropology. Unpublished.

Linton, Adelin, and Charles Wagley   1971   *Ralph Linton*. New York: Columbia University Press.

Linton, Ralph   1936   *The Study of Man*. New York: Appleton-Century.

Linton, Ralph   1947   *The Cultural Background of Personality*. London: Routledge.

Lipset, David   1980   *Gregory Bateson: The Legacy of a Scientist*. Englewood Cliffs, New Jersey: Prentice-Hall.

Locke, John   1960   *An Essay Concerning Human Understanding*.

Lounsbury, Floyd G.   1956   "A Semantic Analysis of the Pawnee Kinship Usage." *Language* 32(1):158–194.

Lowie, Robert   1915   "Psychology and Sociology." *American Journal of Sociology* 21(2):217–229.

Lowie, Robert   1917   *Culture and Ethnology*. New York: Boni & Liveright.

Lowie, Robert   1920   *Primitive Society*. New York: Boni & Liveright.

Lowie, Robert   1937   *The History of Ethnological Theory*. New York: Rinehart.

Lubbock, John (Lord Avebury)   1912 (1870)   *The Origin of Civilization and the Primitive Condition of Man*. London: Longmans.

Lurie, Nancy Oestreich   1966   "Women in Early American Anthropology." In *Pioneers of American Anthropology*, June Helm, ed., pp. 31–81. Seattle: University of Washington Press.

Lutz, Catherine   1983   "Goals, Events and Understanding: Towards a Formal Model of Ifaluk Emotion Theory." Paper presented to Conference on Folk Models, Institute for Advanced Study, Princeton, New Jersey, May 1983.

Lyell, Charles   1830   *Principles of Geology*.

McArthur, Margaret   1974   "Pigs for the Ancestors: A Review Article." *Oceania* 45(2):87–123.

McGonigle, Brendan O.   1980   "Sign, Symbol and Syntax in the Language of Apes." *Nature* 286 (5775):761–762.

McHugh, Tom   1972   *The Time of the Buffalo*. New York: Knopf.

Mahdi, Muhsin   1971   *Ibn Khaldun's Philosophy of History*. Chicago: University of Chicago Press.

Maine, Henry   1861   *Ancient Law*.

Mair, Lucy   1934   *An African People in the Twentieth Century*. London: Routledge.

Malefijt. *See* Waal Malefijt, Annemarie de.

Malinowski, Bronislaw   1927   *Sex and Repression in Savage Society*. London: Routledge.

Malinowski, Bronislaw   1929   *The Sexual Life of Savages in Northwestern Melanesia*. London: Routledge.

Malinowski, Bronislaw   1931   "Culture." *Encyclopedia of the Social Sciences* 4:621–646.

Malinowski, Bronislaw   1935   *Coral Gardens and Their Magic*, 2 vols. London: Allen & Unwin.

Malinowski, Bronislaw   1939a   "The Group and the Individual in Functional Analysis." *American Journal of Sociology* 44:938–964.

Malinowski, Bronislaw   1939b   "Review of Six Essays on Culture by Albert Blumenthal." *American Sociological Review* 4:588–592.

Malinowski, Bronislaw 1944 *A Scientific Theory of Culture*. Chapel Hill: University of North Carolina Press.

Malinowski, Bronislaw 1945 *The Dynamics of Culture Change*. P. M. Kaberry, ed. New Haven, Connecticut: Yale University Press.

Malinowski, Bronislaw 1959 *Crime and Custom in Savage Society*. Paterson, New Jersey: Littlefield, Adams & Co. (first published 1926, Routledge, London).

Malinowski, Bronislaw 1967 *A Diary in the Strict Sense of the Term*. New York: Harcourt.

Marrett, R. R. 1909 *The Threshold of Religion*. London: Methuen.

Marrett, R. R. 1932 *Faith, Hope and Charity in Primitive Religion*. New York: Macmillan.

Marrett, R. R. 1936 *Tylor*. London: Chapman & Hall.

Marshall, Mac 1979 *Weekend Warriors: Alchohol in a Micronesian Culture*. Palo Alto: Mayfield.

Mason, Otis T. 1894 "Technogeography, or the Relation of the Earth to the Industries of Mankind." *American Anthropologist* 7(2):137–161.

Mason, Otis T. 1895 "Influence of Environment upon Human Industries or Arts." In Annual Report of the Smithsonian Institution, pp. 639–665.

Mason, Philip P., ed. 1962 *The Literary Voyager or Muzzeniegun*. East Lansing, Michigan: Michigan State University Press.

Mason, Stephen F. 1962 *A History of the Sciences*. New York: Collier Books.

Mauss, Marcel 1954 *The Gift*, I. Cunnison, trans. New York: Free Press (originally published in French, 1924).

Mead, Margaret 1928 *Coming of Age in Samoa*. New York: Morrow.

Mead, Margaret 1930 *Growing Up in New Guinea*. New York: Morrow.

Mead, Margaret 1934 "Kinship in the Admiralty Islands." American Museum of Natural History *Anthropological Papers* 34(2).

Mead, Margaret 1935 *Sex and Temperament in Three Primitive Societies*. New York: Morrow.

Mead, Margaret 1939 *From the South Seas*. New York: Morrow.

Mead, Margaret 1942 *And Keep Your Powder Dry*. New York: Morrow.

Mead, Margaret 1947 "The Concept of Culture and the Psychosomatic Approach." *Psychiatry* 10:57–76.

Mead, Margaret 1949 *Male and Female*. New York: Morrow.

Mead, Margaret 1951 *Soviet Attitudes toward Authority*. New York: McGraw-Hill.

Mead, Margaret 1956 "The Cross-Cultural Approach to the Study of Personality." In *Psychology of Personality: Six Modern Approaches*, J. L. McCary, ed., pp. 203–252. New York: Logos Press.

Mead, Margaret 1958 "Cultural Determinants of Behavior." In *Behavior and Evolution*, Roe and Simpson, eds., 1958, pp. 480–504.

Mead, Margaret 1959 "Apprenticeship under Boas." In *The Anthropology of Franz Boas*. Memoir 87, American Anthropological Association, Walter Goldschmidt, ed., pp. 29–45.

Mead, Margaret 1963 "Socialization and Enculturation." *Current Anthropology* 4(2)184–188.

Mead, Margaret 1964 *Continuities in Cultural Evolution*. New Haven,

Mead, Margaret *(continued)*
Connecticut: Yale University Press.

Mead, Margaret   1973   Preface to the 1973 edition of *Coming of Age in Samoa.* New York: Morrow.

Mead, Margaret, and Francis Cook MacGregor   1951   *Growth and Culture: A Photographic Study of Balinese Childhood.* New York: Putnam.

Mead, Margaret, and R. Metraux   1953   *The Study of Culture at a Distance.* Chicago: University of Chicago Press.

Mech, L. David   1970   *The Wolf.* New York: American Museum of Natural History Press.

Meggers, B.   1946   "Recent Trends in American Ethnology." *American Anthropologist* 48:176–214.

Meggitt, Mervyn   1965   *The Lineage System of the Mae Enga of New Guinea.* Edinburgh: Oliver & Boyd.

Metzger, Duane, and Gerald E. Williams   1963   "A Formal Ethnographic Analysis of Temejapa Ladino Weddings." *American Anthropologist* 65:1076–1101.

Miller, George A.   1971   Foreword to *The Cultural Context of Learning and Thinking,* Michael Cole, John Gay, Joseph A. Glick, and Donald W. Sharp. New York: Basic.

Modell, Judith Schachter   1983   *Ruth Benedict: Patterns of a Life.* Philadelphia: University of Pennsylvania Press.

Montagu, M. F. Ashley   1954   *The Direction of Human Development.* New York: Harper.

Montesquieu, C.   1900 (original 1748)   *The Spirit of Laws.* T. Nugent, trans. New York: Colonial Press.

Moore, John H.   1974   "The Culture Concept as Ideology." *American Ethnologist* 1(3):537–550.

Morgan, Lewis H.   1851   *League of the Ho-de-no-sau-nee, or Iroquois.* Rochester, New York: Sage & Broa.

Morgan, Lewis H.   1868   *The American Beaver and His Work.* Philadelphia: Lippincott.

Morgan, Lewis H.   1877   *Ancient Society.* New York: World Publishing.

Munroe, Robert L., and Ruth H. Munroe   1975   *Cross-Cultural Human Development.* Monterey, California: Brooks/Cole.

Munroe, Ruth H., Robert L. Munroe, and Beatrice B. Whiting, eds.   1981   *Handbook of Cross-Cultural Human Development.* New York: Garland.

Murdock, George P.   1949a   "The Science of Human Learning, Society, Culture, and Personality." *Scientific Monthly* 69:377–381.

Murdock, George P.   1949b   *Social Structure.* New York: Macmillan.

Murdock, George P., et al.   1950   *Outline of Cultural Materials.* New Haven: Human Relations Area Files.

Murdock, George P.   1965   *Culture and Society: 24 Essays by George Peter Murdock.* Pittsburgh: University of Pittsburgh Press.

Murdock, George P.   1981   *Atlas of World Cultures.* Pittsburgh: University of Pittsburgh Press.

Murphy, Robert F. 1972 *Robert H. Lowie.* New York: Columbia University Press.

Nadel, S. F. 1942 *A Black Byzantium.* London: Oxford University Press.

Nadel, S. F. 1951 *The Foundations of Social Anthropology.* London: Cohen & West.

Napier, John 1969 "Five Steps to Man." In *Evolutionary Anthropology,* Hermann K. Bleibtreu, ed., pp. 156–162. Boston: Allyn & Bacon.

Nisbet, Robert A. 1974 *The Sociology of Emile Durkheim.* New York: Oxford University Press.

Novak, Maximillian E., and Edward Dudley, eds. 1972 *The Wild Man Within.* Pittsburgh: University of Pittsburgh Press.

Oakley, Kenneth Page 1964 *The Problem of Man's Antiquity.* Bulletin of the British Museum (Natural History) 9(5), London.

Obeyesekere, Gananath 1981 *Medusa's Hair.* Chicago: University of Chicago Press.

Opler, Morris 1945 "Themes as Dynamic Forces in Culture." *American Journal of Sociology* 51(3):198–206.

Opler, Morris 1964 "Tylor's Views of Culture and Evolution." *Southwestern Journal of Anthropology* 20(2)(Summer, 1964):123–144.

Parsons, Elsie Clews, ed. 1922 *American Indian Life.* Lincoln: University of Nebraska Press.

Patterson, F. 1978 "The Gestures of a Gorilla: Sign Language Acquisition in Another Pongid Species." *Brain and Language* 5:72–97.

Paul, Robert A. 1982 *The Tibetan Symbolic World.* Chicago: University of Chicago Press.

Peacock, James L. 1975 *Consciousness and Change.* New York: Wiley.

Peirce, C. S. 1931 *Collected Papers.* 8 vols. Cambridge, Massachusetts: Harvard University Press.

Penniman, T. K. 1935 *A Hundred Years of Anthropology.* London: Duckworth.

Penniman, T. K. 1974 *A Hundred Years of Anthropology.* New York: Morrow (original edition 1935, London: Duckworth.)

Perry, W. J. 1923 *Children of the Sun.* London: Methuen.

Pfeiffer, John E. 1969 *The Emergence of Man.* New York: Harper.

Pfeiffer, John 1984 "Early Man Stages a Summit Meeting in New York City." *Smithsonian* 15(5):50–57.

Piaget, Jean 1969 "Genetic Epistemology." *Columbia Forum* 12:4–11.

Piaget, Jean 1970 *Structuralism.* New York: Basic.

Piaget, Jean 1974 "Need and Significance of Cross-Cultural Studies in Genetic Psychology." In *Culture and Cognition: Readings in Cross-Cultural Psychology,* J. W. Berry and P. R. Dasen, eds., pp. 299–309. London: Methuen.

Pike, Kenneth 1954 *Language in Relation to a Unified Theory of the Structure of Human Behavior,* vol. 1. Glendale, California: Summer Institute of Linguistics.

Pitt-Rivers, A. L.-F. 1906 *The Evolution of Culture and Other Essays,* J. L.

Pitt-Rivers, A. L.-F. *(continued)*
   Myres, ed. Oxford: Clarendon Press.
Polanyi, Karl   1944   *The Great Transformation*. New York: Holt.
Pollard, Sidney   1971   *The Idea of Progress*. Baltimore: Penguin.
Pouillon, J., and P. Maranda, eds.   1970   *Echanges et Communications*, 2 vols.
   Paris and The Hague: Mouton.
Premack, A. J., and David Premack   1972   "Teaching Language to an Ape."
   Scientific American 227(4):92–99.
Premack, David   1971   "On the Assessment of Language Competence in
   Chimpanzees." In *Behavior of Non-Human Primates*, Alan M. Schreier,
   Harry F. Harlow, and Fred Stollnitz, eds. New York: Academic Press.
Premack, David   1976   *Intelligence in Ape and Man*. Hillsdale, N.J.: Lawrence
   Erlbaum Associates.
Price-McGough, Laurie   1983   "Illness Stories: Cultural Knowledge in Natural
   Discourse." Paper presented to Conference on Folk Models, Institute for
   Advanced Study, Princeton, New Jersey, May, 1983.
Price-Williams, D. R.   1975   *Explorations in Cross-Cultural Psychology*. San
   Francisco: Chandler & Sharp.
Quinn, Naomi   1982   "Commitment." In "American Marriage: A Cultural
   Analysis," *American Ethnologist*, 9(4):775–798.
Radcliffe-Brown, A. R.   1922   *The Andaman Islanders*. Glencoe, Illinois: Free
   Press.
Radcliffe-Brown, A. R.   1938   Letter to Robert Lowie, unmailed. Reprinted
   from *History of Anthropology Newsletter* 3(2):6, 1976.
Radcliffe-Brown, A. R.   1952   *Structure and Function in Primitive Society*.
   London: Cohen & West.
Radcliffe-Brown, A. R.   1957   *A Natural Science of Society*. Glencoe, Illinois:
   Free Press.
Radin, Paul   1920   *The Autobiography of an American Indian*. University of
   California Publications in American Archaeology and Ethnology, 16(7).
   Berkeley: University of California Press.
Radin, Paul   1926   *Crashing Thunder, the Autobiography of An American
   Indian*. New York: Appleton.
Radin, Paul   1927   *Primitive Man as Philosopher*. New York: Appleton.
Radin, Paul   1953   *The World of Primitive Man*. New York: Schuman.
Rappaport, Roy A.   1963   "Aspects of Man's Influence upon Island Ecosystems:
   Alteration and Control." In *Man's Place in the Island Ecosystem*, F. R.
   Fosberg, ed. Honolulu: Bishop Museum.
Rappaport, Roy A.   1967   *Pigs for the Ancestors: Ritual in the Ecology of a
   New Guinea People*. New Haven, Connecticut: Yale University Press.
Rappaport, Roy A.   1984   *Pigs for the Ancestors: Ritual in the Ecology of a
   New Guinea People*. New Enlarged Edition. New Haven, Connecticut: Yale
   University Press.
Ratzel, F.   1896   *The History of Mankind*. A. J. Butler, trans. (originally pub-
   lished in German, 1885–1888).
Redfield, Robert   1941   *The Folk Culture of Yucatan*. Chicago: University of
   Chicago Press.

Redfield, Robert   1953   *The Primitive World and Its Transformations.* Ithaca, New York: Cornell University Press.

Redfield, Robert   1955   *The Little Community: Viewpoints for the Study of a Human Whole.* Chicago: University of Chicago Press.

Reid, Mayne   1861   *Odd People: Being a Popular Description of Singular Races of Man.*

Resek, Carl   1960   *Lewis Henry Morgan: American Scholar.* Chicago: University of Chicago Press.

Richards, Audrey I.   1954   *Economic Development and Tribal Change.* New York: Cambridge University Press.

Richards, Audrey I.   1957   "The Concept of Culture in Malinowski's Work." In *Man and Culture,* Raymond Firth, ed. pp. 15–32. New York: Harper.

Rivers, W. H. R.   1920   *Instinct and the Unconscious: A Contribution to a Biological Theory of the Pyscho-neuroses.* New York: Cambridge University Press.

Rivers, W. H. R.   1926   *Psychology and Ethnology.* London: Routledge.

Roe, Anne, and George Gaylord Simpson, ed.   1958   *Behavior and Evolution.* New Haven, Connecticut: Yale University Press.

Roheim, Geza   1945   *The Eternal Ones of the Dream.* New York: International Universities Press.

Roheim, Geza   1971 (originally 1943)   *The Origin and Function of Culture.* New York: Anchor.

Rohner, Ronald P., ed.   1969   *The Ethnography of Franz Boas.* Chicago: University of Chicago Press.

Rosaldo, Michelle Z.   1980   *Knowledge and Passion: Ilongot Notions of Self and Social Life.* Cambridge: Cambridge University Press.

Rowell, T.   1967   "Variability in the Social Organization of Primates." In *Primate Ethology,* D. Morris, ed., pp. 219–235. Chicago: Aldine.

Rumbaugh, G. W.   1977   *Language Learning by a Chimpanzee: The LANA Project.* New York: Academic Press.

Ryle, Gilbert   1949   *The Concept of Mind.* London: Hutchinson's University Library.

Sahlins, Marshall D.   1976   *Culture and Practical Reason.* Chicago: University of Chicago Press.

Sahlins, Marshall D., and Elman R. Service, eds.   1960   *Evolution and Culture.* Ann Arbor: University of Michigan Press.

Sahlins, Marshall D., and Elman R. Service   1960   "Evolution: Specific and General." In Sahlins and Service, eds., 1960, pp. 12–44.

Sapir, Edward   1916   *Time Perspectives in Aboriginal American Culture, A Study in Method.* Canada Department of Mines, Geological Survey, Ottawa, Government Printing Bureau.

Sapir, Edward   1917   "Do We Need A Superorganic?" *American Anthropologist* 19:441–447.

Sapir, Edward   1924   "Culture, Genuine and Spurious." *American Journal of Sociology* 29:401–429.

Saussure, Ferdinand de   1954   *Course in General Linguistics.* New York: Philosophical Library.

Savage-Rumbaugh, E. Sue, Duane M. Rumbaugh, and Sarah Boysen 1980
  "Do Apes Use Language?" *American Scientist* 68(1):49–61.
Schaller, George B. 1964 *The Year of the Gorilla.* Chicago: University of
  Chicago Press.
Schaller, George B. 1972 *The Serengeti Lion: A Study of Predator-Prey
  Relations.* Chicago: University of Chicago Press.
Schiller, Clare H., ed. 1957 *Instinctive Behavior.* New York: International
  Universities Press.
Schmidt, Wilhelm 1939 *The Culture Historical Method of Ethnology.* S. A.
  Sieber, trans. New York: Fortuny's.
Schneider, David M. 1968 *American Kinship: A Cultural Account.* Engle-
  wood Cliffs, New Jersey: Prentice-Hall.
Schneider, Louis, and Charles Bonjean, eds. 1973 *The Idea of Culture in the
  Social Sciences.* New York: Cambridge University Press.
Schwartz, Theodore 1981 "The Acquisition of Culture." *Ethos* 9(1):4–17.
Sebeok, Thomas A., and Jean Umiker-Sebeok, eds. 1980 *Speaking of Apes: A
  Critical Anthology of Two-way Communication with Man.* New York:
  Plenum Press.
Seligman, Brenda Z. 1927 "Review of *Psychology and Ethnology.*" *British
  Journal of Psychology* 17:370–376.
Seligman, C. G. 1924 "Anthropology and Psychology: A Study of Some
  Points of Contact" (Presidential Address). *Journal of the Royal Anthro-
  pological Institute of Great Britain and Ireland* 54:13–46.
Seligman, C. G. 1932 "Anthropological Perspective and Psychological
  Theory" (The Huxley Memorial Lecture for 1932). *Journal of the Royal
  Anthropological Institute for Great Britain and Ireland* 62:193–228.
Senn, Peter R. 1966 "What Is 'Behavioral Science?'—Notes toward a
  History." *Journal of the History of Behavioral Sciences* 2(2):107–122.
Shalvey, Thomas 1979 *Claude Lévi-Strauss.* Amherst: University of Massa-
  chusetts Press.
Shankman, Paul 1969 "Le Roti et le Bouilli: Lévi-Strauss's Theory of Canni-
  balism." *American Anthropologist,* 71(1):54–69.
Shankman, Paul 1984 "The Thick and the Thin: On the Interpretive Theoret-
  ical Program of Clifford Geertz." *Current Anthropology* 25(3)261–279.
Shweder, Richard A. 1979–1980 "Rethinking Culture and Personality," Parts
  I, II, and III. *Ethos* 7(3):255–278; 7(4)279–311; 8(1):60–94.
Shweder, Richard A., and Robert A. LeVine, eds. 1984 *Culture Theory:
  Essays on Mind, Self, and Emotion.* Cambridge: Cambridge University
  Press.
Silverman, Sydel, ed. 1981 *Totems and Teachers: Perspectives on the History
  of Anthropology.* New York: Columbia University Press.
Simpson, George Gaylord 1949 *The Meaning of Evolution.* New York:
  Mentor.
Simpson, George Gaylord 1958 "The Study of Evolution: Methods and
  Present Status of Theory." In Roe and Simpson, 1958, pp. 7–26.
Singer, Milton 1961 "A Survey of Culture and Personality Theory and

Research." In Kaplan, 1961, pp. 9–90.

Singer, Milton 1978 "For a Semiotic Anthropology." In *Sight, Sound and Sense*, Thomas A. Sebeok, ed., 1978, pp. 202–231. Bloomington, Indiana: Indiana University Press.

Smith, Adam 1776 *An Inquiry into the Nature and Causes of the Wealth of Nations*. New York: Modern Library, 1937.

Smith, George Elliot 1928 *In the Beginning: The Origin of Civilization*. New York: Morrow.

Smith, M. G. 1960 *Government in Zazzau: 1800–1950*. New York: Oxford University Press.

Sperber, Dan 1975 *Rethinking Symbolism*. Cambridge: Cambridge University Press.

Spindler, G. 1955 *Sociocultural and Psychological Processes in Menomini Acculturation*. University of California Publications in *Culture and Society*, vol. 5. Berkeley: University of California Press.

Spindler, G., ed. 1978 *The Making of Psychological Anthropology*. Berkeley: University of California Press.

Spiro, Melford E. 1951 "Culture and Personality: The Natural History of a False Dichotomy." *Psychiatry* 14:19–46.

Spiro, Melford E. 1954 "Human Nature in Its Psychological Dimensions." *American Anthropologist* 56:19–31.

Spiro, Melford E. 1958 *Children of the Kibbutz*. Cambridge, Massachusetts: Harvard University Press.

Spiro, Melford E. 1961a "An Overview and Suggested Reorientation." In Hsu, 1961, pp. 459–492.

Spiro, Melford E. 1961b "Social Systems, Personality, and Functional Analysis." In Kaplan, ed., 1961, pp. 93–127.

Spiro, Melford E., ed. 1965 *Context and Meaning in Cultural Anthropology*. New York: Free Press.

Spiro, Melford E. 1967 *Burmese Supernaturalism*. Englewood Cliffs, New Jersey: Prentice-Hall.

Spiro, Melford E. 1968a "Review of *Purity and Danger*." *American Anthropologist* 70:391–393.

Spiro, Melford E. 1968b "Virgin Birth, Parthenogenesis, and Physiological Paternity." *Man* 3:224–261.

Spiro, Melford E. 1969 Discussions, in *Forms of Symbolic Action: Proceedings of the 1969 Annual Spring Meeting of the American Ethnological Society*, pp. 208–214. Seattle: University of Washington Press.

Spiro, Melford E. 1972 "An Overview and Suggested Reorientation." In Hsu, ed., 1972, pp. 573–607.

Spiro, Melford E. 1978 "Culture and Human Nature." In Spindler, ed., 1978, pp. 331–360.

Spiro, Melford E. 1979 "Whatever Happened to the Id?" *American Anthropologist* 81(1):5–13.

Spiro, Melford E. 1982 *Oedipus in the Trobriands*. Chicago: University of Chicago Press.

Spiro, Melford E.   n.d.   *Melford Spiro: Theoretical Papers.* Compiled and with an Introduction by Benjamin Kilborne and L. L. Langness. Chicago: University of Chicago Press.

Spock, Benjamin McLane   1946   *The Common Sense Book of Baby and Child Care.* New York: Duell.

Spradley, James P.   1970   *You Owe Yourself a Drunk: An Ethnography of Urban Nomads.* Boston: Little, Brown.

Spradley, James P.   1972   *Culture and Cognition: Rules, Maps, and Plans.* New York: Chandler.

Spuhler, J. N., ed.   1959   *The Evolution of Man's Capacity for Culture.* Detroit, Michigan: Wayne State University Press.

Stanton, William   1960   *The Leopard's Spots: Scientific Attitudes toward Race in America 1815–59.* Chicago: University of Chicago Press.

Steward, Jane C., and Robert F. Murphy, eds.   1977   *Evolution and Ecology: Essays on Social Transformation by Julian H. Steward.* Urbana: University of Illinois Press.

Steward, Julian   1955   *Theory of Culture Change.* Urbana: University of Illinois Press.

Stocking, George W., Jr.   1963   "Matthew Arnold, E. B. Tylor, and the Uses of Invention." *American Anthropologist* 65:783–799. As reprinted in Stocking, 1968.

Stocking, George W., Jr.   1964   "French Anthropology in 1800." *Isis* 55:134–150. As reprinted in Stocking, 1968.

Stocking, George W., Jr.   1965   "From Physics to Ethnology: Franz Boas' Arctic Expedition as a Problem in the Historiography of the Behavioral Sciences." *Journal of the History of the Behavioral Sciences* 1(1):53–66. As reprinted in Stocking, 1968.

Stocking, George W., Jr.   1968   *Race, Culture, and Evolution: Essays in the History of Anthropology.* New York: Free Press.

Stocking, George W., Jr., ed.   1974   *The Shaping of American Anthropology 1883–1911: A Franz Boas Reader.* New York: Basic.

Stocking, George W., Jr., ed.   1983   *Observers Observed.* Madison: University of Wisconsin Press.

Stocking, George, W., Jr., ed.   1984   *Functionalism Historicized.* Madison: University of Wisconsin Press.

Street, B. V.   1975   *The Savage in Literature.* London: Routledge.

Sturtevant, W.   1964   "Studies in Ethnoscience." *American Anthropologist* 66(2)99–131.

Sweetser, Eve   1983   "The Definition of *LIE:* An Examination of the Folk Theories Underlying a Semantic Prototype." Paper presented to Conference on Folk Models, Institute for Advanced Study, Princeton, New Jersey, May, 1983.

Tax, Sol, ed.   1960   *Evolution after Darwin.* Chicago: University of Chicago Press.

Terrace, H. S.   1979a   "How Nim Chimsky Changed My Mind." *Psychology Today* 13(6):65–91.

Terrace, H. S.   1979b   *Nim: A Chimpanzee Who Learned Sign Language.* New

York: Knopf.

Tinbergen, Nikolaas 1953 *Social Behaviour in Animals: with Special Reference to Vertebrates.* London: Methuen.

Titiev, Mischa 1964 "Enculturation." In *A Dictionary of the Social Sciences,* Julius Gould and William L. Kolb, eds., p. 239. Glencoe, New York: Free Press.

Toynbee, Arnold J. 1973 "The Genesis of Pollution." *Horizon* 15(3):4–9.

Turgot, A. R. J., Baron de Laune 1750 *On the Historical Progress of the Human Mind.* (In Latin.)

Turner, Victor 1967 *The Forest of Symbols.* Ithaca, New York: Cornell University Press.

Tyler, Stephen A. 1969 *Cognitive Anthropology.* New York: Holt.

Tylor, Edward Burnett 1861 *Anahuac or Mexico and the Mexicans, Ancient and Modern.* London: Longmans.

Tylor, Edward Burnett 1903 *Primitive Culture: Researches into the Development of Mythology, Philosophy, Religion, Language, Art and Custom,* 2 vols. London: John Murray (originally published 1871).

Vaidyanathan, A., K. N. Nair, and Marvin Harris 1982 "Bovine Sex and Species Ratios in India." *Current Anthropology* 23:365–383.

Van den Berg, J. H. 1961 *The Changing Nature of Man.* New York: Norton.

Vayda, Andrew 1961 "Expansion and Warfare among Swidden Agriculturalists." *American Anthropologist* 63:346–358.

Voget, Fred W. 1960 "Man and Culture: An Essay in Changing Anthropological Interpretation." *American Anthropologist* 62:943–965.

Voget, Fred W. 1975 *A History of Ethnology.* New York: Holt.

Waal Malefijt, Annemarie de 1974 *Images of Man: A History of Anthropological Thought.* New York: Knopf.

Wagner, Roy 1975 *The Invention of Culture.* Englewood Cliffs, New Jersey, Prentice-Hall.

Waitz, T. 1863 *Introduction to Anthropology.* London: Longmans.

Wallace, Anthony F. C. 1952 *The Modal Personality Structure of the Tuscarora Indians, as Revealed by the Rorschach Test.* Bulletin 150, Bureau of American Ethnology. Washington, D.C.: Smithsonian Institution.

Wallace, Anthony F. C. 1970 *Culture and Personality.* New York: Random House.

Webb, Malcolm C. 1968 "The Culture Concept and Cultural Change in the Work of Margaret Mead." *The Proceedings of the Louisiana Academy of Science* 31:148–165.

Weber, Max 1930 *The Protestant Ethic and the Spirit of Capitalism.* New York: Scribner.

White, Andrew D. 1955 *A History of the Warfare of Science with Theology in Christendom.* New York: Braziller (originally published 1895).

White, Hayden 1972 "The Forms of Wildness: Archaeology of an Idea." In Novak and Dudley, 1972, pp. 3–38.

White, Leslie A. 1925 "Personality and Culture," *Open Court* 39:145–149.

White, Leslie A. 1940 *Pioneers in American Anthropology: The Morgan-Bandelier Letters 1873–1883.* Albuquerque: University of New Mexico Press.

White, Leslie A. 1969 *The Science of Culture*, 2nd ed. New York: Farrar.

White, Leslie A. 1975 *The Concept of Cultural Systems: A Key to Understanding Tribes and Nations*. New York: Columbia University Press.

White, Leslie A., with Beth Dillingham 1973 *The Concept of Culture*. Minneapolis, Minnesota: Burgess.

Whiting, Beatrice B., ed. 1963 *Six Cultures: Studies of Child Rearing*. New York: Wiley.

Whiting, John W. M. 1941 *Becoming a Kwoma: Teaching and Learning in a New Guinea Tribe*. New Haven, Connecticut: Yale University Press.

Whiting, John W. M. 1964 "Effects of Climate on Certain Cultural Practices." In *Explorations in Cultural Anthropology*, Ward H. Goodenough, ed., pp. 511–544. New York: McGraw–Hill.

Whiting, J. W. M., E. H. Chasdi, H. F. Antonovsky, and B. C. Ayres 1966 "The Learning of Values." In *People of the Rimrock: A Study of Values in Five Cultures*, E. Vogt and E. Albert, eds. Cambridge, Massachusetts: Harvard University Press.

Whiting, John W. M., and Irvin L. Child 1953 *Child Training and Personality*. New Haven, Connecticut: Yale University Press.

Whiting, J. W. M., R. Kluckhohn, and A. S. Anthony 1958 "The Function of Male Initiation Ceremonies at Puberty." In *Readings in Social Psychology*, E. E. Maccoby, T. Newcomb, and E. Hartley, eds., pp. 359–370. New York: Holt.

Wiener, Norbert 1954 *The Human Use of Human Beings: Cybernetics and Society*. New York: Doubleday.

Williams, Thomas Rhys 1972 *Introduction to Socialization: Human Culture Transmitted*. St. Louis, Missouri: Mosby.

Wissler, Clark 1906 "A Psycho-Physical Element in Primitive Art." Reprint, *Boas Anniversary Volume: Anthropological Papers Written in Honor of Franz Boas*, Berthold Laufer, ed., pp. 189–192. New York: Stechert.

Wissler, Clark 1912 "The Psychological Aspects of the Culture-Environment Relation." *American Anthropologist* 14(2):217–225.

Wissler, Clark 1914 "Influence of the Horse in the Development of Plains Culture." *American Anthropologist* 16:1–25.

Wissler, Clark 1916 "Psychological and Historical Interpretations of Culture." *Science* 43:193–201.

Wissler, Clark 1923 *Man and Culture*. New York: Thomas Y. Crowell.

Wissler, Clark 1926 *The Relation of Nature to Man in Aboriginal America*. New York: Oxford University Press.

Wissler, Clark 1938 *The American Indian*. 1st edition, 1917. New York: Oxford University Press.

Wokler, Robert 1978 "Perfectible Apes in Decadent Cultures: Rousseau's Anthropology Revisited." *Daedalus*, Summer 1978, pp. 107–134.

Wolfgang, Marvin E. 1960 "Cesare Lombroso." In *Pioneers in Criminology*, Hermann Mannheim, ed., pp. 168–227. Chicago: Quadrangle Books.

Young, Michael W., ed. 1979 *The Ethnography of Malinowski: The Trobriand Islands 1915–18*. London: Routledge.

Notices of Copyright and Literary Property

251

Author Index

Subject Index